Expanding Job Opportunities in Ghana

DIRECTIONS IN DEVELOPMENT
Human Development

Expanding Job Opportunities in Ghana

Maddalena Honorati and Sara Johansson de Silva

WORLD BANK GROUP

Contents

Boxes

Figures

Map

Tables

Acknowledgments

This report was prepared by Maddalena Honorati and Sara Johansson de Silva under the overall guidance of Kathleen Beegle (Program Leader), Stefano Paternostro (Practice Manager, Social Protection and Labor), Pablo Fajnzylber (Practice Manager, Poverty and Equity), and Henry Kerali (Ghana Country Director). Liz Foster and Federica Alfani provided excellent research assistance for the analysis of household survey data. Invaluable inputs were supplied by Vasco Molini and Pierella Paci (poverty analysis), Marco Ranzani (Africa structural transformation data analysis), David Francis (enterprise survey analysis), Deryck Brown (public employment), Johannes Jansen (agricultural development), Theo Awanzam (wage analysis), and Dan Pavelesku (household enterprise analysis). The report benefitted greatly from comments and suggestions from Omar Arias and Tomomi Tanaka and from its peer reviewers Dino Merotto and Roberta Gatti from the World Bank. The team is much indebted to Priscilla Twumasi Baffour, Department of Economics, University of Ghana, for her extremely useful comments. The report was edited by Nancy Morrison.

Abbreviations

ES	Enterprise Survey
GLSS	Ghana Living Standard Survey
GSS	Ghana Statistical Service
HHE	household enterprise
ICT	information and communications technology
ILO	International Labour Organization
LEED	Legal and Economic Empowerment Database
LESDEP	Local Enterprises and Skills Development Program
MDGs	Millenium Development Goals
MDG1	Millenium Development Goal no.1
MELR	Ministry of Employment and Labor Relations
MSME	micro, small, and medium enterprise
NAP	National Apprenticeship Program
NEP	National Employment Policy
NGO	nongovernmental organization
SME	small and medium enterprise
SSNIT	Social Security National Insurance Trust
STEP	Skills towards Employment and Productivity
TVET	technical and vocational training and education
UN	United Nations
WDI	World Development Indicators

Currency equivalents:
All monetary amounts are U.S. dollars unless otherwise indicated.
US$1.00 = Ghana cedi, GH¢2.9 (Average 2014)

Government fiscal year:
January 1–December 31

Overview

Jobs Matter for Ghana

Ghana was, until very recently, a success story on the African continent, achieving high and sustained growth and impressive poverty reduction. The country's economic growth rate has consistently outperformed that of its African peers since the early 1990s and has further accelerated in the past decade, bringing the country into lower-middle-income status. Economic growth has been fueled by strong price increases in its main commodity exports (cocoa and gold, for which prices more than tripled between 2000 and 2010) and the start of commercial oil production in 2011. In tandem with the expanding economy, poverty fell dramatically. Ghana met the Millennium Development Goal (MDG) of halving poverty ahead of the target period, with the share of the population living in poverty decreasing from 52 percent in 1991 to 24 percent in 2012 (GSS 2014a; Molini and Paci 2015). Significant progress has also been made in health, education, and other areas important to individual and social well-being.

In the same period, Ghana also created a considerable number of jobs while increasing total labor productivity, especially between 2005 and 2012. Job creation averaged 3.2 percent per year between 1991 and 2005, and rose to 4 percent per year between 2005 and 2012, at a time when gross domestic product (GDP) growth increased to 8 percent per year.[1] Labor force participation for 15- to 64-year-olds remained high (at 80 percent of the total population), even as the share of youth (15- to 24-year-olds) enrolled in school increased from 21 percent to 31 percent, and unemployment rates fell from 4 percent to 2 percent between 2005 and 2012. Labor productivity increased from 1991 to 2005 following the boom in the service sectors (mostly in financial, communication, and storage services), and was even higher from 2005 to 2012, driven by the rapid increase in value added in the extractive and construction sectors.

Growth and job creation were accompanied by rapid urbanization and a gradual structural transformation of Ghana's economy, as agricultural work has largely given way to services jobs and to a lesser degree, to industry. Since 1991, the populations of the two major cities, Accra and Kumasi, have more than doubled, gaining over 2.4 million inhabitants. Secondary cities also expanded significantly. There are now more people living in urban areas than rural ones, and the urban population is expected to rise from slightly more than 50 percent to 70 percent of the total population by 2050 (UN 2014). In parallel, the share of agriculture in value added and employment fell from 36 percent and 61 percent in 1991, to 24 percent and 43 percent, respectively, in 2012, while the share of services expanded from 36 percent to 48 percent between 1991 and 2005, and then remained constant.

As the economy has undergone this sectoral transformation, employment also shifted toward self-employment off the farm (especially in urban areas) and, to a lesser extent, to private wage employment. Over the last two decades, the share of off-farm self-employment in total employment has increased from 26 percent to 36 percent. Private wage employment nearly tripled, from 6 percent to 16 percent, while the share of public wage work fell from 9 percent to 6 percent. In the last decade, half (1.5 million) of the new jobs have been created in the off-farm self-employment sector and in urban areas—especially Greater Accra and Kumasi. By contrast, job creation was more balanced between urban and rural areas from 1991 to 2005.

Ghana is now facing major challenges in diversifying its economy, sustaining growth, and making it more inclusive. Ghana's growth model has become increasingly dependent on natural resources—and even more so since 2011, with the start of commercial oil production. As a result, the mining industry, construction, and the services sectors have expanded, whereas the manufacturing sector has stagnated. While this growth model has generated more jobs, most of the new jobs in the past decade have been created in low-earning, low-productivity trade services, the demand for which increased with rapid urbanization. Two in five Ghanaians still work in agriculture, and one in four in the trade services sector. The mismatch between the relatively low growth in high-value added jobs in the mining industry and the rapid increase in jobs in low-value added services is likely one reason why growth has been much less able to reduce poverty since 2005, compared to earlier decades.

The current period of economic instability is seriously hampering the development of the private sector and the creation of jobs. Ghana is living through a significant fiscal and economic crisis, including an energy crisis, which is directly curtailing private sector activity. Since 2012, Ghana has faced major macroeconomic challenges with slower growth, high internal and external imbalances, high inflation, a depreciated currency (cedi), and lack of energy supply, providing very poor circumstances for supporting investments that could create jobs. The crisis is simultaneously heightening the need for urgent reforms while limiting the room to maneuver and increasing pressure for a careful prioritization of policy actions.

Inequalities have increased along many dimensions, and disparities have increased between urban and rural areas, within urban areas, and across different regions of the country. High growth and poverty reduction have been accompanied by widening inequality in household consumption. The distribution of increased prosperity has worsened, with the consumption share of the poorest groups decreasing and the share of the top quintile increasing slightly. Despite the increase, the Gini index in Ghana (measuring inequality of consumption) compares favorably with the rest of Sub-Saharan Africa. Poverty has fallen below 20 percent in the more dynamic regions in the south and center, while poverty rates remain above 60 percent in the northern and western parts of Ghana (Molini and Paci 2015).

The limited diversification and growing inequities in Ghana's labor markets make it harder to create more, better, and inclusive jobs. Ghana's economy needs to create about 300,000 new jobs per year between now and 2020 to absorb a growing population if it is to avoid increasing unemployment or inactivity (those who are not in school and are not looking for work). Although the challenge of creating more jobs has been comfortably met in the past, the strong and growing inequities in job opportunities suggest that past patterns of employment creation will not be sufficient. Employment needs to expand in both urban areas, which will continue to grow rapidly according to projections, and rural areas, where poverty is still the highest. More jobs need to be created in higher-productivity sectors in the industry and trade services, and productivity needs to be increased in lower-productivity sectors in services and agriculture, in order to increase the earnings potential for the many poor who still work there. In particular, Ghana's youth and women need help in connecting to these jobs, through relevant skills development and services that target gaps in information about job opportunities. Even with significant effort, most of Ghana's population will continue to work in jobs characterized by low and fluctuating earnings for the foreseeable future. They will need safety nets that help them manage vulnerability to income shortfalls.

More productive and inclusive jobs will be necessary to move to a second phase of structural transformation and help Ghana develop into a modern middle-income economy. Job opportunities are central to Ghana's challenges. Although access to jobs is high in Ghana, where one works is strongly linked to poverty; more than 70 percent of the poorest 20 percent work in self-employment activities on the farm. More productive jobs, accessible to the entire population, are necessary to continue to shift Ghana's poor out of subsistence agriculture and help low-productivity workers expand their earning opportunities and access better-quality jobs. While Ghana has been successful in moving people from agriculture to off-farm self-employment activities, the future challenge will be to increase the productivity of the increasing share of the self-employed, reduce their income vulnerability, foster more wage work, and create a middle-income class of workers. More productive jobs are central to sustainable economic growth and economic modernization, and to political and social stability.

In this context, *Expanding Job Opportunities in Ghana* provides an analysis of the landscape of jobs in Ghana. The report is intended as a jobs diagnostic, analyzing key trends and characteristics of workers and work in Ghana, highlighting key features and constraints that are relevant to Ghana's jobs challenges, and identifying policy options going forward. A detailed strategy for job creation necessarily encompasses many sectors, requiring industrial/sectoral policies as well as policies related to macroeconomic management, trade, education, and social protection, among other areas. It is beyond the scope of this report to provide detailed sectoral policy suggestions; rather, it aims at presenting general policy directions. The report draws on labor information from household data: particularly Rounds 3, 5, and 6 of the Ghana Living Standard Survey (GLSS3, 5, and 6); two rounds of the World Bank Enterprise Surveys (ES); and information on household enterprises from the GLSS6.

Challenges and Constraints to Expanding Job Opportunities

The Ghanaian labor market is characterized by high levels of labor participation and low levels of unemployment. Most people work in Ghana; in 2012, 77 percent of the adult population was employed, and only 2 percent of the active population was unemployed. Most jobless are inactive rather than unemployed: some 200,000 adults are unemployed, while 3 million are inactive. Half of the inactive are students, but the remainder are not in school and are not actively looking for work.

Most jobs are in low-productivity self-employment activities that generate limited earnings. The problem is not a lack of jobs per se, but the quality of jobs. In the absence of scaled-up social safety nets and because most jobs pay poorly, adults (and some children) are obliged to make a living; they cannot rely on their families or the state to provide for them. Four out of five workers work in farm and off-farm household enterprises. As in many Sub-Saharan African countries, agriculture remains the single largest employer, accounting for two out of five jobs. Outside of agriculture, another 36 percent of jobs are in the form of self-employment in off-farm activities. Most of these household enterprises are made up of one person (an own-account worker), and as such do not create wage employment. The wage sector accounts for only 22 percent of all jobs, and most of it is informal, offering little job security. Some jobs offer much better opportunities than others: wage work is better paid than self-employment; work outside agriculture is better paid than farm work; and only the public sector consistently offers social security to its workers. In addition, job and social security are considerably higher in the public sector than the private wage employment sector. In spite of increasing prosperity in urban areas, many jobs are in low-productivity sectors (informal trade). Job markets in rural areas are marked by limited diversification out of the agricultural sector, where productivity is still low, and vulnerability to climatic changes is high and increasing.

Most jobs in Ghana are also low skill, requiring limited use of cognitive skills like reading and writing. The low earnings potential of jobs is mirrored in the limited use of skills in the jobs. Only urban formal sector workers use reading and writing skills regularly. By contrast, less than half of informal wage workers, and less than one-third of the self-employed, use these skills. Jobs are also characterized by a low technology content overall.

Access to job opportunities differs across Ghana's regions, which significantly worsens gaps in income and poverty. Urbanization is both a cause and consequence of widening gaps in job opportunities across Ghana's regions. National averages mask vastly different employment structures, which reflect a lack of diversification in production and employment in the northern and rural areas of Ghana. More than half of workers in formal firms are in Accra and larger urban areas. In Accra, private wage work accounts for 40 percent of employment. By contrast, less than 10 percent of the population has access to wage work in the Northern region. Agriculture accounts for less than half of employment in the regions in the south, compared to over 70 percent in the upper west region.

Women have less access to productive jobs than men do. First, women are more likely to be inactive than men, largely because of family or household responsibilities that claim much of their time (when these unremunerated activities are counted as "work," women work more hours than men). Second, women dominate Ghana's large sector of self-employment outside of farm activities. Less than 10 percent of women work in wage jobs, compared to one-third of men. Whether as self-employed or wage workers, women tend to work in less productive activities and earn less than men.

Youth are also disproportionately barred from better jobs and will present an even bigger challenge, given the bulge in young labor market entrants expected in the next five years. Youth are less likely than older adults to be working: in 2012, 52 percent of people aged 15–24 were employed, compared to 77 percent for the entire population. Part of this discrepancy is due to schooling: nearly one-third of youth are inactive because of studies. Nonetheless, youth also make up nearly half of all the inactive who are not in school, although they account for only one-third of the adult population. Youth who drop out of school early in order to work end up in poorly paying activities, with more than half employed in agriculture. This suggests that early dropout from school is primarily a rural phenomenon and/or that youth from poorer families must leave school early to make a living. The growth in the youth population (15–24 years of age) will be peaking in the coming decade, adding pressures on both education systems and job creation for less-educated youth.

While access to formal education has increased in Ghana, the quality of education remains a problem. Education levels have increased in Ghana, and gender disparities are falling in the younger generation. However, two out of five women still have no more than a primary education, one in four young women (ages 15–24) cannot read and write, and less than half of women older than 25 are literate. Transition from school into productive jobs is too slow, especially for girls who bear the burden of family duties. The highly educated are concentrated in the public sector, which pays the highest salaries, and in the private wage sector.

There may be barriers to income diversification. Households generally derive their labor income from *either* farm *or* off-farm sectors, but are not diversified across this divide. Less than 20 percent of households are diversified along the farm–off-farm divide, in the sense of having at least one individual engaged in an off-farm job and at least one in farm activity. Job diversification is also more common among households in the poorest quintiles as a strategy to cope with low labor income. However, there is significant diversification within the off-farm sector; most households have family members working in both wage employment and self-employment.

There are signs of dynamism in the private formal sector, although analysis is hampered by limitations in firm-level data. Private sector formal employment is a tiny share of total employment (about 2 percent) compared to informal firms and household enterprises, which account for 54 percent of total employment (about 6 million people). A vast majority (91 percent) of formal firms are microenterprises. The bulk of formal employment in 2012 was in large and old firms. The private formal sector is dynamic, yet segmented, World Bank Enterprise Surveys suggest. The share of new entrants and young firms is relatively high. Formal firms also experienced positive growth in employment and robust growth in labor productivity between 2010 and 2012, mostly driven by large firms and microenterprises. However, the formal enterprise sector suffers from a "missing middle": large firms appear to prosper, offer higher wages, are more productive, and account for more job creation, whereas small and medium enterprises (SMEs) struggle to grow. While the Enterprise Survey data were the only firm-level data available at the time of writing this report, they have their own limitations. Firm census data would be needed to support sound empirical analysis of the demand for jobs.

However, formalization has not been happening as would be expected, given the past high economic growth and the increasing share of workers engaged in household enterprises and small-scale entrepreneurship. The small size of the formal sector points to severe constraints to formalization: the majority (87 percent) of household enterprises are not registered with any government agency. Lack of knowledge about the potential benefits (and costs) of formalization, rather than monetary and time costs, seems to keep microenterprises in the informal sector. However, more analysis is needed to better understand why firms do not formalize, as would be expected given the economic development in Ghana in the past decade.

Firms of all sizes, formal and informal, rate access to finance as the major business constraint; however, the constraint is most severe for microenterprises and household enterprises. Real interest rates are high in Ghana, and credit is prohibitively expensive and not accessible to most firms, particularly microenterprises and informal enterprises that lack collateral and proper documentation. More than half of microenterprises and small registered firms report access to finance as the top obstacle to grow their business. Similarly, the vast majority of household enterprises operate without access to external finance. As a consequence, firms end up sourcing funds internally for both working capital and further investments. The lack of access to external finance also affects the ability of firms to manage liquidity, making them vulnerable to even small financial shocks and unable to invest in innovative activities. Competitiveness in export markets also suffers because they are unable to cover the higher costs associated with trade logistics.

Inadequate electricity supply is the second most commonly cited major constraint mentioned by firms of all sizes, leading to higher costs to firms and sporadic use of information and communication technologies (ICTs). Lack of regular power supplies creates major problems for firms of all sizes and especially for microentrepreneurs in rural areas, where access to electricity is very limited. The implications for firms' profitability and competition are huge, preventing them from producing during dark hours; reducing the development of modern capital-intensive technologies; and most important, preventing firms from exploiting the potential of ICT. Manufacturing is the most affected sector. In a 2015 survey, 27 percent of chief executive officers (CEOs) planned to cut jobs in the following six months, were the power crisis to persist. (AGI 2015).

Priorities and Possible Solutions

Going forward, Ghana will need to consider an integrated jobs strategy that addresses barriers in the business climate, deficiencies in skills, lack of competitiveness of job-creating sectors, problems with labor mobility, and comprehensive labor market regulation. Building on the positive results in reducing poverty, the development challenge for Ghana will be to continue its structural transformation into a modern economy, continue moving people out of poverty, and boost the earnings of all, especially the poor and vulnerable. This will require an integrated jobs strategy to increase the productivity of agriculture jobs and of the growing number of off-farm self-employment jobs, create more wage jobs in a modern and competitive private sector, and facilitate the labor and geographical mobility of workers to maximize the benefits of rapid urbanization. Although public wage jobs are the best paid in Ghana, expanding public sector employment is not a viable long-term vehicle for job creation, given the current difficulties with the unsustainable level of public expenditures on the wage bill—which has grown rapidly since 2010, and was still around 10 percent of GDP in 2015 (World Bank 2016).

Ghana needs to diversify its economy through gains in productivity in sectors like agribusiness, transport, construction, energy, and ICT services. Rapid urbanization has generated increased demand for processed food products in terms of both quantity and quality (certified products). The agroprocessing sector is underdeveloped to meet local (and global) demand and offers opportunities to create productive jobs, increase exports, and reduce the tremendous post-harvest losses that hurt farmers and traders. Besides manufacturing of processed food, trade and the logistics of moving these products to meet market demand will be important to consider when tackling job creation, given that the majority of off-farm jobs are actually in trade services. Importantly, the "post-processing" (packaging, logistics, and marketing services) sectors offer opportunities to employ youth that are more attractive than farming (for the many young Africans who do not want to be the farmers their grandparents were).

A more inclusive growth strategy is needed to generate more and productive jobs for all. While addressing the current macroeconomic challenges through the stabilization program supported by the International Monetary Fund (IMF), the World Bank, and other development partners, it is crucial for Ghana to promote diversification and economic growth in sectors other than the extractive industries (oil and gold); instead, sectors with high potential to create jobs should be prioritized (World Bank 2016). Channeling resources from high-value added sectors to sectors with high potential to create jobs should be considered as a policy toward making growth more inclusive. The manufacturing sectors, which are traditionally more labor intensive, have been particularly vulnerable to the recent high inflation, depreciation of the cedi, and relatively high cost of labor with respect to China (Ceglowsky et al. 2015). However, industries such as agribusiness may have positive spillovers on nonmanufacturing jobs up and down the supply chain, supporting the creation of financial, transport, and logistical services.

Encouraging the competitiveness of its exports would help Ghana tap into markets abroad. Given the economic slowdown since 2012, it is important for Ghana to find alternative sources of demand for its products on global markets. The depreciated cedi might help mitigate the effects of the "Resource Curse": a slowdown in tradable sectors beyond natural resources because of an appreciation of the real exchange rate, hampering economic diversification. However, it must be recognized that building export competitiveness will be challenging, given the international environment for trade. A clear priority is identifying key issues for consideration to promote agro-based industrialization in global and regional trade corridors.

Expanding firms' connectivity to local, regional, and global markets would help increase their competitiveness, product sophistication, and exports. Whereas foreign markets could be a source of demand for Ghana's products and services, natural resources (cocoa, gold, oil) accounted for an overwhelming share (87 percent) of exports in 2014; other exports (free on board) accounted for only 12 percent of GDP. Overall, only 8 percent of registered firms were exporting in 2013, and most of them were large firms. This suggests the need for reforms to improve trade logistics and strengthen linkages with neighboring trade partners. Policies aiming at developing value chains are viable policy options, including capacity building; extension; transfer of knowledge; and tools to help micro and small and medium enterprises (MSMEs) involved in the value chain locate new buyers and markets, improve basic business practices, develop logistical supply programs with buyers, and expand contract farming to enhance the links with smallholders. For example, the agroprocessing sector, which processes raw materials into market-ready products, offers opportunities to develop value chains, create productive jobs, and retain value locally (instead of exporting raw products).

Facilitating access to finance and ensuring reliable access to electricity and ICT are the top policy priorities for private firms in Ghana. Investment in the production and distribution of energy to ensure a consistent power supply would be a major step toward reducing constraints facing the industry sector, particularly manufacturing. Strengthening the financial sector to improve access to finance, primarily to MSMEs, needs to be prioritized. Furthermore, MSMEs, especially in the capital-intensive manufacturing sector, require longer-term financing, such as equity investments (World Bank 2015). Identifying innovative financing mechanisms that can build on existing initiatives (such as the Ghana Climate Innovation Center and donor partner activities) and leveraging a relatively small amount of finance are key to reforming the financial sector.

Investing in urban policies to stimulate internal demand and jobs in secondary towns would help reduce the jobs gap between major and minor cities and between regions. Urbanization in Ghana has not been restricted to Accra and Kumasi (GSS 2014b). Additional research is needed to better understand the challenge of generating jobs, and good jobs, across cities and regions, and to identify secondary towns through which industrial and migration strategies could spread the gains of more and better jobs across the country—and in particular to regions in the north that have benefitted less from the structural transformation that has occurred in the past few decades.

Improving agricultural productivity will be especially important to reach Ghana's poor. Ghana's jobs strategy needs to focus on how to make these jobs better. Despite the structural transformation that is taking place in Ghana, agriculture remains the dominant form of income for the bottom 40 percent of the population, employs 42 percent of workers, and will very likely continue to be a net job contributor in the foreseeable future. Unlocking Ghana's agricultural potential will require investments in the infrastructure—notably irrigation schemes—and modern production methods. More productive agricultural jobs will hinge on commercialization, both by helping smallholder farmers enter value chains and upgrading their skills, including literacy and numeracy levels, modernizing production technologies, and increasing access to digital technologies. Mobile/digital technology, for example, can be used to provide extension services, coordinate distribution of inputs, provide early warning systems for climatic shocks, and reduce search costs related to sales.

Enforcing ownership regulations would foster agricultural investment and labor mobility. Lack of property rights that define land ownership increases the risks of investing in agriculture and discourages mobility; for example, if land cannot be safely leased or sold, smallholders cannot readily migrate. The weak and unclear system of land rights also impedes seasonal and more permanent migration. There is a need to develop the system of land tenure so as to increase land property rights. Currently, material investment in improving and upgrading land is held back by a lack of clear ownership rules (GIZ 2011). Lack of property rights (land and assets) may be particularly constraining for women, affecting their economic and entrepreneurial opportunities. The Ghana legal framework does not impose particular restrictions on women (Hallward-Driemeier and others 2013).

However, qualitative evidence suggests that women often lack the title to property of their household enterprises, further limiting their access to finance (ISSER 2015).

Policies to improve access to credit and saving, upgrade skills and technology, and improve access to markets and links with formal firms are all possible instruments to increase the productivity of informal enterprises and eventually boost their rates of formalization. Informal entrepreneurs and workers suffer from similar but more severe constraints than formal firms, including lack of assets, no access to credit or modern technology, limited access to markets and value chains, lower skill levels and few opportunities to develop skills, and no social security coverage. Reduced mobility and family duties add to the burdens of female entrepreneurs. Policies aimed at facilitating access to finance and savings, and upgrading technical skills—as well as financial literacy, business management and practices, and socioemotional skills—through certified training and apprenticeships would help increase the productivity of the informal sector.

Informal jobs in Ghana also require greater security; incentives are needed to increase participation in the informal social security scheme. While informal workers are entitled to social security benefits through the voluntary third pillar of the Social Security National Insurance Trust (SSNIT), its coverage is very low. Coverage of informal workers is higher under the other public social protection instrument, the National Health Insurance Scheme, and it is sponsored by the government for poor people and workers.

Urban policies to improve the occupational health and safety conditions of informal workers are also needed. Urban policies should safeguard public space and property rights and not constrain household enterprises that operate in urban areas. Regulating these activities can help protect them from violence and theft and create the space and infrastructure for them to thrive. Improved urban planning will also need to be part of a broader strategy to manage urbanization and labor mobility. Involving street vendors in city planning and enhancing the dialogue between policy makers and urban street vendors would not only facilitate ownership of policies but also ensure that their needs are met, fostering industrial harmony.

Skills play an important role in labor market outcomes in Ghana, but their quality needs to be upgraded and their content adapted to the new jobs. While educational attainment has improved over time, education and training policies need to consider how to best strengthen the quality of basic education to ensure that key cognitive and socioemotional skills are imparted. At the post-secondary level, technical and vocational education and training (TVET), job training programs, and in particular apprenticeship training with private sector informal firms could expand labor market opportunities for young people by providing them with relevant on-the-job experience and market-ready skills (Adams, Johansson de Silva, and Razmara 2013; Honorati 2015). To increase the quality and effectiveness of programs to develop job-relevant skills, it is important to incentivize firms to train their staff, involve employers in the design of training curricula, and introduce certification of occupational standards. "Traditional," unregulated apprenticeships in informal enterprises are a common entry point for junior high school–aged youth into self-employment in Ghana. To increase the quality of these apprenticeships, it is important to link them to the formal, government-managed national apprenticeship system, which offers standard curricula, tests learning, and certifies master craftsmen.

Note

1. The reference period of 1991 to 2012 is linked to the availability of data for employment, as reported by three rounds of the Ghana Living Standard Survey (1991, 2005, 2012).

References

Adams, A. V., S. Johansson de Silva, and S. Razmara. 2013. *Improving Skills Development in the Informal Sector: Strategies for Sub-Saharan Africa*. Directions in Development: Human Development. Washington, DC: World Bank.

AGI (Association of Ghana Industries). 2015. Business Barometer, 1st Quarter 2015. www.agighana.org.

Ceglowsky, J., A. Aly Mbaye, S. S. Golub, and V. Prasand. 2015. "Can Africa Compete with China in Manufacturing? The Role of Relative Unit Labor Costs." Working Paper 201504, Development Policy Research Unit, World Bank, Washington, DC.

GIZ (Deutsche Gesellschaft für Internationale Zusammenarbeit, German International Cooperation). 2011. *Financing Agricultural Value Chains in Africa: Focus on Pineapples, Cashews and Cocoa in Ghana*. Eschborn, Germany: GIZ.

GSS (Ghana Statistical Service). 2014a. "Poverty Profile in Ghana (2005–2013)." GSS, Accra, Ghana (August).

———. 2014b. "Ghana Living Standard Survey Round 6 (GLSS6). Main Report." GSS, Accra, Ghana.

Hallward-Driemeier, M., T. Hasan, J. Kamangu, E. Lobti, and M. Blackden. 2013. "Women's Legal and Economic Empowerment Database for Africa (Women LEED Africa)." Development Economics, World Bank, Washington, DC.

Honorati, M. 2015. "The Impact of Private Sector Training and Internship on Urban Youth in Kenya." Policy Research Working Paper 7404, World Bank, Washington, DC.

ISSER (Institute of Statistical, Social and Economic Research). 2015. "Public Policy and Enterprise Development in Ghana." ISSER Policy Brief No. 2, University of Ghana (August).

Molini, V., and P. Paci. 2015. "Poverty Reduction in Ghana: Progress and Challenges." World Bank, Washington, DC.

UN (United Nations). 2014. World Urbanization Prospects: The 2014 Revision (database). Population Division, Department of Economic and Social Affairs (accessed September 2015–January 2016), https://esa.un.org/unpd/wup/.

World Bank. 2015. "Ghana Manufacturing Competitiveness." World Bank, Washington, DC.

———. 2016. "Ghana Public Expenditure Review 2016. Fiscal Consolidation for Growth and Employment." World Bank, Washington, DC.

CHAPTER 1

The Context for Job Creation in Ghana

Main Messages

In the past 20 years, Ghana has achieved tremendous reductions in poverty. Ghana's success story is underpinned by high and sustained economic growth. In the past 10 years, in particular, there has been a significant change in the composition of value added and employment, from agriculture to services. During this structural transformation from farm to off-farm activities, the urban population has increased rapidly because of migration from rural areas, as well as natural demographic growth.

During the past decade, economic growth has accelerated compared to the previous decade, and poverty has fallen further; however, economic growth has also become less *efficient* in reducing poverty, as most of the growth has been driven by sectors that do not generate much employment, such as mining and construction. Instead, jobs have been created in low-productivity sectors like trade. Inequalities across regions, and between poor and nonpoor households, have increased. Moreover, the current macroeconomic crisis threatens to unravel some of the gains in reducing poverty.

These facts suggest that while Ghana has experienced high economic growth in the past decade, the economy has not created enough productive jobs, and now faces the challenges of reinstating macroeconomic stability and confidence in the economy and fostering more inclusive growth during a time of economic slowdown.

The Ghana Success Story: Two Decades of High Growth and Significant Poverty Reduction

In the past 20 years, Ghana's economic growth has outpaced that of most African lower-middle-income peers (figure 1.1); the country achieved middle-income status in 2011. Economic growth has been consistently high, and has accelerated in the past 10 years. Real gross domestic product (GDP) growth rates averaged

Figure 1.1   Economic Growth in Ghana as Compared with Its African Peers

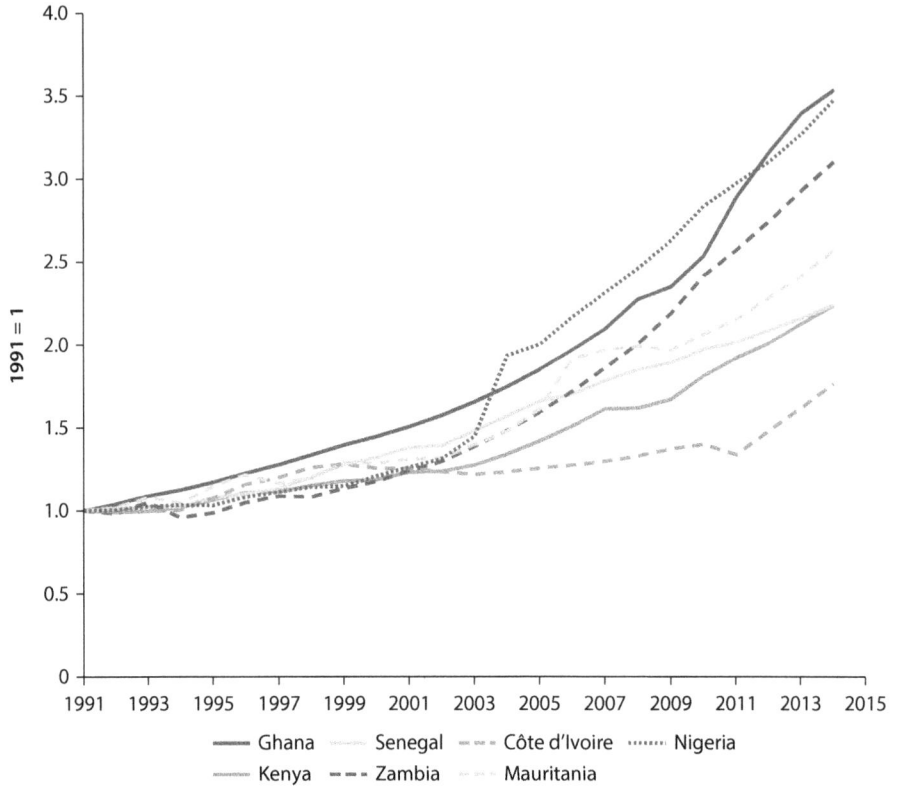

Source: World Development Indicators (WDI).

more than 4.3 percent between 1991 and 2000, increased to around 5 percent
between 2000 and 2005, and accelerated further to 8 percent between 2006 and
2012, peaking at 14 percent in 2011, when Ghana started producing oil. In 2012,
the GDP growth rate slowed down, and it fell to 4 percent in 2014. GDP growth
is projected to fall further to about 3 percent in 2015, as energy rationing, high
inflation, and ongoing fiscal consolidation continue to undermine economic
activity in all sectors (figure 1.2, panel a) (World Bank 2016a).

Ghana's growth performance has been driven by natural resources and has
been characterized by a rapid expansion in the services sector (especially in
recent years), while the contribution of agriculture has steadily declined.
Economic growth has been fueled by strong price increases in its main commodity exports, cocoa and gold, for which prices more than tripled between 2000 and
2010 (figure 1.2, panel b) and the start of commercial oil production in 2011,
which sparked consumption and investment booms. Whereas oil production has
increased, gold production has recently suffered considerably, as several gold
mines closed as a result of the reversion in international prices after 2012.
The share of services in GDP increased dramatically from less than one-third of

GDP (32 percent) in 2005 to 50 percent in 2012 (figure 1.3, panel a). The increase in the share of services represents increases in information and communications technology (ICT), transport, finance, and the increasing number of microenterprises operating retail and wholesale activities. The contribution of industry to growth comes from commercial oil production and construction, rather than from manufacturing (figure 1.3, panel b).

Figure 1.2 Natural Resources as Drivers of Growth

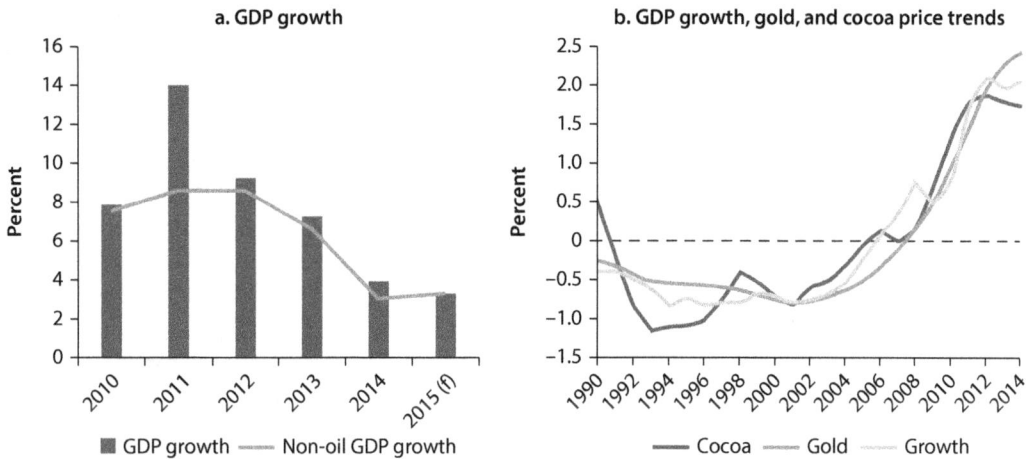

a. GDP growth

b. GDP growth, gold, and cocoa price trends

Sources: Aykut and Herrera 2015 and World Bank 2016a.
Note: For panel b, five-year moving averages, normalized, percent. 2015(f) = forecast.

Figure 1.3 Economic Structure and Contribution to Growth, by Sector

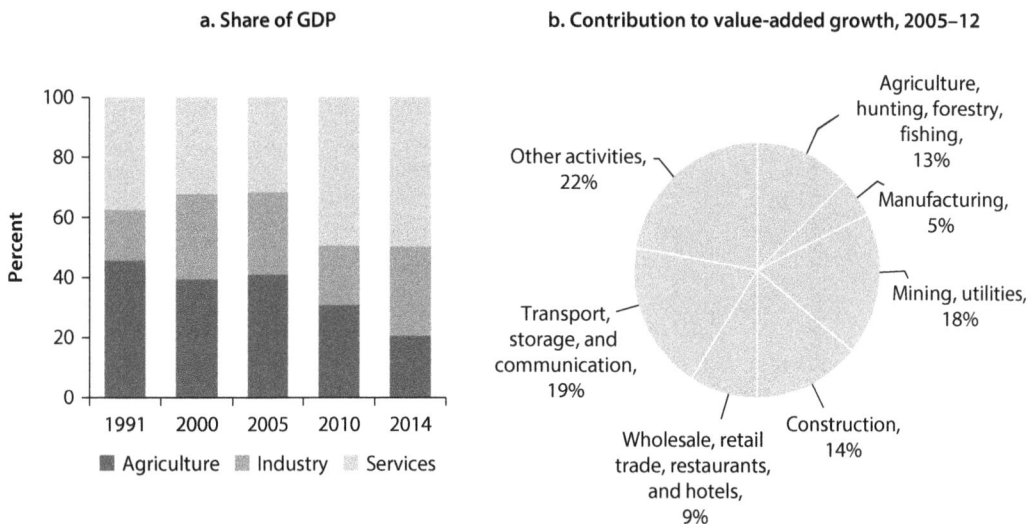

a. Share of GDP

b. Contribution to value-added growth, 2005–12

Sources: WDI; national accounts (UN 2014b).

Expanding Job Opportunities in Ghana • http://dx.doi.org/10.1596/978-1-4648-0941-5

The manufacturing sector has been "the missing middle" in the recent growth process. As in other African countries, the share of the manufacturing sector has been declining over time. Between 2005 and 2012, the manufacturing sector contributed only 5 percent to the total increase in value added. The higher cost of inputs has undermined the already low competitiveness of the sector (Ceglowsky and others 2015). A recent report from the United Nations (UN) Economic Commission for Africa shows that the African manufacturing sector, traditionally including the more labor-intensive industries, provides only 6 percent of all jobs, compared to 16 percent in Asia (UN 2015). Unlike in Asian countries, the structural transformation in Ghana skipped the intermediate stage of moving from agriculture to traditional manufacturing industries. Workers leaving agriculture have been absorbed mostly in the services sector, and mostly in urban areas, accommodating the higher demand created by the recent rapid rise in urbanization.

Ghana has made remarkable progress in increasing living standards and reducing poverty and deprivation along many dimensions. Extreme poverty was halved in the past two decades and MDG1 met. In 1991, around one out of two Ghanaians (53 percent) lived in poverty, and nearly two out of five (38 percent) lived in extreme poverty. By 2012—only two decades later—one in five Ghanaians (21 percent) lived in poverty, and one in ten (10 percent) in extreme poverty (GSS 2014; Molini and Paci 2015). Other social indicators such as life expectancy, child mortality, and hunger now approach those of countries with higher average levels of income (figure 1.4, table 1.1). Educational attainment has also increased.

Figure 1.4 Decline in Poverty Rates in Ghana

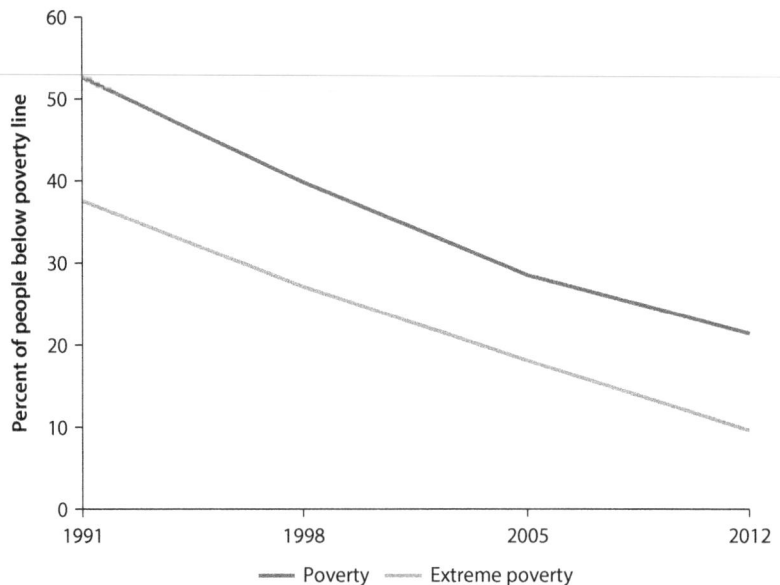

Source: Molini and Paci 2015.

Table 1.1 Social Indicators in Ghana as Compared with Middle-Income Countries and Sub-Saharan Africa

	Ghana	Cameroon	Côte d'Ivoire	Kenya	Nigeria	Mauritania	Congo, Rep.	Senegal	Zambia	Sub-Saharan Africa
GDP per capita ($, 2014)	1,442	1,407	1,546	1,358	3,203	1,275	3,147	1,067	1,722	1,776
Life expectancy at birth (years)	61	55	51	61	52	63	62	66	59	58
Maternal mortality ratio (modeled est., per 100,000)	319	596	645	510	814	602	442	315	224	547
Under-5 mortality rate (per 1,000)	62	88	93	49	109	85	45	47	64	83
Prevalence of undernour-ishment (% of pop.)	5	11	15	24	6	7	32	17	48	19
Adult literacy rate (% of pop. 15+)	71	71	41	72	51	46	79	43	61	60
Improved water source (% of rural pop. with access)	84	53	69	57	57	57	40	67	51	56

Sources: FAO 2015; WDI, latest available 2006–15.
Note: est. = estimate; pop. = population.

New Challenges: Less Inclusive Growth and Macroeconomic Imbalances

While poverty has continued to fall, economic growth has become less pro-poor in recent years. Significant progress was made on poverty between the early 1990s and 2005, when the headcount index fell from 53 percent to 29 percent of the population. While poverty has continued to fall since 2005, from 29 percent to 21 percent, the rate of poverty reduction has slowed down—in a period when economic growth has accelerated considerably. The average poverty-to-growth elasticity (the percentage change in poverty given a percentage change in consumption growth) fell from over 2.0 percent in 1991–2005 to 0.7 percent in 2005–12 (GSS 2014; Molini and Paci 2015).

Poverty reduction has been accompanied by growing inequality in terms of income levels and across regions. At the national level, inequality increased; the Gini index rose by almost 9 percent, from 37.5 in 1991 to 40.8 in 2012. Moreover, the poverty rate in the northern part of the country has declined much

less than in the rest of the country, largely reflecting the northern area's dependence on low-productivity subsistence farming. In 2012, more than one-third of
national poverty was concentrated in the three northern regions, where only
17 percent of the population lives. The concentration of Ghana's very poor grew
from 25 percent to 40 percent from 1991 to 2012 in the north (Molini and
Paci 2015). There are also significant disparities in other social indicators across
income quintiles and between the north and south, for example in access to basic
health and education services (World Bank 2016b).

Large macroeconomic imbalances now threaten growth and continued
poverty reduction. The major drivers of the large fiscal deficit have been the
rapidly growing public wage bill, interest payments on public debt, energy
subsidies, lower growth, and higher inflation. The government of Ghana
(GoG) has been addressing these imbalances, but as of late 2014, significant
imbalances remained, including a fiscal (cash) deficit of about 9.5 percent of
GDP, driven in part by the high public wage bill, interest payments, and
energy subsidies. The fiscal consolidation effort in 2015 included the reduction of energy subsidies, a new tax on petroleum products, and more decisive
containment of the wage bill. Media reports suggest that, together with the
lingering effects of a power crisis, some of the measures to increase government income have increased the cost of doing business and have led to job
cuts across industry and services sectors, including the manufacturing sector
and the telecom business.[1] The large macroeconomic imbalances reduce
Ghana's attractiveness for investment and reduce the resources available for
reforms.

Growing Working-Age Population and Significant Urbanization

The share of Ghana's working-age population has increased relative to dependent children. Ghana's growth period has also been accompanied by demographic changes that are both the cause and effect of the nature of economic
growth. Ghana's population growth is still high (2.5 percent per year between
2000 and 2014), but has fallen since the mid-1980s, when it reached over 3
percent. As a result of this transition, the working-age population—adults who
are between 15 and 64 years of age—is increasing as a share of total population,
from 49 percent in 1991 to 56 percent in 2012, while the share of dependent
children is falling. The share of young adults (15- to 24-year-olds) increased less,
from 17 to 19 percent, in the same period. Compared to Sub-Saharan Africa as
a whole, Ghana now has an older population with a lower share of children and
youth. These numbers translate into an increase of 7.4 million people in the
adult population between 1991 and 2012, or around 350,000 people per year
(figure 1.5).

The urban population has increased rapidly because of internal migration and
natural demographic factors. Around 1.5 million people flowed into urban areas
in 1991–98; 1.9 million in 1998–2005; and 4.7 million in 2005–12. In 1991, 70
percent of Ghana's population was living in rural areas. As of 2009, however,

Figure 1.5 Ghana's Population, by Age and Gender

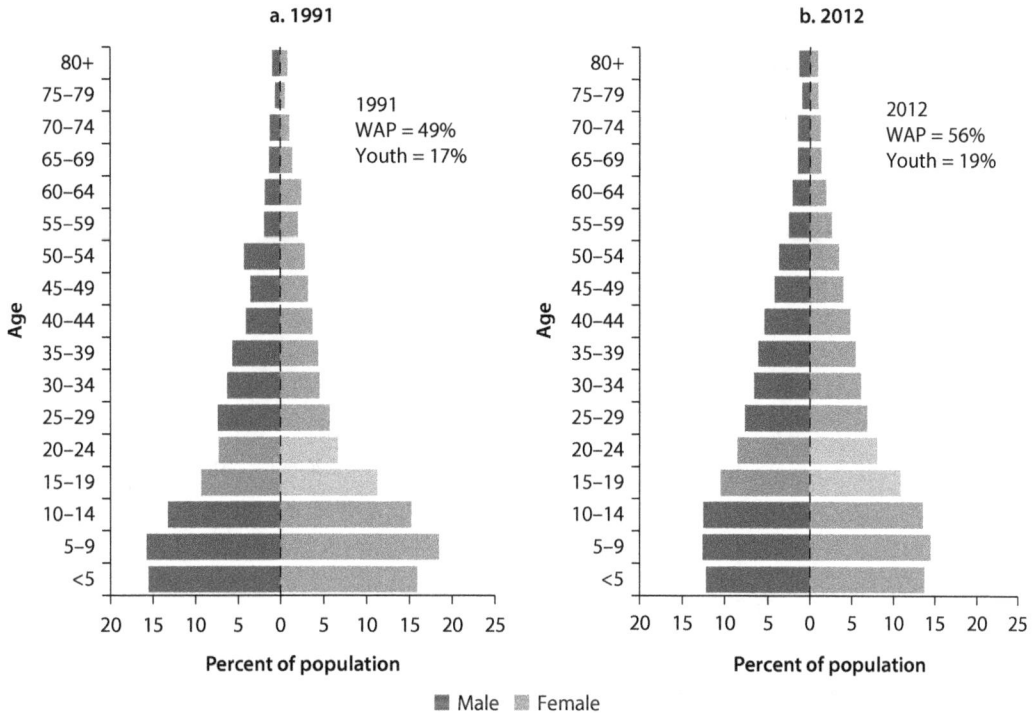

a. 1991

1991
WAP = 49%
Youth = 17%

b. 2012

2012
WAP = 56%
Youth = 19%

Percent of population

Percent of population

■ Male ▨ Female

Source: Estimates based on Ghana Living Standards Surveys (GLSS), Rounds 3 and 6.
Note: WAP = working-age population.

Ghana's urban population has overtaken the rural population, although both urban and rural populations continue to expand (figure 1.6). The share of urban population is expected to rise from slightly more than 50–70 percent by 2050 (UN 2014a). Since 1991, Accra and Kumasi have more than doubled, gaining over 2.4 million inhabitants each. In addition to migration, other demographical phenomena are contributing to the growth in the urban population, such as a rapid increase of household size and lower mortality rates in urban areas (Jedwab, Christiansen, and Gindelsky 2014). These demographic trends have resulted in markedly different population structures between rural and urban areas; the share of dependents (children) relative to adults is higher in rural areas, which is likely to contribute to differences in poverty (figure 1.7).

Urbanization has brought opportunities to Ghana's population, but also comes with its own set of challenges. Urban growth has been surprisingly balanced, in the sense that it has happened across all regions and across all sizes of towns and cities (box 1.1). The inflow of workers in cities coincided with a fall in unemployment, and urban areas have significantly lower poverty rates and better access to services. Nonetheless, urban areas are suffering from lack of planning and insufficient infrastructure investments, which in

Figure 1.6 Growth of Urban and Rural Populations

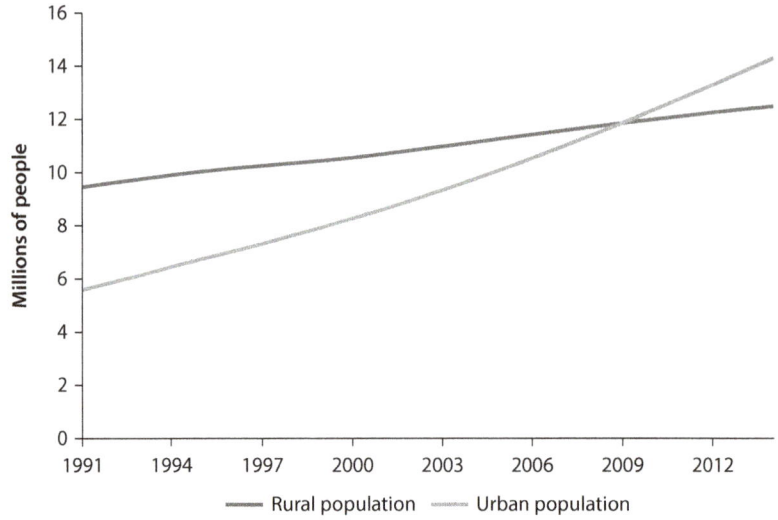

Source: WDI.

Figure 1.7 Urban and Rural Population, by Age and Gender, 2010

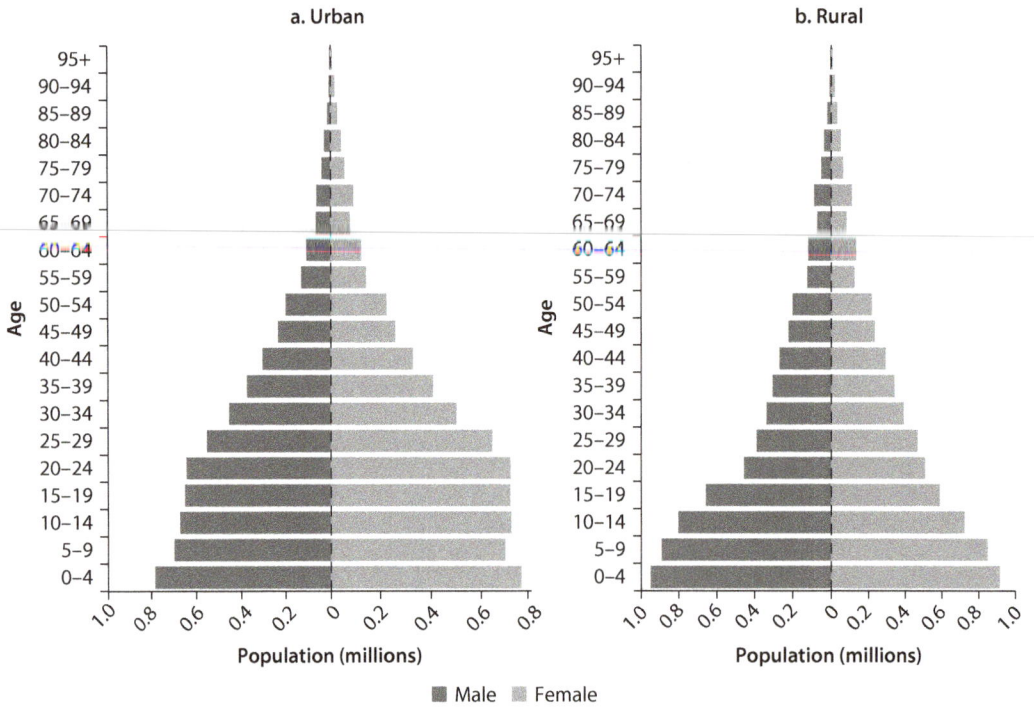

Source: 2010 Population and Housing Census (GSS 2013).

Box 1.1 Opportunities and Challenges of Urbanization

Urbanization has accelerated in Ghana, especially in the past seven years, when the share of urban population surpassed rural population. Currently, 51 percent of Ghana's population lives in urban areas. A particular feature of recent years is that urban growth has been surprisingly balanced: all regions of the country have experienced urbanization, and all types of cities—from small towns to metropolitan areas—have expanded. In fact, urban population growth has been faster in smaller cities than in larger ones. Accra's share of urban population fell from one-fourth in 1984 to about one-sixth in 2010. Urbanization has taken place in a context of high economic growth and the promise of better job opportunities and living conditions. Since 2005, in a period when the urban population has increased by nearly 50 percent, urban unemployment rates nonetheless have fallen.

Urban growth and the concentration of population in urban areas are necessary conditions for accelerated growth and shared prosperity. However, they are not sufficient conditions, as many African countries have demonstrated. Urbanization is traditionally seen as an intrinsic part of a structural transformation process that involves workers moving out of agriculture and into more productive tradable and nontradable sectors that flourish in "production cities." However, while Ghana has an urbanization rate similar to that of China, Indonesia, and Thailand, it is considerably poorer, and has a different economic structure. The differences between Africa and Asia appear to stem from different growth models underpinning the urbanization processes. In Asia, urbanization has been the result of productivity increases in agriculture and manufacturing, resulting in high employment in the tradable sector, with widespread benefits. In many African countries, including Ghana, urbanization has instead resulted from higher income from commodities and natural resource exports, which has spilled over into high demand for nontradables, largely services, resulting in "consumption cities." African countries are consequently becoming more and more urbanized—without becoming more industrialized.

Urbanization has brought benefits to Ghana: poverty rates are much lower in urban than rural areas. Moreover, access to secondary and tertiary education has increased significantly, as the concentration of the population is facilitating access to educational institutions, as well as support services. Quality of life has also improved, in terms of access to services, such as access to electricity, solid and liquid waste disposal, toilet facilities, and piped water.

Urbanization has also brought more jobs, mostly in the trade sector; these have been characterized by self-employment rather than wage jobs. The share of manufacturing in Ghana's economy has shrunk dramatically over time, consistent with the framework of "consumption cities." Urbanization has consequently offered increasing job opportunities for Ghana's growing urban populations, but has not provided significantly more productive jobs, or jobs in sectors where productivity can be expected to grow rapidly over time.

Urbanization has also brought new challenges to Ghana, and its benefits have not been fully reaped in terms of productivity, social inclusion, and poverty reduction. Since rapid growth has been occurring at a relatively early stage of development, urbanization has been happening without sufficient urban planning and infrastructure investments to increase

box continues next page

Box 1.1 Opportunities and Challenges of Urbanization *(continued)*

benefits of agglomeration and manage negative externalities. As a result, slums are spreading, environmental degradation is increasing, and other negative pressures from urbanization are rising. Uncoordinated spatial expansion results in limited connectivity within urban cities, and insufficient infrastructure investments means that there is also limited connectivity between cities. Moreover, an increasing number of urban residents do not have access to urban services, particularly toilet facilities in some form.

The government of Ghana identifies several challenges from the urbanization process in terms of *productivity* (such as weak transportation planning and traffic management, inadequate land use, and weak rural-urban linkages); *inclusion* (more specifically increasing insecurity, slums, environmental deterioration, weak infrastructure, and lack of services); and *institutions* (including weak urban governance and lack of urban-specific data and information for results-based decision making).

As suggested by the Ghana Urbanization Review, Ghana can foster more economically productive and socially inclusive urbanization by addressing the following areas: (a) strengthening land markets, through stronger land use management and planning; (b) improving connectivity within and between cities, by establishing efficient transport infrastructure; and (c) exploring sustainable ways of financing these reforms and enhancing institutions and coordination as they relate to issues of urbanization.

Sources: Gollin, Jedwab, and Vollrath 2013; Freire, Lall, and Leipziger 2014; World Bank 2008a, 2015.

---

turn results in slum development and negative environmental effects. More specifically, "urbanization" has not been connected with "industrialization" in Ghana, suggesting that some of the potential benefits of agglomeration have not been reaped.

Labor Productivity and Job Creation in Ghana: Quality versus Quantity of Jobs

Growth does not necessarily translate into poverty reduction; the different forces that underpin growth matter—in particular, whether economic growth translates into more productive jobs for the poor. The link between economic growth and job creation depends on the extent to which growth generates employment, while the poverty-reducing effects of employment generation depend on the type of jobs that responded to growth: notably on the extent to which poor workers benefit from the new jobs. Thus the poverty-reducing effect of economic growth depends on the quantity and quality of jobs created from growth.

Generally, labor income is by far the most important source of livelihood for the poor, who have few assets other than their own work to draw on to make a living. Whether economic growth trickles down to the labor income of the poor depends on how and where it takes place. This process is not necessarily connected to the creation of jobs per se, but to the creation of jobs that offer better earnings for poor people. More specifically, there is evidence that the labor income of the poor benefits from growth processes that involve increases in labor productivity in low-productivity sectors, and shifts of workers from low-productivity to higher-productivity sectors (World Bank 2008b, 2008c).

In recent years, job creation has more than kept up with the growth of the working-age population. Annual job creation growth averaged 3.2 percent a year between 1991 and 2005, according to data from the Ghana Living Standard Survey (GLSS). However, this was not sufficient to keep up with the 3.8 percent per year increase in the potential workforce—the population aged 15–64. By contrast, as of 2005, growth in employment significantly outpaced the growth in the working-age population. While annual job creation reached 4.0 percent between 2005 and 2012, annual growth in the working-age population fell back to 2.6 percent.

For a given level of economic growth, however, the Ghanaian economy has created relatively few jobs. Between 2005 and 2012, average economic growth increased 8.0 percent per year, while average annual employment growth grew 4.0 percent per year, meaning that every 1.0 percent increase in economic growth was associated with 0.5 percent increase in job growth, regardless of the type of job. In this period, growth increased significantly compared to the 1991–2005 period, while employment increased only marginally. As a result, the employment-growth elasticity (the percentage change in employment given a 1.0 percentage point change in growth) dropped to 0.5 from an average of 0.7 in the 15 preceding years. This suggests a marginal slowdown in job creation in response to economic growth that was driven by sectors that generate low employment: mining and commercial oil production. The Ghana employment-growth elasticity is below the Africa average (0.72) and aligned with the average for lower-middle-income countries (0.6) (figure 1.8). This lower elasticity implies fewer jobs for a given level of economic growth. Conversely, it is also a sign of higher growth in labor productivity.

In tandem with a strong urbanization process, the structure of both value added and employment has changed over time. In particular, both value added and employment have shifted from agriculture into services, although value added has also increased in the mining industry, especially in the past decade. The boom in service value added happened between 1991 and 2005, while the increase in its share of employment took place after 2005. Within the industry and services sectors, more complex changes have been occurring. Mining and construction have become more important than manufacturing in terms of value added, but have become comparatively less labor intensive. While the trade sector share in value added has remained relatively constant over time, its share in employment has increased quite significantly since 2005 (table 1.2).

The share of agriculture in GDP and employment has declined steadily—especially in the past decade—as in several other countries in Sub-Saharan Africa, but agriculture remains the mainstay for many of the poor. Agriculture is declining in terms of its contribution to total output (as well as employment). Nonetheless, the agricultural sector still has specific significance as a

Figure 1.8 Ghana's Employment-Growth Elasticity Compared with Other Lower-Middle-Income Countries

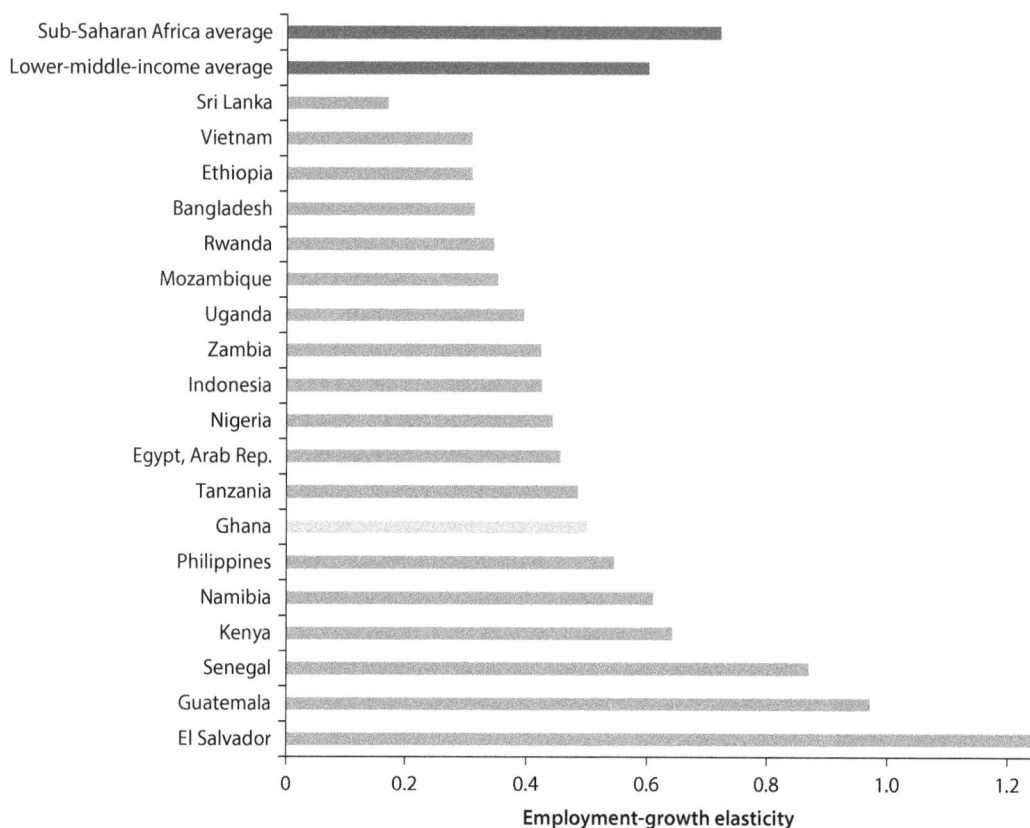

Sources: WDI; GLSS 5 and GLSS6 for Ghana.
Note: The employment to GDP growth elasticity refers to average annual employment growth and GDP growth between 2005 and 2012.

Table 1.2 Value Added and Employment, by Economic Sector

	Value added			Employment		
	1991	2005	2012	1991	2005	2012
Agriculture, hunting, forestry, fishing	36	32	24	61	53	43
Industry	28	20	27	11	15	14
Manufacturing	21	10	8	9	12	9
Mining, utilities	3	4	10	1	1	2
Construction	4	6	9	1	2	3
Services	36	48	48	29	31	43
Wholesale, retail trade, restaurants, and hotels	8	11	10	17	18	25
Transport, storage, and communication	12	16	17	2	3	4
Other activities	16	21	21	10	10	14

Source: Estimates based on national accounts from UN 2014b (value added) and GLSS3, GLSS5, and GLSS6 (employment, 15- to 64-year-olds).

key source of livelihood for many of the poor (box 1.2). The share of value added from mining increased from 3 percent to 10 percent, and the share of value added from construction grew from 4 percent to 9 percent between 1991 and 2012; this is a structural change that is not reflected in an increased employment share. Conversely, the share of wholesale and trade in total employment increased substantially, especially between 2005 and 2012, while its share of value added remained almost the same. Manufacturing, which was the leading subsector within industry until 2005, experienced a drop in its share of value added to less than half of what it was in 1991—bringing its share below those of mining and construction—while its share in total employment remained constant.

Most job creation in recent years has taken place in economic sectors with relatively low labor productivity, and in urban self-employment, rather than wage employment. The main source of jobs creation has been the trade services sectors. However, employment also increased in other services activities such as financial and business services and public administration. In total, Ghana's economy created nearly 3 million jobs between 2005 and 2012, of which most were in urban areas and nearly half were in the trade sector (figure 1.9). The agriculture sector, while shrinking in relative terms, continued to create a significant number of jobs in absolute terms. With the exception of construction, the industry sector created very few jobs, however. Thus, more than half of all jobs were created in the two economic sectors with the lowest levels of labor productivity, as measured by value added per worker (figure 1.10).

Thus the overall poverty-reducing effects of Ghana's economic growth slowed down in the past decade, in part because the growing self-employment in trade and retail services offered limited productivity gains compared to agriculture. The limited productivity gains associated with employment shifts out of agriculture—in particular, the low labor productivity associated with the expansion of jobs in the trade sector—is hence one of the determinants for the decrease in the rate of reduction in poverty for a given level of growth (poverty elasticity) in recent years. The role of returns to worker characteristics (education, access to infrastructure) in explaining poverty reduction declined substantially between 2005 and 2012, as opposed to the period between 1991 and 2005, when the transformation from farming to off-farming activities was paying a higher premium (Molini and Paci 2015). A breakdown (Shapley decomposition) (box 1.3) of the contributions of productivity, employment, and demographics to growth, measured as growth in value added per capita, also sheds light on the dynamics within and between sectors in the two periods when the economy experienced major structural changes (1991–2005 and 2005–12).[2]

Between 1991 and 2005, growth was equally driven by labor productivity and demographic increases. The labor productivity increases, in turn, were mainly due to the structural transformation of the economy: that is, the intersectoral shift out from agriculture and into more productive sectors like transports and construction.

Box 1.2 The Role of Agriculture in Structural Change and Poverty Reduction in Africa

The views of the role of agriculture in growth and poverty reduction, globally and in Sub-Saharan Africa, have varied greatly. Development planning in the 1960s and 1970s focused on industrialization, resulting in an "urban bias" in development. However, a shift toward focusing on poverty reduction in addition to growth led to a renewed interest in the role of agriculture: it is generally the sector where most of the poor, and the most poor, work, but also a sector that has a potentially strong direct and indirect impact on economic growth.

In poor economies, agricultural productivity growth is critical to both structural change and poverty reduction. Agricultural productivity tends to be significantly lower than in other sectors. African workers in the nonagricultural sector are six times as productive as agricultural workers, according to national accounts data (value added/total employment). However, new evidence from microdata suggests that these productivity differences are largely due to underemployment (fewer hours worked); productivity differences are much smaller on the basis of per hour worked.

Higher productivity in agriculture raises family incomes and increases demand for products and services in the nonagricultural sector. The role of agriculture in poverty reduction goes far beyond its direct impact on farmers' incomes. There is evidence that increasing agricultural productivity has benefitted millions through higher incomes, through more plentiful and cheaper food, and by generating patterns of development that are employment-intensive and benefit both rural and urban areas. Thus, a reduction in agricultural employment results in a structural change toward more productive jobs as (if) underemployed workers, equipped with the right skills and other assets, can take up jobs in the nonagricultural sector. In Sub-Saharan Africa, unlike Asian countries in an earlier era, this structural change has resulted in new jobs in the services sector rather than the manufacturing industry.

In Ghana, policies, investment, and institutional reforms in the 1990s and since have helped improve agricultural productivity and increase domestic food and cocoa production. Ghana is the third largest producer of cocoa in the world and the second largest exporter after Côte d'Ivoire (cocoa beans represent almost 30 percent of export revenues). Small-scale farmers, especially cash crop growers, have benefitted from increasing agricultural productivity and rising incomes and consumption.

Globally, agricultural growth has been shown to be significantly more effective for poverty reduction among the very poorest (those living on less than $1 per day) than nonagricultural growth because more of the poorest are working in agriculture. However, for the next level of poverty ($2 per day), growth in the nonagricultural sectors is more effective. No poor country has ever successfully reduced poverty through agriculture alone, but almost none have achieved it without first increasing agricultural productivity.

Sources: DFID 2005; Christiansen, Demery, and Kuhl 2011; Ghana, Ministry of Food and Agriculture 2013; McCullough 2015.

Figure 1.9 Total Employment Creation, by Economic Sector, 2005–12
Thousands

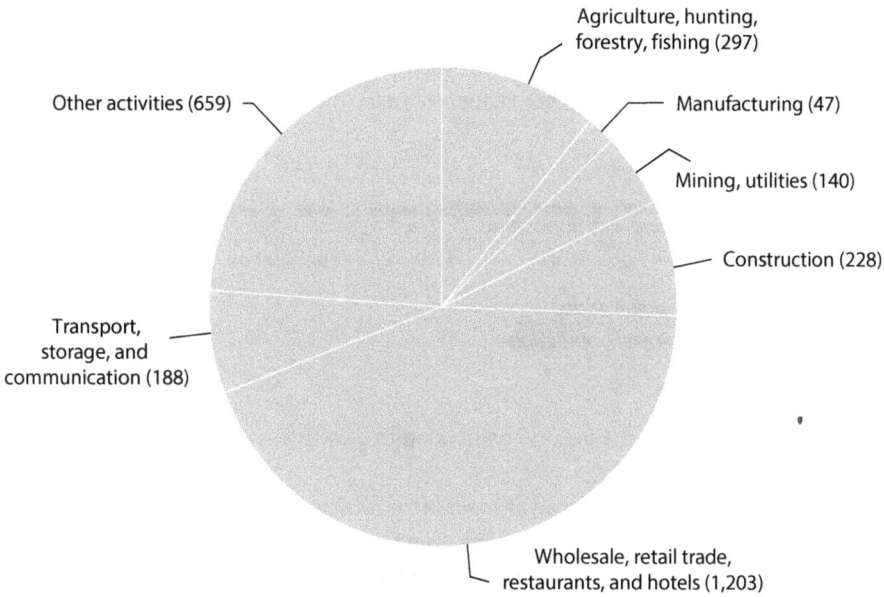

- Agriculture, hunting, forestry, fishing (297)
- Manufacturing (47)
- Mining, utilities (140)
- Construction (228)
- Wholesale, retail trade, restaurants, and hotels (1,203)
- Transport, storage, and communication (188)
- Other activities (659)

Source: Estimates based on GLSS5 and GLSS6.
Note: Number of additional jobs created between 2005 and 2012 are in parentheses (thousands).

Figure 1.10 Value Added per Worker, by Economic Sector and Year

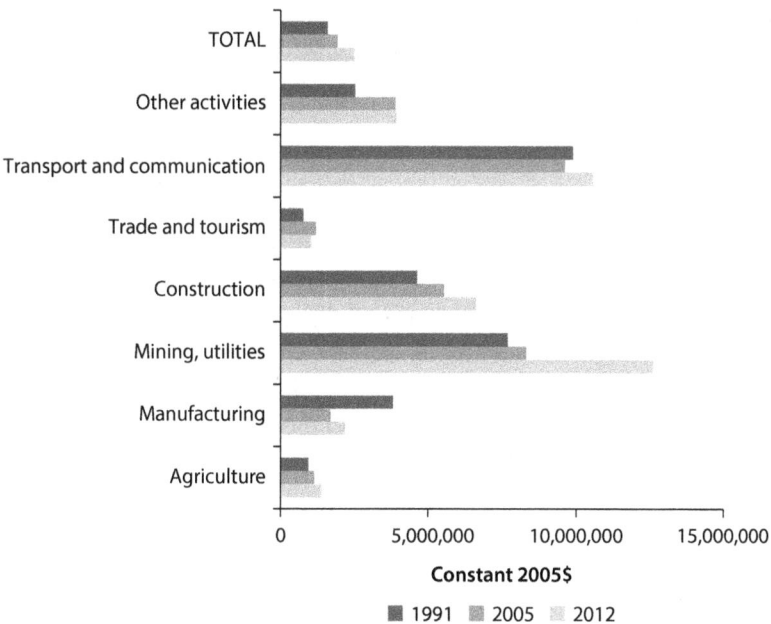

Source: Estimates based on UN 2014b, GLSS3, GLSS5, and GLSS6.

Box 1.3 Separating Out the Drivers of Growth

A so-called Shapley decomposition helps separate out the various contributions to economic growth (increases in value added per capita) over time from demographics, employment, and productivity dynamics, holding other factors constant. The underlying relationship can be described as follows:

$$\frac{Value\ added}{Population} = \frac{Working\text{-}age\ population}{Population} \times \frac{Employed\ population}{Working\text{-}age\ population} \times$$

$$\frac{Value\ added}{Employed\ population}$$

Considered separately, the factors contributing to growth in value added per capita are defined as follows:

Demographic changes. An increase of adults in the total population, increasing the share of potential workers relative to dependents. The contribution of demographics to growth is thus the contribution to value added per capita of an increase in the share of the working-age population in the total population, if employment rates and labor productivity had remained constant.

Changes in employment rates. Changes in the share of employed workers in the working-age population

Changes in labor productivity. The change in value added per worker.

The contributions of total labor productivity growth can further be separated into contributions through *within-sector growth* in value added per worker versus increases that arise from the flow of workers from less productive sectors to more productive sectors.

The employment effect, however, was negative, because the relative reduction in agricultural work was not compensated for by rapid job creation elsewhere. These developments coincided with a substantial fall in labor productivity in the manufacturing sector—or, put differently, an increase in labor intensity (table 1.3).

Since 2005, growth has been largely driven by increased labor productivity within sectors and by an intersectoral shift to more productive sectors (mining, construction, and services outside of trade). Per capita growth in value added between 2005 and 2012 was twice as high as in the previous period. The increase in labor productivity represented almost all (98 percent) of the change in value added per capita. Labor productivity was driven by intersectoral shifts, as well as increases in within-sector output per worker, and by an increase in employment-to-population ratios in different sectors. The highest sectoral contributions to growth came from mining (21 percent), other services (19 percent), transport and communication (16 percent), and

Table 1.3 Growth Decomposition in Ghana, by Sector

Sector Contribution	1991–2005 Percent contribution total growth in GDP				2005–12 Percent contribution to total growth of GDP			
	Within-sector changes in output per worker	Changes in employment	Intersectoral shifts	Total	Within-sector changes in output per worker	Changes in employment	Intersectoral shifts	Total
Agriculture, hunting, forestry, fishing	29	−49	12	−8	14	−15	12	11
Industry	−48	14	18	−16	18	4	18	40
Manufacturing	−53	10	7	−36	6	−4	1	3
Mining, utilities	1	1	5	8	8	3	10	21
Construction	4	3	6	12	4	5	7	16
Services	50	3	21	74	0	37	8	45
Wholesale, retail trade, restaurants, and hotels	18	1	−3	16	−4	22	−8	10
Transport, storage, and communication	−2	4	23	25	4	3	9	16
Other services	34	−2	1	33	0	12	7	19
Subtotal	31	−33	52	51	33	27	38	98
Demographic component	n.a.	n.a.		49	n.a.	n.a.		2
Total				100				100
Total % change in value added per capita, 1991–2005	26				Total % change in value added per capita, 2005–12	44		

Source: GLSS4, GLSS5, GLSS6; UN 2014b.

Note: n.a. = not applicable

construction (16 percent). The trade services sector, despite its gains in terms of job creation, has been the smallest net contributor to aggregate output, behind manufacturing. For the agricultural and manufacturing sectors, productivity growth has been linked to a relative shift of workers out of these sectors to mostly retail trade and other service activities. However, the sector that created the most jobs—trade—experienced a reduction in labor productivity. Declines in labor productivity in sectors that receive many new workers are not a problem per se, as long as labor productivity overall is higher than in the sectors in which employment shares are declining. However, the trade sector does not offer measurably higher-productivity jobs than agriculture (both sectors contribute the same amount to labor productivity growth: 9 percent). This may explain why the current growth model, driven by sectors that have low labor intensity, such as natural resources and construction, has had a lower effect on poverty compared to previous years.

In summary, increased labor productivity growth (measured as value added per worker) has been the main driver of Ghana's growth over the last decade, more than demographic components. In turn, the increased labor productivity has been driven by limited jobs creation in more productive economic sectors (mining, construction, transport), and by the movement of jobs from low- to higher-productivity sectors (out of agriculture), including other services such as financial and ICT services. The main transformation has been the reduction in the number of jobs in agriculture, which were essentially jobs in rural areas, and the emergence of new jobs in urban areas, mainly in services. The large inflow of mainly low-skilled labor into the trade sector explains the low productivity gains after 2005, when the trade sector had less capacity to absorb the increasing supply of workers, and thus paid decreasing returns.

The lower employment and poverty effects of Ghana's economic growth in the past decade, coupled with rising inequality, call for greater investment in a more inclusive growth strategy. The changing structure of growth and employment signal the need to redirect resources to increase the productivity of sectors with high potential to create jobs, such as agriculture and manufacturing—and especially to those industries linked to agriculture (such as agribusiness) to ensure that smallholder farmers are benefitting. The challenge for Ghana in the near future is to promote the growth of economic sectors that can generate more and productive jobs for all.

Note

1. http://www.ghanaweb.com/GhanaHomePage/economy/artikel.php?ID=414868, accessed February 16, 2016.
2. The choice of the two periods is in part dictated by the availability of employment data through the different rounds of the GLSS and in part due to the different factors that characterized Ghana before and after 2005. Results are consistent with the growth decomposition between 1991 and 2012 in Molini and Paci (2015).

References

Aykut, D., and S. Herrera. 2015. "Long-Run Growth in Ghana: Determinants and Prospects." Policy Research Working Paper 7115, World Bank, Washington, DC.

Ceglowsky, J., A. Aly Mbaye, S. S. Golub, and V. Prasand. 2015. "Can Africa Compete with China in Manufacturing? The Role of Relative Unit Labor Costs." Working Paper 201504, Development Policy Research Unit, World Bank, Washington, DC.

Christiansen, L., L. Demery, and J. Kuhl. 2011. "The (Evolving) Role of Agriculture in Poverty Reduction: An Empirical Perspective." *Journal of Development Economics* 96: 239–54.

DFID (Department for International Development). 2005. *Growth and Poverty Reduction: The Role of Agriculture*. London: Department for International Development.

FAO (Food and Agriculture Organization). 2015. *The State of Food Security in the World*. Rome: FAO.

Freire, M. E., S. Lall, and D. Leipziger. 2014. "Africa's Urbanization: Challenges and Opportunities." Working Paper 7, The Growth Dialogue, Washington, DC.

Ghana, Ministry of Food and Agriculture. 2013. "Agriculture in Ghana, Facts and Figures (2012)." Statistics, Research and Information Directorate, Ghana Ministry of Food and Agriculture, Accra, Ghana.

Gollin, D., R. Jedwab, and D. Vollrath. 2013. "Urbanization with and without Industrialization." Working Paper 21013-290-26, Department of Economics, University of Houston.

GSS (Ghana Statistical Service). 2013. *2010 Population and Housing Census: National Analytical Report*. Accra, Ghana.

———. 2014. *Poverty Profile in Ghana (2005–2013)*. GSS, Accra, Ghana.

Jedwab, R., L. Christiansen, and M. Gindelsky. 2014. "Rural Push, Urban Pull and ... Urban Push? New Historical Evidence from Developing Countries." Working Paper 2014-4, Institute for International Economic Policy, Elliott School of International Affairs, The George Washington University, Washington, DC.

McCullough, E. 2015. "Labor Productivity and Employment Gaps in Sub-Saharan Africa." Policy Research Working Paper 7234, World Bank, Washington, DC.

Molini, V., and P. Paci. 2015. *Poverty Reduction in Ghana: Progress and Challenges*. Washington, DC: World Bank.

UN (United Nations). 2014a. *World Urbanization Prospects: The 2014 Revision (database)*. Population Division, Department of Economic and Social Affairs.

———. 2014b. "National Accounts Main Aggregates Database." United Nations (accessed September 2015), https://unstats.un.org/unsd/snaama/Introduction.asp.

———. 2015. "Industrializing through Trade." United Nations Economic Commission for Africa.

World Bank. 2008a. *World Development Report 2009: Reshaping Economic Geography*. Washington, DC: World Bank.

———. 2008b. *Making Work Pay in Bangladesh: Employment, Growth and Poverty Reduction*. Washington, DC: World Bank.

———. 2008c. *Making Work Pay in Nicaragua: Employment, Growth and Poverty Reduction*. Washington, DC: World Bank.

———. 2015. *Rising through Cities in Ghana: Ghana Urbanization Review, Overview Report*. Washington, DC: World Bank.

————. 2016a. *Ghana Public Expenditure Review 2016. Fiscal Consolidation for Growth and Employment.* Washington, DC: World Bank.

————. 2016b. *Ghana: Social Protection Assessment and Expenditure Review.* Washington, DC: World Bank.

————. WDI (World Development Indicators) 2016 (database). World Bank, Washington, DC, http://data.worldbank.org/data-catalog/world-development-indicators.

CHAPTER 2

A Profile of Jobs in Ghana: Where and How Do People Work?

Main Messages

Most working-age people in Ghana work—and work relatively long hours, and for a relatively long period of their working lives—but in low-productivity sectors and in jobs that require very limited use of cognitive or other skills. Most jobless are inactive (in school, disabled, or otherwise not looking for work), rather than unemployed.

The problem is not a lack of jobs per se, but the quality of jobs. While job creation has increased, the structural transformation is still too slow to make a further dent in poverty. Better-paying and more secure jobs are needed, since poverty is still related to where people work, rather than if they work. At the same time, poverty also contributes to high rates of employment in low-productivity activities. In the absence of at-scale public safety nets and private transfers, most adults are compelled to work.

Households are not using diversification as a strategy to improve incomes and well-being. Households generally derive their labor income from either farm or off-farm sectors, but are not diversified across this divide. However, diversification is significant in the off-farm sector; most households have family members who work in both wage employment and self-employment.

What Is a Good Job?

Creating more good jobs—and make the existing ones better—will be important to improve living conditions in Ghana. For these reasons, it is important to identify both what might constitute a good job, and how current jobs and workers in Ghana compare against this measure. This chapter presents a profile of the actual and potential workforce and jobs landscape in Ghana. It discusses how opportunities differ between young and old, women and men, poor and wealthy, and depending on where one lives, using information from Ghana's household surveys (box 2.1).

Who is a worker? What is a job? And what is "good" job in the context of Ghana? A job is here defined as an economic activity that is remunerated in cash or kind. Being employed (being a worker) is synonymous with holding a job. Those who would like a job but cannot find one are considered unemployed, while those who are not looking for a job are inactive. (Definitions of key terms pertaining to the labor market are provided in box 2.2.)

Box 2.1 Sources of Data for the Profile of Labor Status

The analysis in this chapter draws significantly on information from the Ghana Living Standard Surveys from 1991, 2005, and 2012 (GLSS3, 5, and 6), with an emphasis on the dynamics in recent years (2005–12).

The GLSS is a nationally representative multipurpose household survey administered by Ghana Statistical Survey (GSS), which serves to collect detailed information on individual and household characteristics. The first GLSS was launched in 1987. Six rounds of data have been collected. GLSS3 to GLSS6 use the same questionnaire, and thus provide comparable data, making Ghana one of few African countries for which it is possible to provide an analysis over two decades. However, in this report, GLSS4 is excluded from the analysis because of difficulties with data on economic activity reported for 15- to 24-year-olds.

Box 2.2 Definitions of Labor Market Indicators

In analyzing jobs and development in Ghana, this report uses the following definitions:

Job: An economic activity that is remunerated in cash or in kind, and does not violate human rights (World Bank 2012). Apart from wage jobs, it includes income generated at the household (rather than individual) level, whether from farming or off the farm. While it includes the production of goods for consumption within the household, the provision of services (cleaning, food preparation, care of one's children, and the like) is not included in the definition of economic activities.

Productive job. A broad term linked to the quality of jobs, primarily their productivity and earnings capacity and the security of earnings over time. Productivity generally refers to the value added each worker generates. From the perspective of poverty reduction, "productive jobs" can be considered employment opportunities that generate sufficient income to bring people out of poverty and contribute to productivity growth in the economy. The agricultural sector, together with the trade sector, have the lowest levels of labor productivity, measured as value added per worker; they are both dominated by self-employment.

Working-age population. The population between 15 and 64 years of age.

Labor force. Consists of the employed and unemployed. The *labor force participation rate* is the share of the active labor force in the working-age population.

box continues next page

Box 2.2 Definitions of Labor Market Indicators *(continued)*

The employed. Those who reported, in the relevant survey, having worked for pay or for profit for at least one hour in the previous week. The *employment-to-population ratio* is the share of employed in the population.

Wage workers. Those who work for somebody else in exchange for a salary, daily wage, or "per-task" pay.

Formal wage workers. Those who either have a written contract or who benefit from any type of social security or health insurance benefits, including paid sick leave, maternity leave, old-age pensions, and occupational injury coverage (see box 2.3 for more details).

Self-employed. To work for oneself, making income from the profits of one's own activity. The distinction in a household between self-employment and unpaid, contributing family workers can be blurred. Thus the report considers as self-employed all workers reporting themselves as employers, working on their own account, or those who are contributing family workers in a household enterprise.

Unemployed. Those who do not hold a job but are actively looking for one and available to take it up should they find one. This definition is in accordance with the approach established by the International Labour Organization (ILO). *Unemployment rates* are the share of unemployed in the active population. In a country with a small wage sector and relatively high poverty rates like Ghana, the ILO definition is not sufficient as an indicator of poor labor outcomes or exclusion. Other factors also matter, such as social barriers to looking for a job in the first place, or limited access to good jobs.

The inactive. Those who do not work and who are not looking for work. They include students, discouraged workers (who have given up looking for jobs), people engaged in household work, sick people, and the elderly.

NEETs. Those who are Not in Employment, Education or Training: that is, the inactive who are not in school in any form.

Labor market. The market for work, where employers find workers, workers find jobs, and the wage rate is determined. In the case of Ghana, the labor market is not a good term for labor status or jobs, since most work is not found in labor markets. Most people hire themselves, and the wage sector is small.

Decent work. Following the ILO definition, decent work involves productive jobs, fair income, equality of opportunity in the work place, safe and fair working conditions, right to social protection, and freedom of organization.

Focusing only on access to a job is not enough to understand the impact of labor markets on individual and household welfare because many jobs provide insufficient means to prevent poverty. The definition of a "good job" ultimately may differ, depending on personal circumstances and preferences. Some job characteristics are nonetheless highly relevant indicators of the opportunities offered by a job: high income (which in turn is often linked to high job productivity), and the security of that income. When asked about what they considered "good jobs," young Africans in both rural and urban areas describe work that offers good earnings and status; "bad jobs" are those that offer low and insecure pay, are dangerous, or are illegal (Filmer and Fox 2014). For employees, income security involves long-term contractual relationships and benefits like sick leave and retirement pay. In the discussion that follows, jobs are defined in terms of three main different sectors (or occupations) of work:[1]

Self-employment in farming. This category includes mostly smallholder farmers—typically family farms, which occupy the majority of agricultural land and represent the backbone of the agricultural sector. Family farms are very diverse in terms of size, access to markets, and household characteristics. Some are subsistence farms, mostly producing for their own consumption, while others produce for local and domestic markets. In this report, this category excludes larger farms in the commercial agriculture sectors producing for international markets.

Self-employment in an off-farm household enterprise. This category includes employers, those working on their own account, and unpaid family workers. Typically, these family- and household-based firms are very small firms, operating from or close to the household location, involving (mostly) a single entrepreneur, and sometimes family members who do not receive wages; instead, the profits of the enterprise accrue to the household.

Wage work in the off-farm sector. This group of employees encompasses very varied job situations, ranging from informal workers paid by the task or on a daily basis, to salaried formal sector workers with paid vacations, sick leave, and other benefits, working mostly in the industrial and services sectors (but also on large farms in the commercial agriculture sector). The analysis that follows separates out private and public wage workers.

These sectors differ in the opportunities they offer, although there is significant overlap between them. In general, productivity and household earnings are lowest in the farm sector, dominated by smallholder subsistence farming. The household enterprise sector operating off the farm generally offers higher profits than the agricultural sector, and diversified households are generally better off than those relying only on farm work. The wage sector tends to offer better earnings than self-employment, on average.

The 2012 Snapshot of Jobs

There Is No Lack of Employment

Many are employed and few are unemployed in Ghana. Out of Ghana's 26 million people, 15 million are "of working age": between 15 and 64 years. Of these adults, nearly 12 million people are active, and a vast majority (11 million of the active population) is employed (figure 2.1). By contrast, official unemployment is negligible, affecting around 200,000 people. Among the employed, almost 5 million are engaged in family farming, with another nearly 4 million working for themselves or their family in household enterprises outside of agriculture. Fewer than 3 million workers are actually wage employees. Some 2 million wage workers are in the private sector, and fewer than 1 million are public sector employees. In short, most people work in Ghana, but for themselves,

Figure 2.1 Labor Status of the Population in Ghana, 2012
Millions

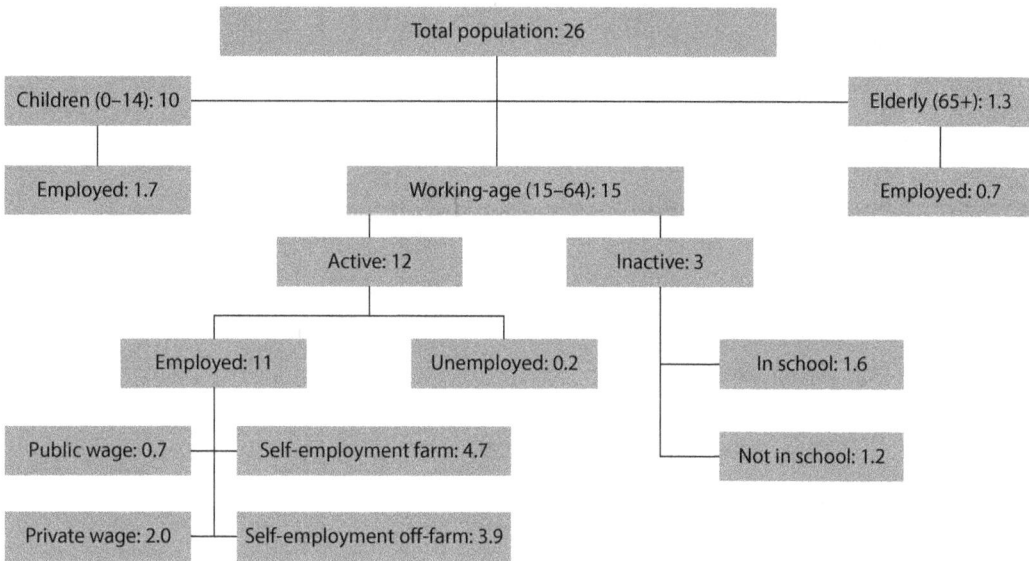

Source: Estimates based on GLSS6.

and in occupations offering comparatively low productivity and earnings opportunities. Lacking access to a comprehensive social safety net system at scale, and with a low labor demand for jobs that offer better earnings, a majority of Ghanaians are simply not able to wait for an appropriate job opportunity, but must create their own employment.

Another 3 million adult Ghanaians are inactive. A majority of adults who are neither working nor looking for work (1.6 million) are students in school, but there are also more than 1 million adults who are not working or actively looking for a job. This group of jobless NEETs (those Not in Employment, Education or Training) is several times larger than the group of unemployed.

Children and the elderly also work. Ghana's population is young; 10 million Ghanaians are children under 15 years of age. Although the report focuses mostly on the adult population between 15 and 64 years, it is important to note that there are 1.7 million children (between ages 7 and 14) who work in some capacity, a majority of them while attending school.

These numbers translate into high levels of labor force participation and low rates of unemployment. Four out of five adult Ghanaians (79 percent) are active, and only one in fifty (2 percent) of this active labor force is unemployed (table 2.1). Both men and women are active, and unemployment rates are similar across gender. The only exception are children (aged 7–14) and youth (aged 15–24), whose activity rates are lower because many of them are still enrolled in education, and the elderly, some of whom have retired from working life. Nonetheless, 30 percent of children, 55 percent of youth, and 58 percent of the elderly are working. Although indicators are quite similar across gender,

Table 2.1 Activity and Employment Rates, by Age Group
Percent

	Working age 15–64	Age groups				
		7–14	15–24	25–39	40–64	65+
Labor force participation rate[a]	79	29	55	91	92	58
Male	81	29	57	94	94	65
Female	77	29	53	87	90	52
Unemployment rate[b]	2	0	4	2	1	0
Male	2	0	4	2	1	0
Female	2	0	5	2	1	0
Inactive, in school[a]	11	67	31	2	0	0
Male	12	67	32	2	0	0
Female	10	67	30	1	0	0
Inactive, not in school[a]	10	4	14	8	8	42
Male	7	3	11	3	6	35
Female	13	4	17	11	10	48

Source: Estimates based on GLSS6.
a. As share of total population in respective age group.
b. As share of active population in respective age group.

women, and especially young women, are more likely than men to be inactive but not in school.

The share of employed adults is high across gender, age, and region. High activity rates and low unemployment rates reflect the fact that most people are compelled to work if they are able, in the absence of other assets to draw upon, or safety nets that could provide temporary or long-term compensation for income shortfalls. The share of employed in the population—the employment-to-population ratio—is high for adults between ages 25 and 64, for men and women, and across Ghana's different regions. Even for youth, half the population is employed, as well as a nonnegligible share of children and elderly (figure 2.2).

The Structure of Employment Indicates a Lack of Good Job Opportunities

Most jobs are in low-productivity self-employment activities that generate little earnings. In general, employment in Ghana takes place outside of the labor market, as most people work for themselves or their families. For their primary jobs, four out of five workers work in farm and off-farm household enterprises, and only one in five is a wage worker (and thus actually employed and receiving a wage from a firm or person). The differences between rural and urban areas are significant: wage employment is insignificant in rural areas, but accounts for one in four jobs in urban areas (figure 2.3, panel a). Self-employment dominates in both rural and urban areas; unsurprisingly, rural self-employment is largely in the farm sector, whereas urban self-employment is largely in off-farm activities. The high share of urban self-employment outside agriculture is witness to the importance of jobs in the low-productivity wholesale and retail trade sector in urban areas. Overall, the industrial sector is limited in terms of employment,

Figure 2.2 Employment-to-Population Ratios, by Age Group, Gender, and Region

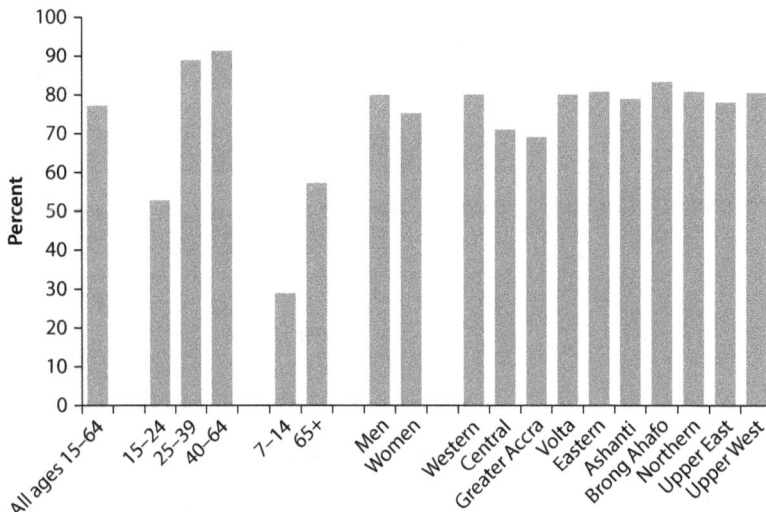

Source: Estimates based on GLSS6.

even in urban areas: it absorbs about 19 percent of the workforce there, while the services sector employs two out of three urban workers (figure 2.3a, panel b).

The structure of employment in Ghana is similar to countries with a similar income level, but differs significantly from that of more advanced economies. In Sub-Saharan Africa's lower-middle-income countries, agriculture continues to absorb more than half of all employment, and wage employment remains subdued compared to self-employment in the off-farm sector. The structure contrasts sharply with that of upper-middle-income countries, where the structural transformation away from both farm and self-employment has come much further, and wage employment has become the dominant form of job (figure 2.3, panels c and d).

Most jobs in Ghana are also low skill, requiring limited use of cognitive skills like reading and writing. Numeracy is a basic functional skill used regularly by all workers, and is necessary for street vendors who charge for their produce, as well as for public sector servants. Other cognitive skills, however, are much less used. Only in the urban formal sector are workers actually using reading and writing skills regularly. By contrast, less than half of informal wage workers, and less than one-third of the self-employed, use these skills. Jobs are also characterized by a low technology content overall. Even among formal wage workers, less than half use computers to some degree at work. There is a further digital divide: very few informal wage workers,[2] and virtually none of the self-employed (that is, a majority of workers) use a computer at all (figure 2.4, panel a). The dominance of low-skill and undigitalized jobs is very different from more advanced economies: in the member countries of the Organisation for Economic

Figure 2.3 Employment

a. Employment in rural and urban regions, by sector of work

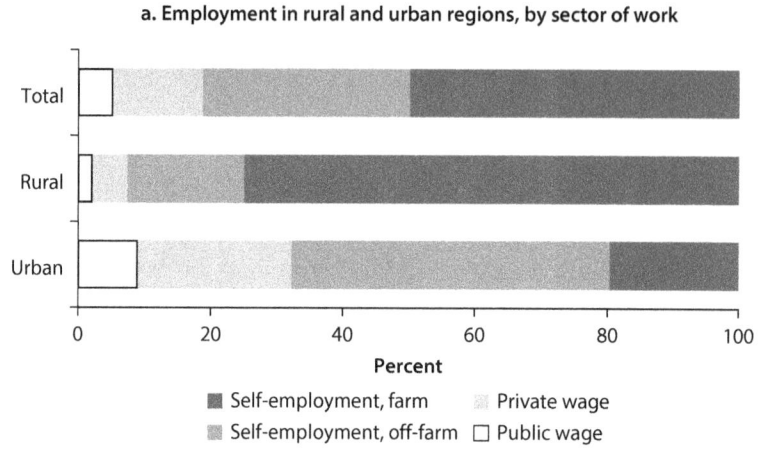

Legend:
- ■ Self-employment, farm
- ▨ Self-employment, off-farm
- ░ Private wage
- □ Public wage

b. Employment in rural and urban regions, by economic sector

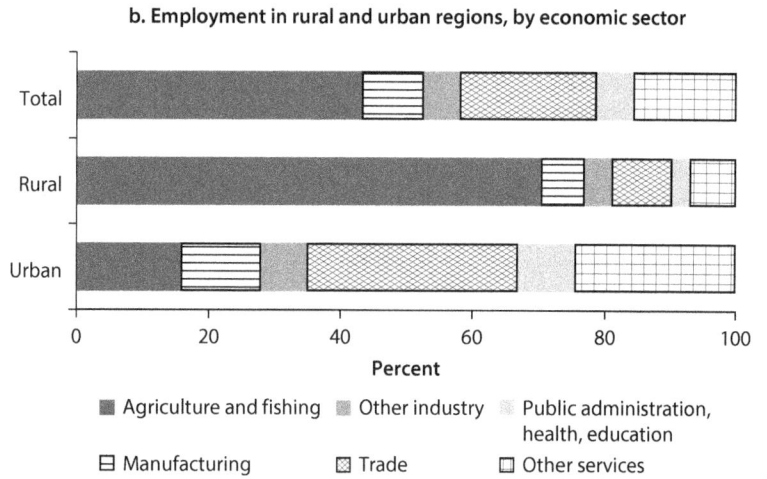

Legend:
- ■ Agriculture and fishing
- ▨ Other industry
- ░ Public administration, health, education
- ⊟ Manufacturing
- ⊠ Trade
- □ Other services

c. Employment structure in Ghana and Sub-Saharan Africa, by country type

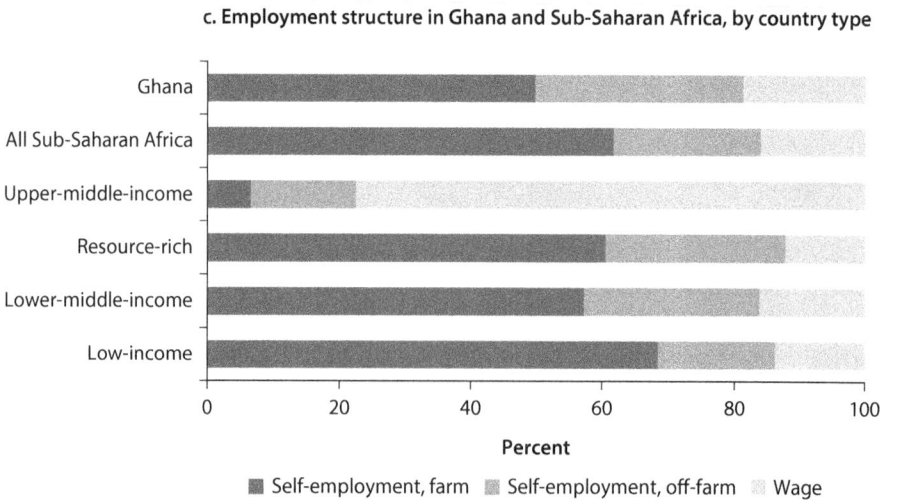

Legend:
- ■ Self-employment, farm
- ▨ Self-employment, off-farm
- ░ Wage

figure continues next page

Figure 2.3 Employment *(continued)*

d. Employment structure in Ghana and Sub-Saharan Africa, by sector of work

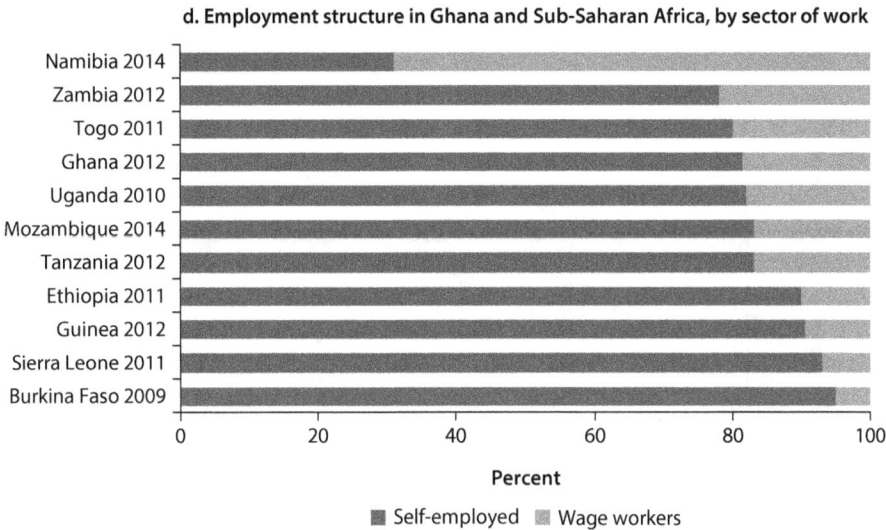

■ Self-employed ▨ Wage workers

Source: Estimates based on GLSS6 for Ghana, Filmer and Fox 2014 (panel c) and standardized and harmonized household and labor force surveys under the World bank Africa SHIP project (panel d).

Co-operation and Development (OECD), nearly 70 percent of all workers use computers regularly on the job (OECD 2015).

The prevalence of low-skill jobs is mirrored in the low education levels among the employed. Two in five workers have no more than primary education, and only one in five has more than basic education. In Ghana as in many poorer countries, education levels are lower among the employed than among the unemployed or inactive. The lower level of schooling among the employed is a reflection of the need to work to support oneself, especially for those from low-income households, who also are likely to have completed fewer years of school. These individuals cannot afford to be unemployed and wait for a sufficiently good job opportunity to come about; conversely, many of them cannot afford further schooling (figure 2.4, panel b). An analysis of labor market participation and selection into different employment sectors using the urban worker survey data from 2004 to 2006 shows a clear preference by educated workers for formal sector employment, particularly in the public sector. Higher levels of education reduce the likelihood of being self-employed and increase the probability of formal sector employment. In addition, individuals with secondary education prefer to wait in unemployment for formal sector jobs rather than enter into self-employment (Twumasi-Baffour 2015).

Jobs Quality Is Reflected in Earnings and Income Security

Some jobs offer more opportunities than others simply because they offer higher earnings. What one earns on the job is, of course, a key aspect of job quality: jobs that offer higher earnings make households less vulnerable to poverty. These opportunities may be related not only to higher earnings, but also to the scope

Figure 2.4 Jobs Skills and Educational Attainment

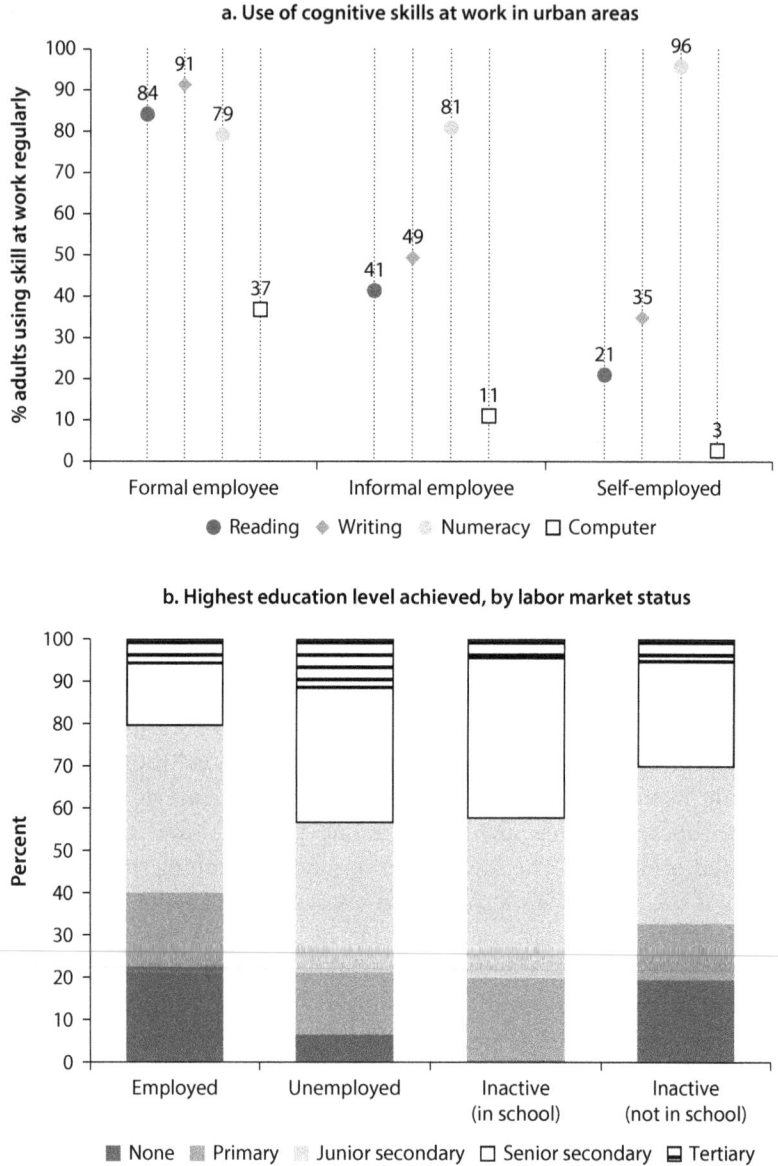

a. Use of cognitive skills at work in urban areas

b. Highest education level achieved, by labor market status

Source: Darvas, Favara, and Arnold 2016, based on the STEP household survey (panel a); estimates based on GLSS6 (panel b).
Note: "Informal employee" refers to wage workers without access to social security.

for full-time employment (and thus a lower risk of underemployment) and a lower volatility of earnings. Different sectors of work differ significantly in the quality of jobs they offer, considering earnings as a benchmark for quality (figure 2.5). Most clearly, the public wage sector offers higher wages, and a public sector premium is present at all ages and levels of education. Work in

Figure 2.5 Median Monthly Earnings, by Sector of Work

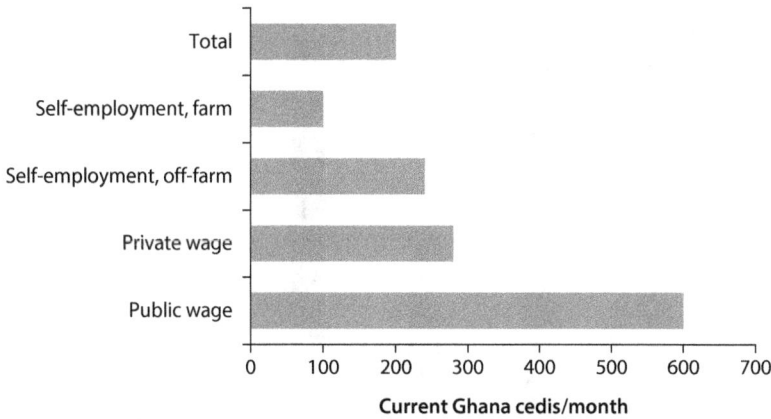

Source: Estimates based on GLSS6.
Note: Figure includes only earnings, which is not strictly comparable across the four employment categories, as they reflect wages for public and private wage workers and labor income for the self-employed.

farming, on the other hand, pays the least.[3] The private wage sector also offers higher wages than off-farm self-employment, but the differences are quite small.

In addition, job and income security is considerably higher in the public wage sector than in the private wage sector. Job and income security make up important aspects of wage work. The ability to take paid sick leave or maternity leave and retain both job and income, for example, reduces household exposure to health or pregnancy risks. Access to a pension reduces the risk of income shortfalls in old age. The existence of a written contract implies contractual obligations on the part of both employer and employee, and thus some measure of job security. From this perspective, it is clear that the public wage sector has far more to offer than the private wage sector. A majority of public sector employees have access to paid holidays, pension contributions, and sick leave, and two out of five have access to subsidized health care as an extra benefit. Less than 5 percent lack a contract. By contrast, in the private wage sector, 30 percent of workers, or fewer, have access to any form of social security, and less than 30 percent have a written contract. The low levels of social security coverage or formal contracts suggest that informal work is the norm in Ghana, even in the wage sector (figure 2.6 and box 2.3.).

The public-private wage differential in Ghana may crowd out other types of employment and increase unemployment among the higher-skilled workers. Ghana experienced an increase in both the size of government employment and the wage bill during the 2000s, although the civil service has contracted since the mid-2000s. The higher wages, greater job security, and more generous provision of nonwage benefits make jobs in the public sectors very attractive for prospective entrants in the labor market. In Ghana, public sector workers on average earn about twice as much as workers in the private sector, after controlling for

Figure 2.6 Job Security and Benefits, by Sector of Work

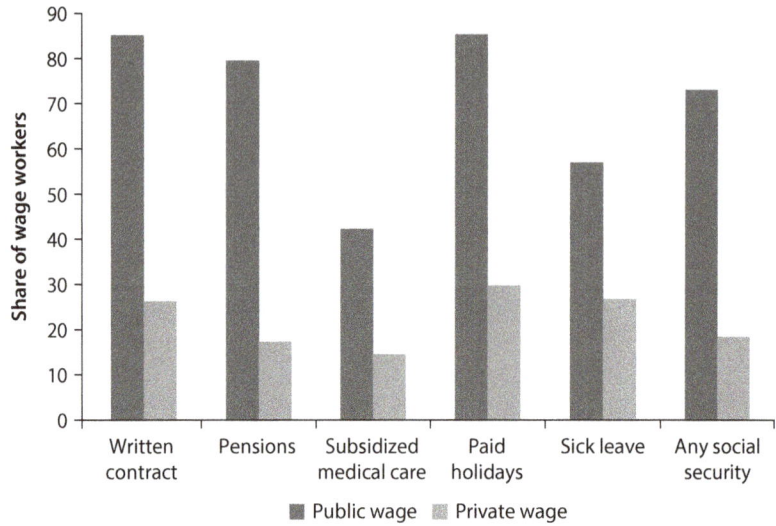

Source: Estimates based on GLSS6.

the double selectivity into wage and public employment (Falco and others 2011). Moreover, individuals in districts with a larger share of public workers are more likely to be unemployed, suggesting that new entrants in the labor market prefer to wait and queue for a public sector job (Ranzani and Tuccio, forthcoming). Public employment is also more geographically concentrated than private wage employment, and accounts for 10 percent of total employment in only a few districts in Ghana, most particularly in Accra (map 2.1).

Access to full-time employment also differs across sectors, further increasing the gaps in effective pay. Most of the employed work relatively long hours; two-thirds of Ghanaians work more than 30 hours per week. But there are noticeable differences across the four main sectors (figure 2.7). Unsurprisingly, there is a higher tendency among the self-employed to work fewer hours. In some cases, this may reflect voluntary choices and be a motivation for choosing self-employment; in other cases, it may reflect involuntary underemployment due to lack of sufficiently good business opportunities. Those engaged in the farm sector, in particular, work fewer hours than those in other sectors. The low income levels and higher poverty levels of individuals working in the farm sector suggest that underemployment may be involuntary. Moreover, these differences imply that total wage differences are larger across wage and self-employment sectors than the hourly wages suggest.

There May Be Barriers to Diversifying Opportunities to Generate Income
The low productivity and lack of income security of jobs is not mitigated by efforts to diversify opportunities to generate income at the individual level. Low household-level earnings could conceivably be mitigated by individuals taking

Map 2.1 Public and Private Wage Workers, Share of Total Employment, by District

a. Private wage workers   b. Public wage workers

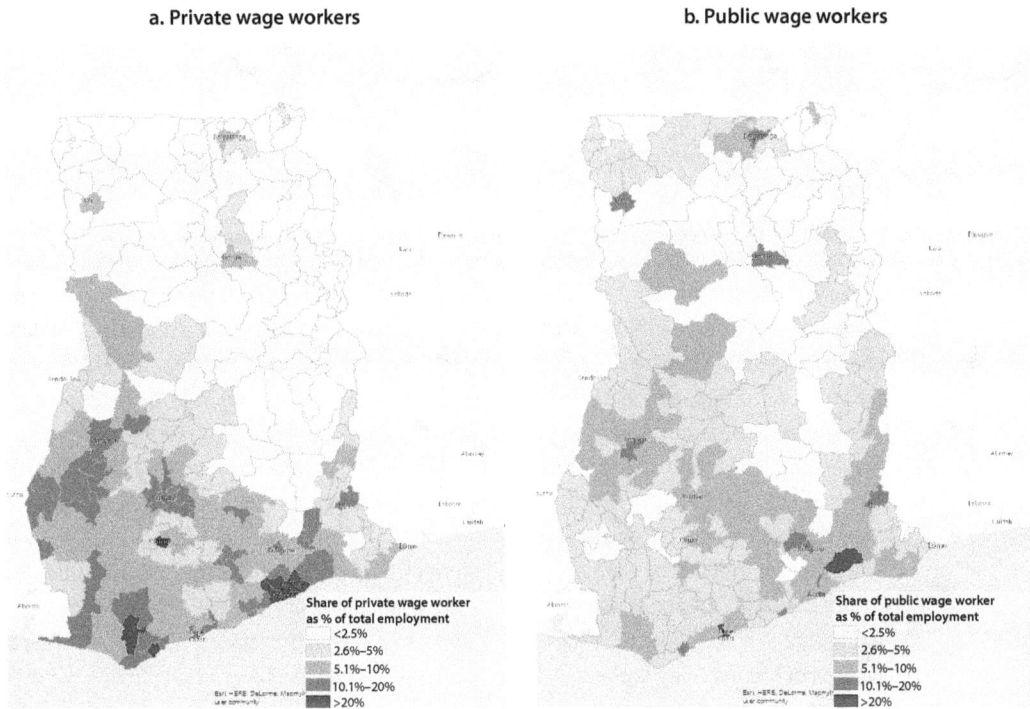

Share of private wage worker
as % of total employment
<2.5%
2.6%–5%
5.1%–10%
10.1%–20%
>20%

Share of public wage worker
as % of total employment
<2.5%
2.6%–5%
5.1%–10%
10.1%–20%
>20%

Sources: Population Census 2010; GSS 2013.

Box 2.3 Estimating Informality in Ghana's Labor Markets

Conceptually, this report refers to *informal employment* as employment in the production of goods and services that are legal, but where there is noncompliance in some legal aspects of employment or the production process. The concept of informality is defined in different ways within the economics literature, pointing to the continuum of dimensions that characterizes informality (Loayza and Rigolini 2006; Schneider 2014). It can refer to all those working in the informal sector (firms that are not formal, such as those not registered with the authorities, or that do not pay taxes), as well as to those who work in formal firms but whose employment conditions are informal (that is, they do not comply with labor laws).

In practice, household surveys can be used to approximate informal and formal employment using information on employment conditions that convey some measure of income security, such as access to social security or contractual relations. Information on household enterprises can be used to identify firms that are not registered with government agencies and authorities or that do not offer social security benefits to their employees (Gatti and Honorati 2008).

In this report, *informal enterprises* are defined as firms managed by the self-employed, whether own-account workers, unpaid family workers, or employers. This includes all household enterprises, whether they are registered or not (in fact, as seen in chapter 4, only about

box continues next page

Box 2.3 Estimating Informality in Ghana's Labor Markets *(continued)*

13 percent of off-farm household enterprises are registered with the authorities). Nearly 6 million Ghanaians can be considered informal workers who are engaged in off-farm household enterprises.

Informal wage workers are those who do not enjoy a regularized work status. The GLSS surveys provide several options to characterize the extent of informality. The lowest level of informality is obtained using access to paid holidays as an indication of regularized working conditions (some 30 percent of private wage workers, and 85 percent of public wage workers, do have paid holidays). Another definition involves the existence of a written contract between employee and employer; the shares of workers are similar. According to this definition, 1.4 million workers are informally employed as wage workers. The most stringent definition involves access to pensions (less than 20 percent of private wage workers have access to pensions). According to this definition, 1.6 million wage workers are informally employed. Focusing on the existence of a written contract, the rate of informality in Ghana's jobs, both wage employment and self-employment, is high: about 90 percent of workers are informal. Focusing only on off-farm work (both wage employment and self-employment), the rate of informality still reaches 87 percent.

Informality is driven by both pull and push factors. Informality, at least in low- and middle-income countries, may be a natural "first step" in the launching of a firm and should not be seen as illegality. In some contexts, informality is opportunity-driven or at least a conscious choice because of the flexibility it offers (witness the many women in Ghana who combine work in informal household enterprises with the main family responsibilities) or because access to social security and other formal services is not seen as valuable or worth attaching oneself to (Perry and others 2007). However, informality is also a reflection of lack of opportunities in better jobs because of lack of labor demand, or because people in the informal sector lack the necessary skills or necessary connections to enter better-paid jobs in the formal sector.

---

on second jobs ("moonlighting"), by more household members entering work, or by trying to involve household members in different sectors. However, only a minority of those employed (some 15 percent) also hold second jobs. Most of them are informal workers in agriculture or nonagricultural occupations. Given the fact that most people work relatively long hours, it is not surprising that few hold second jobs in addition to their primary occupation. The shares of workers holding additional jobs are similar for women and men, but lower for youth than for older workers. Overall, farm work is the most common sector for additional work, reflecting the need to involve more household members on the family farm. Farm workers predominantly work in self-employment in off-farm activities as a second job. Wage employees are less likely than others to hold additional jobs, and conversely, additional jobs are almost exclusively in self-employment, with very few options in wage work (table 2.2).

In general, households do not diversify income across the farm and off-farm sectors by having family members engaged in both sectors. Less than 20 percent of households are diversified along the farm–off-farm divide, in the sense of having at least one individual engaged in an off-farm job and at least one in farm activity

Figure 2.7 Hours Worked per Week in Primary Activity, by Sector of Work

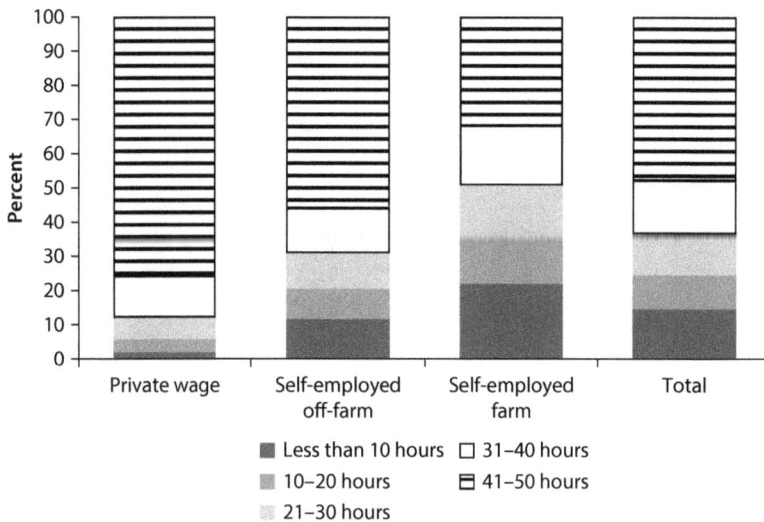

Source: Estimates based on GLSS6.

Table 2.2 Percent of the Employed Holding a Second Job, by Sector of Work

Percent

		Employed in a second job			
	All	Self-employment farm	Self-employment off-farm	Wage employment	No additional job
All employed	15	7	7	1	85
Self-employment, farm	7	2	4	1	36
Self-employment, off-farm	6	4	2	0	30
Wage employment	2	1	1	0	19

Source: Estimates based on GLSS6.

(figure 2.8, panel a). One-third of households are engaged only in farming, while half of the households consist of individuals who all work in off-farm activities (whether as self-employed or wage workers). The share of diversified households among the poorest quintiles is higher than for households belonging to the richer quintiles: diversification is a strategy for some poor households to cope with low labor income in the farm or off-farm sector.

In households that depend on farming, more people (proportionally) need to work to make ends meet. Households depending exclusively on farming also have considerably higher employment rates (here meaning the share of all adults in the household who are employed) than diversified households or those relying only on off-farm jobs, indicating the need to employ all possible labor (figure 2.8, panel b). In light of the more persistent underemployment (and seasonality) of the farm sector, some household diversification would seem beneficial. The fact that farm

Figure 2.8 Household Diversification across Farm and Off-Farm Sectors

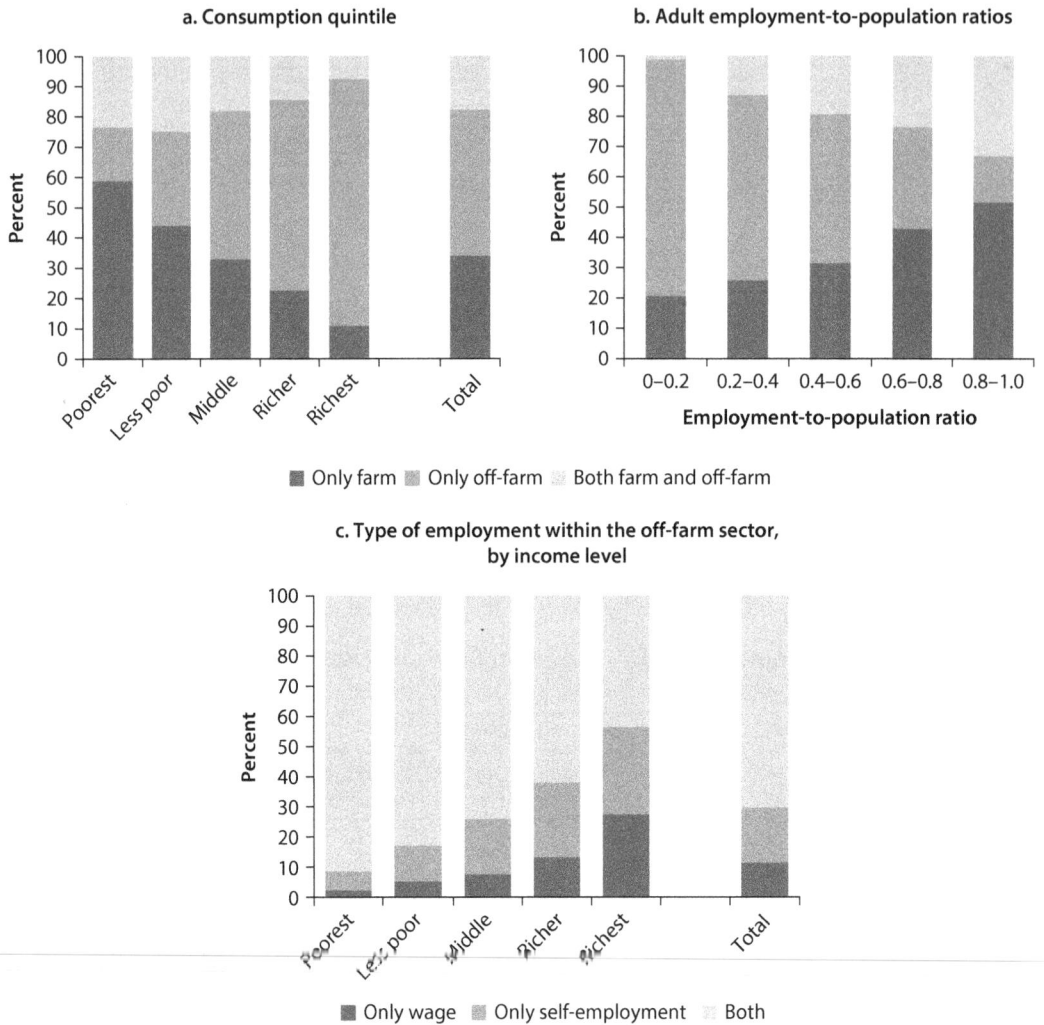

a. Consumption quintile

b. Adult employment-to-population ratios

■ Only farm ▨ Only off-farm ▧ Both farm and off-farm

c. Type of employment within the off-farm sector, by income level

■ Only wage ▨ Only self-employment ▧ Both

Source: Estimates based on GLSS6.
Note: Only farm (or off-farm) refers to undiversified households where all employed individuals are working in the farm (or off-farm) sector. Only wage (or self-employment) refers to undiversified households in the off-farm sector, where all employed individuals are working in the wage (or self-employment) sector.

households are not in general able to generate additional income in off-farm activities suggests that barriers to such diversification need to be removed.

A majority of households operating outside of agriculture derive income from both wage employment and self-employment, however. Households that derive all their income from off-farm activities are largely diversified, in the sense of simultaneously having family members who work as wage employed and as self-employed (figure 2.8, panel c). Seventy percent of households in the off-farm sector are diversified, according to this definition. Diversified households are generally worse off than those that can depend on only wage employment and those that can depend on only self-employment.

Who Are the Jobless?

Most of those out of a job in Ghana are inactive and are thus not looking for, and not available for, a job. As discussed, the number of inactive is much higher than the number of unemployed, who make up only 6 percent of the jobless. Nearly half of the inactive—47 percent—consists of young people who are still in school. Half of the jobless, however, are inactive for other reasons than education; most of them are at least 25 years of age (figure 2.9, panel a).

Figure 2.9 Composition of the Jobless Population

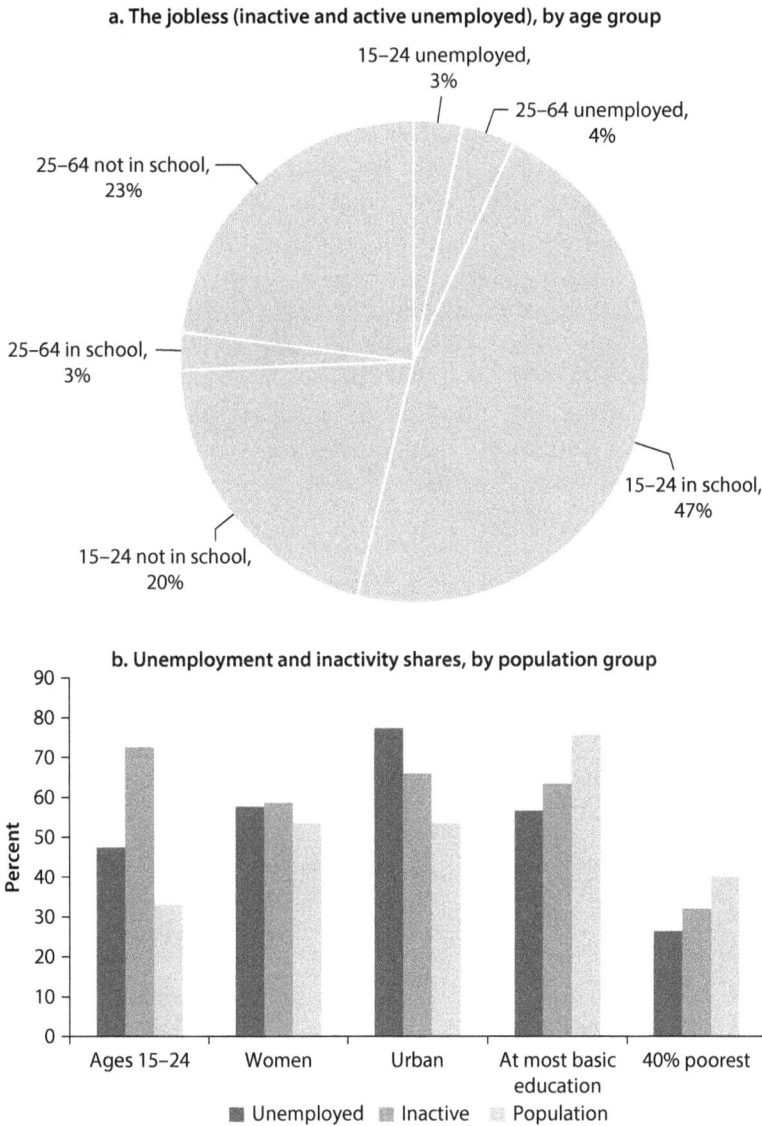

a. The jobless (inactive and active unemployed), by age group

- 15–24 unemployed, 3%
- 25–64 unemployed, 4%
- 25–64 not in school, 23%
- 25–64 in school, 3%
- 15–24 in school, 47%
- 15–24 not in school, 20%

b. Unemployment and inactivity shares, by population group

■ Unemployed ▨ Inactive ▨ Population

Source: Estimates based on GLSS6.
Note: At most basic education = has finished at the most lower secondary school.

The young, women, urban residents, those with more than basic education (junior secondary school), and those who do not live in poor families are over-represented among the jobless, in the sense that their share of inactivity and unemployment is higher than their share of the population (figure 2.9, panel b). The profile of the jobless underscores the message that much of employment is distress work, necessary to secure household income. Those with higher levels of education and from more wealthy households and living in urban areas where there are more interesting job opportunities may prefer to wait for a specific job opportunity that suits their aspirations, and they have the means to do so.

Early family formation affects young women's entry in labor markets. At any specific age, inactive women are more likely to be married than inactive men, irrespective of age (figure 2.10, panel a). Inactive women are not idle; they are occupied with time-consuming but unpaid chores in the household. The division of labor within households—with married men supporting families with labor income, and married women occupied with children and household chores—is contributing to keeping women outside what are counted as economic activities. A recent time use survey provides evidence of a distinct gender dimension in terms of access to remunerated activities (figure 2.10, panel b). Compared to men, Ghanaian women spend less time on remunerated activities, as well as on leisure activities, and more on unpaid household service work (three times as much as men, in fact). Adult women are in charge of fetching water and firewood in 70 percent and 60 percent of Ghana's households, respectively. They have the main responsibility for childcare and food preparation. When such household-based services are included, women spend, on average, as much time as men working during any given day (GSS 2012).

Figure 2.10 Inactivity Types and Levels of Economic Activity, by Gender

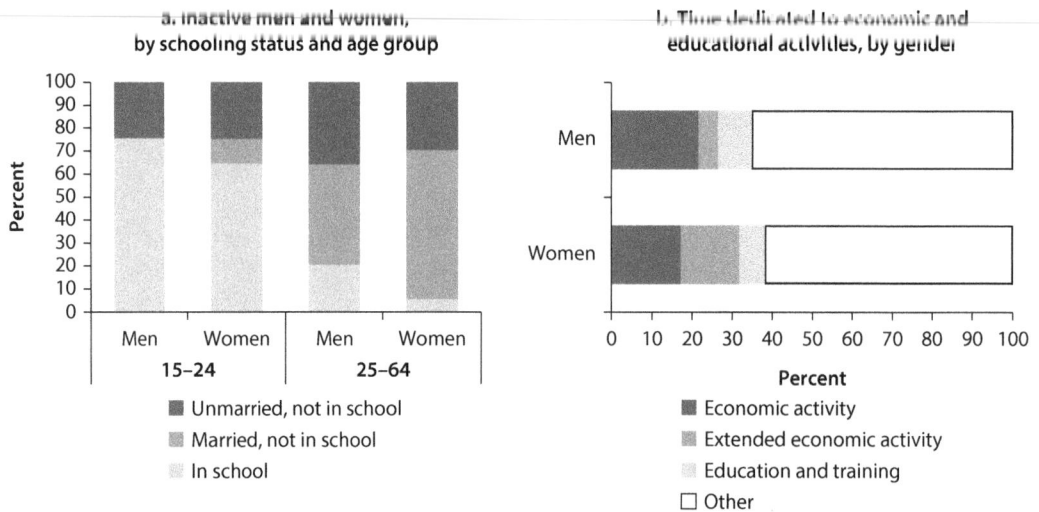

Source: Estimates based on GLSS6 (panel a) and GSS (2012) (panel b).

Who Lacks Access to Better Jobs? The Challenges of Creating More Inclusive Jobs

Given high employment ratios across gender, region, and poverty status, the greatest welfare losses are likely to stem from lack of access to more productive sectors and jobs. In particular, the youngest, women, those in northern and rural locations, and those lacking education have fewer chances of accessing more productive opportunities. The opportunities offered by different sectors of work are very different, and access to these opportunities depends on different social and economic barriers.

Young people who exit school early are predominantly working in low-productivity activities, namely agriculture. Among the 52 percent of 15- to 24-year-olds who are employed, a majority are working in low-productivity activities in the farm sector. This suggests that early dropout from school is primarily a rural phenomenon, and that those who leave school early end up in less productive employment, and/or that youth from poorer families must leave school early to make a living. Few of the young who are working—less than 20 percent—are employed in the wage sector, especially the public sector, where education requirements are higher than elsewhere (figure 2.11).

There are also remarkable differences between men and women in terms of access to wage jobs. Women are significantly more likely than men to be working for themselves in nonagricultural activities; a majority (70 percent) of Ghana's self-employed in the off-farm sector are women. Compared to young men, young women are less likely to be involved in farming. Overall, women have much less access to wage work than men. The share of women in wage work is less than half that of men (figure 2.11).

The lack of diversification in the northern and more rural regions compared to the dynamic southern and urban areas is reflected in regional differences in employment structure. In particular, the region containing Ghana's capital— Greater Accra—stands out because of the negligible share of workers involved in agriculture (2 percent), and the comparatively high share of private wage work (42 percent). Overall, in the regions in the south (Greater Accra, Eastern, Ashanti, Central, and Western regions), agriculture accounts for less than half of employment, compared to over 70 percent in the Upper West region. The southern regions also have higher shares of private wage work, which is very low in other regions (figure 2.12, panel a).

Those with more education are likely to work in higher earning jobs, off the farm, and in wage work. More than half of all workers with a tertiary education are concentrated in the public wage sector. By contrast, those with no or little education are limited to self-employment, especially in the agricultural sector (figure 2.12, panel b).

Education, age, and gender matter for earnings, even when access to different sectors is taken into account. Even within the wage sector, there are differences in earnings between different types of workers, further increasing differences across gender and education, in particular. As shown in figure 2.13,

Figure 2.11 Sector of Employment, by Age Group and Gender

Employment by sector

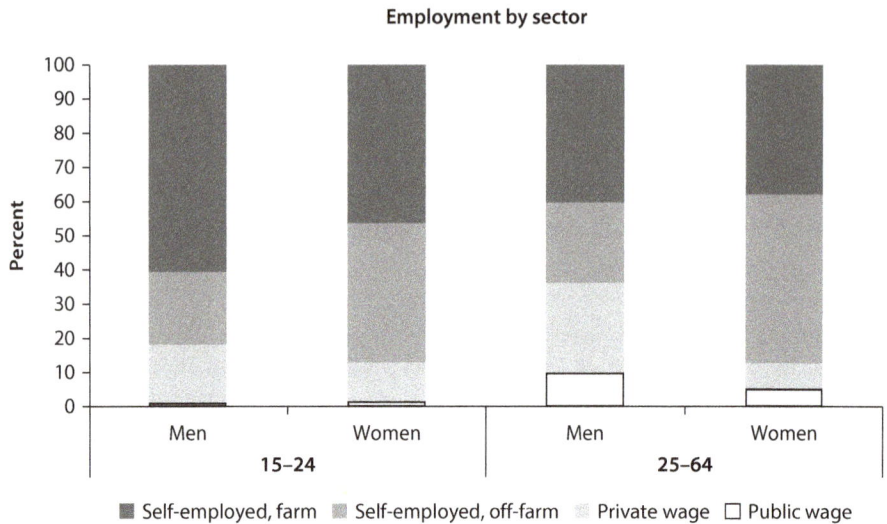

Source: Estimates based on GLSS6.

panel a, women wage employees earn significantly less than men. Although not shown here, the gender gap is consistent across different levels of education—and consequently not only a result of limited access to education for girls. Achieving at least basic education—that is, completing the junior secondary high school level of education—is also important: those with primary levels of education or less clearly tend to earn less than those with at least junior secondary level (figure 2.13, panel b). The exponentially increasing returns to tertiary education may well reflect the concentration of highly educated workers in the public wage sector, where wages are significantly higher than what the private sector can offer (figure 2.13, panel c). However, the differences between tertiary education on the one hand, and lower levels of education on the other, are even more significant (figure 2.13, panel b). Unsurprisingly, wages are lower for 15- to 24-year-olds (the distribution of wages lies to the left of the distribution of wages for older workers). There are significant returns to experience (older wage employees earn more than young ones), although the age-wage gaps may potentially also reflect the cost of entering working life with limited levels of education.

The payoff to an extra year of school in terms of earnings increases exponentially at higher levels of education among wage workers. A comparison of median hourly income suggests that, compared to those without any schooling, or less than primary education, there is only a small payoff to finishing basic education, which includes the majority of the population and thus no longer constitutes a competitive advantage (figure 2.14). Instead, there is a significant premium to attending university, especially in wage employment (which may partly be driven by public wages), as evidenced in a rapid increase in earnings in the wage

Figure 2.12 Regional and Educational Disparities in Sectors of Work

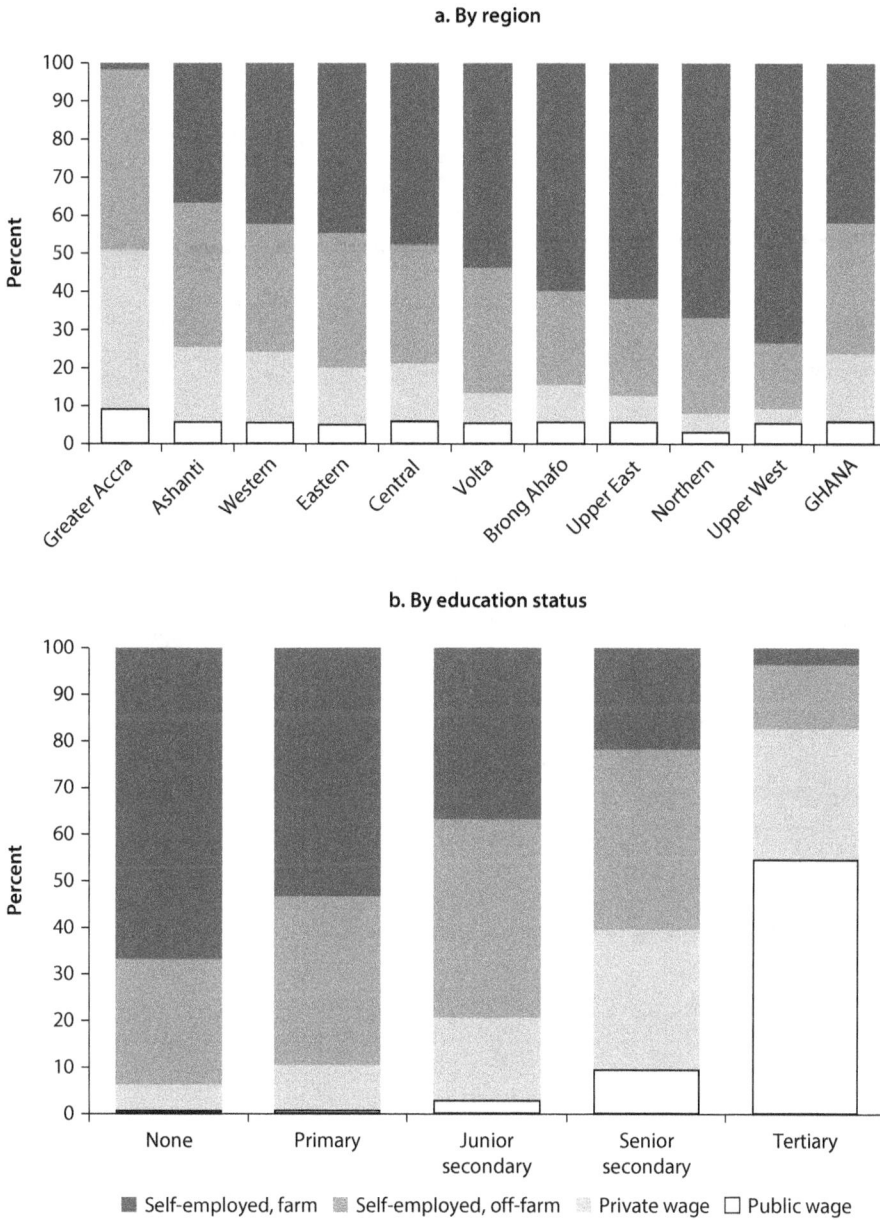

a. By region

b. By education status

■ Self-employed, farm   ▨ Self-employed, off-farm   ▨ Private wage   ☐ Public wage

Source: Estimates based on GLSS6.

sector after 13 years of school and more. In self-employment in the farm and off-farm sectors, there is also a premium to additional years of schooling, although it enters later than for wage employment. The average premium for an additional year of education (based on the Urban Worker Survey of Ghana for 2004–06) is estimated to be highest in the private sector (8.7 percent), followed

Figure 2.13 Wage Distribution by Worker and Job Characteristics

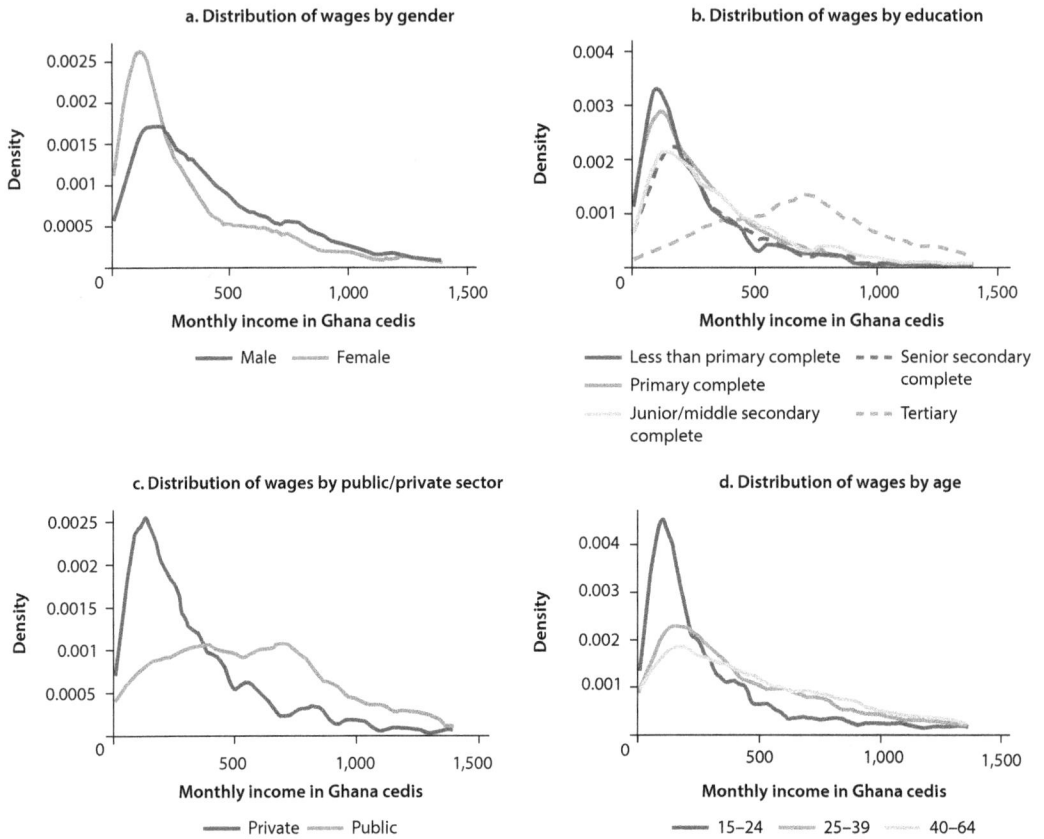

a. Distribution of wages by gender

b. Distribution of wages by education

c. Distribution of wages by public/private sector

d. Distribution of wages by age

Source: Estimates based on GLSS6.

Figure 2.14 Earnings in Relation to Years of Schooling

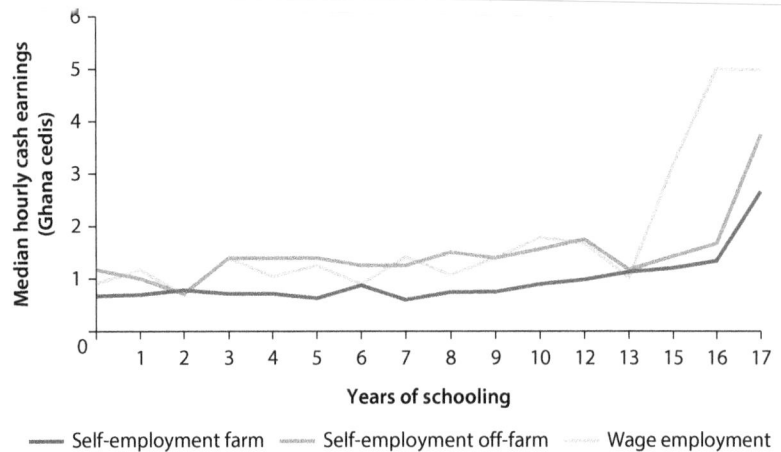

Source: Estimates based on GLSS6.
Note: Earnings (only cash earnings) are not strictly comparable across the employment categories, as they reflect wages for public and private wage workers and labor income for the self-employed.

Figure 2.15 Relationship of Poverty to Sector of Work

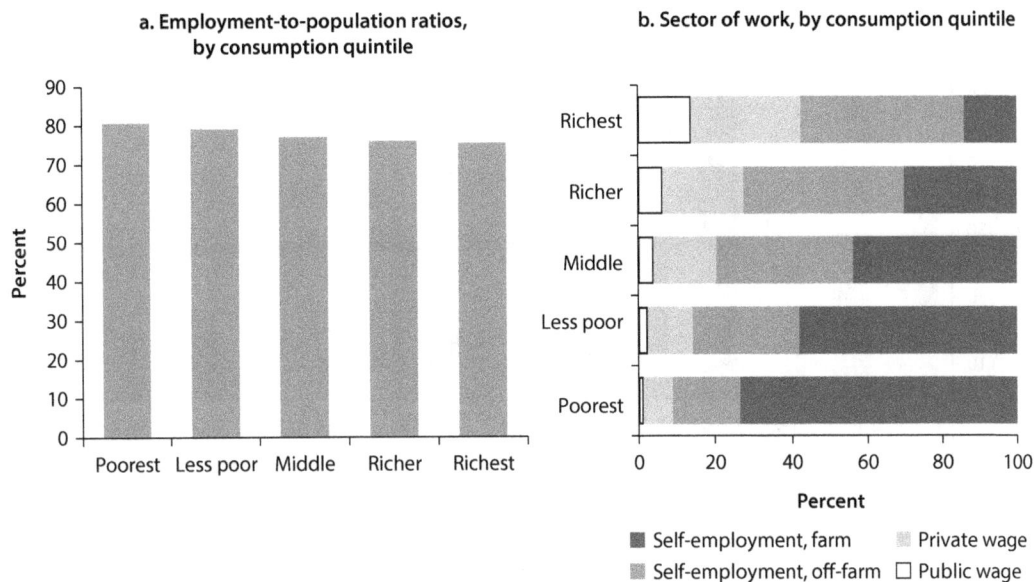

a. Employment-to-population ratios, by consumption quintile

b. Sector of work, by consumption quintile

■ Self-employment, farm
■ Self-employment, off-farm
▨ Private wage
□ Public wage

Source: Estimates based on GLSS6.

by the public sector (8.4 percent), and self-employment (2.3 percent) (Twumasi-Baffour 2015).

Where and how one works matters for welfare levels; it is not enough to have a job. The poor are at least as likely as the nonpoor to hold a job. Again, this is because poorer households generally have few other assets than their labor to rely on for income and survival. Some 80 percent of the poorest 20 percent of the adult population in Ghana are employed: a slightly higher share than those from richer quintiles (figure 2.15, panel a). Access to a job per se is therefore not a ticket out of poverty: what matters is the kind of job one holds. While those in the poorest quintile of households are working, they are overwhelmingly confined to low-productivity activities on the farm, and less than 10 percent hold a wage job. By contrast, the richer the household, the greater the chance that workers will be occupied outside agriculture, in off-farm household enterprises, or—for the most affluent—in wage employment. Over 40 percent of workers from the richest consumption quintile are wage workers (figure 2.15, panel b).

The Transformation of the Landscape of Jobs in Ghana

The rate of job creation and the share of employed persons in the adult population have increased since 1991. After dipping in the mid-2000s compared to 1991, labor force participation rates have reverted to earlier levels, to reach nearly 90 percent for 25- to 64-year-olds, and over 50 percent for 15- to 24-year-olds (figure 2.16, panel a). The increase in labor force participation for

Figure 2.16 Participation of Working-Age Population in the Labor Force

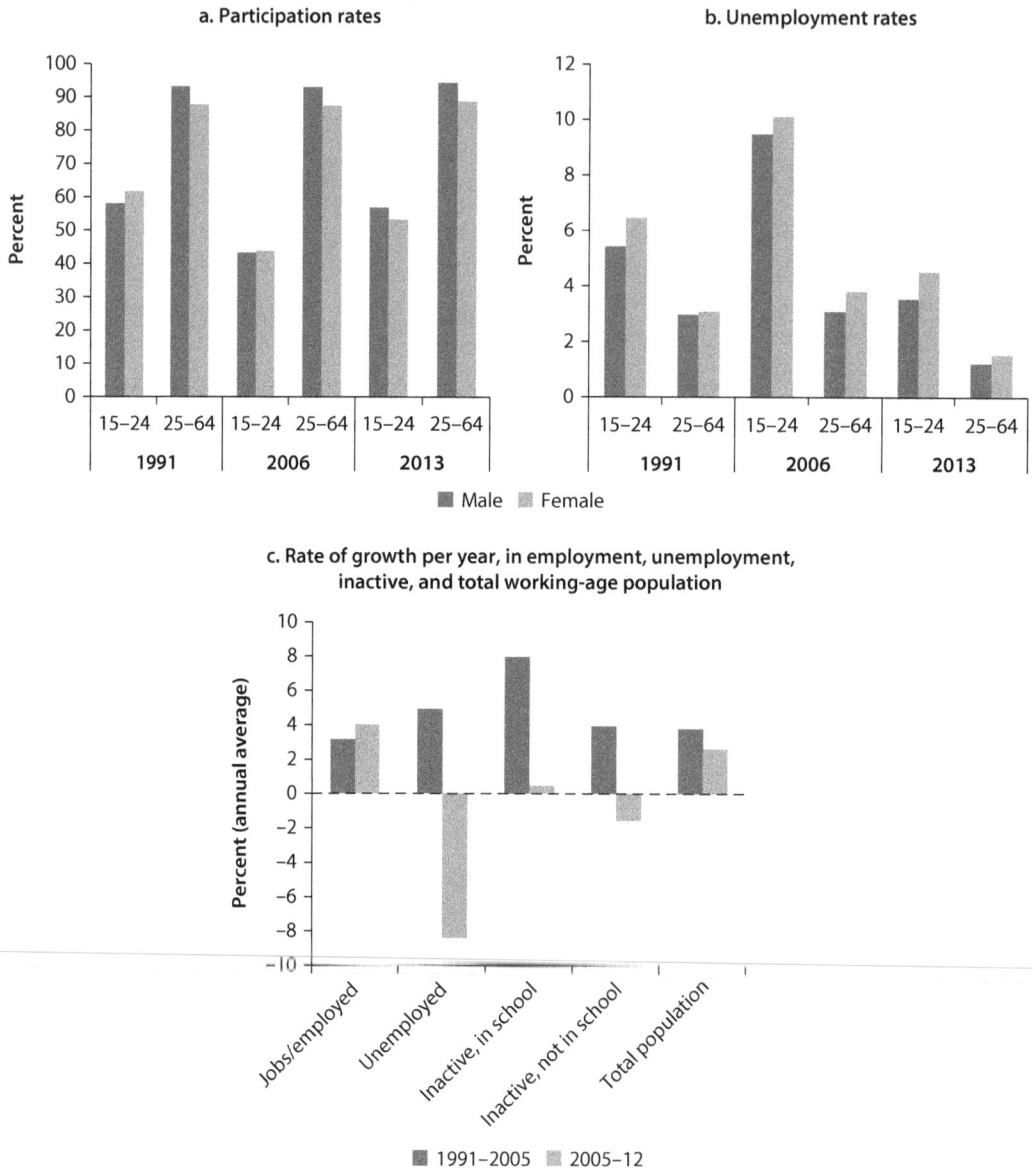

a. Participation rates

b. Unemployment rates

■ Male   ■ Female

c. Rate of growth per year, in employment, unemployment, inactive, and total working-age population

■ 1991–2005   ■ 2005–12

Source: Estimates based on GLSS3, GLSS5, and GLSS6.

youth is significant, as it has taken place at the same time that school enrollment has increased, and unemployment rates have fallen. While around 10 percent of Ghana's active youth were unemployed in 2005, less than 4 percent were unemployed in 2012. The unemployment rate also dropped for workers aged 25–64 (figure 2.16, panel b). Since job creation (at 4 percent per year) outpaced working-age population growth (at 2.6 percent per year) (figure 2.16, panel c), the growth in overall labor force participation between 2005 and 2012 is also reflected in a concomitant increase in employment rates.

The structure of employment has also changed toward off-farm self-employment and to a less extent toward private wage employment, reflecting improvements in poverty reduction and the economic sector contribution to value added. In particular, the share of agricultural employment has fallen from 59 percent to 42 percent of total employment, although agriculture is still the largest job-creating sector in absolute terms (figure 2.17, panel a). As shown in chapter 1, over the last decade, agricultural work has largely given way to services jobs and, to a lesser degree, to industry. The most significant outflow has thus been from farm work, which has given way to predominantly self-employment and to a lesser extent to private wage employment in the nonagricultural sector. Public sector employment has fallen in relative terms. Over the two decades, the share of private wage employment in total employment nearly tripled, from 6 percent to 16 percent, while the share of public wage work fell from 9 percent to 6 percent. Compared with the 1991–2005 period, the transformation of employment accelerated between 2005 and 2012.

All sectors, including agriculture, continue to create new employment. In absolute terms, an additional 400,000 people entered agricultural work between 2005 and 2012, while as many as 1.5 million additional workers took up self-employment in the off-farm sector. In the same period, the private wage sector increased by 700,000 people, compared to 200,000 in the public wage sector (figure 2.17, panel b).

Earnings opportunities have also changed and have diverged across sectors, especially between public sector work and other jobs. While overall earnings have been increasing over time for all categories, earnings growth between 2005 and 2012 was highest in the self-employment sector, in spite of the inflow of workers (figure 2.18). A more disaggregated analysis suggests that earnings did

Figure 2.17 Transformation of the Labor Market over Time, by Sector of Work

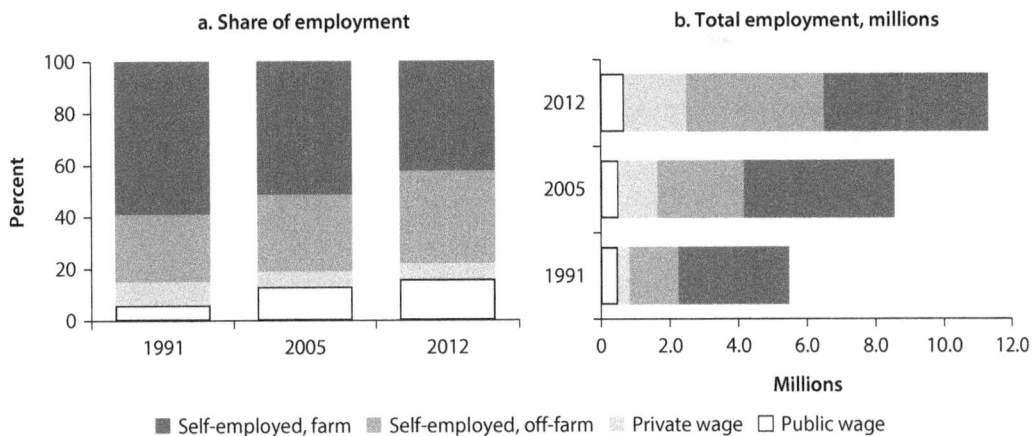

Source: Estimates based on GLSS3, GLSS5, and GLSS6.

Figure 2.18   Increase in Aggregate Income over Time, by Sector of Work

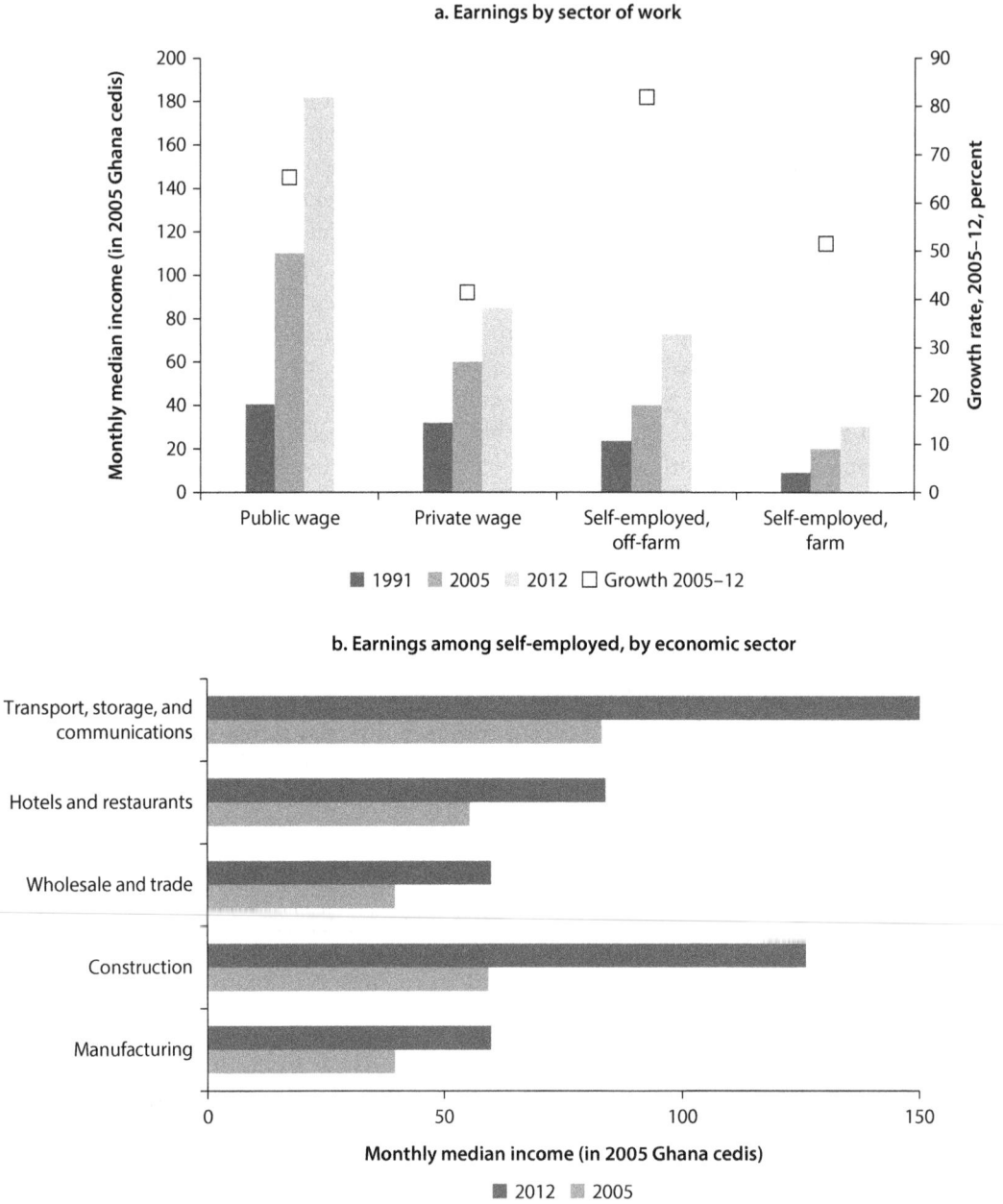

a. Earnings by sector of work

■ 1991   ■ 2005   ■ 2012   □ Growth 2005–12

b. Earnings among self-employed, by economic sector

Monthly median income (in 2005 Ghana cedis)

■ 2012   ■ 2005

Source: Estimates based on GLSS3, GLSS5 and GLSS6.
Note: Earnings (only cash earnings) are not strictly comparable across the employment categories, as they reflect wages for public and private wage workers, and labor income for the self-employed.

not increase significantly among self-employed in the trade sector (which created the most jobs), but instead in other sectors such as transport and other services sectors, where earnings were considerably higher in 2012. In addition, analysis on earnings dynamics between 2004 and 2008, based on the Ghana Urban Household Panel, reveals that, within each sector of employment, increases in wages have been small, especially among low-paid jobs. In the short term, the most effective way of increasing earnings is to change the type of job, such as moving between wage employment and self-employment (Falco and others 2014).

The growth in self-employment between 2005 and 2012 has been accompanied by an improvement in education and aggregate earnings among the self-employed. Analysis based on different rounds of the Ghana Urban Household Panel Survey points to increasing returns to capital and education among the self-employed. Returns to education for the self-employed were lower than for wage workers between 2004 and 2006, but grew faster between 2009 and 2011 (Rankin, Sandefur, and Teal 2010; Twumasi-Baffour 2015; Falco and Haywood 2016). Similarly, the level of education among the self-employed increased between the two periods. This is consistent with the idea that changes in returns are driving changes in the composition of the workforce. Finally, consistent with GLSS data, the panel survey also provides evidence of a decreasing differential between the wage and self-employment premium between 2009 and 2011 (Falco and Haywood 2016). Taken together, the findings support the view that the self-employment sector became an attracting option for relatively higher educated workers.

Education levels among workers increased in all nonagricultural sectors. In 1991, a majority of the self-employed in off-farm activities had completed only primary education, at most. By 2012, nearly two-thirds had at least finished basic education. In parallel, the share of workers in the wage sector with senior secondary education (especially) and tertiary education increased as a result of higher levels of education among incoming youth. Only the farm sector retains a majority of workers with less than basic education. In contrast, the share of tertiary educated workers is increasingly more concentrated in the public sectors (figure 2.19).

Youth accounted for a high share of the new job creation, but mostly in farm work, and the transformation of jobs did not reduce the gender gap. Centering on the most recent and more dynamic period between 2005 and 2012, young men and women accounted for a disproportionate share of new jobs, compared to their share in total employment in 2005. However, young men's work predominantly increased in the farm sector, while young women's work increased in both farm and off-farm self-employment. Men between 25 and 64 were the most significant beneficiaries of the growth in private wage work. As a result of these patterns, the transformation of jobs has not been accompanied by a change in gender gaps. Already in 1991, women were dominant among the self-employed in off-farm activities, and men dominated in the private wage sector (figure 2.20, panels a and b).

Figure 2.19   Level of Education, by Sector of Work

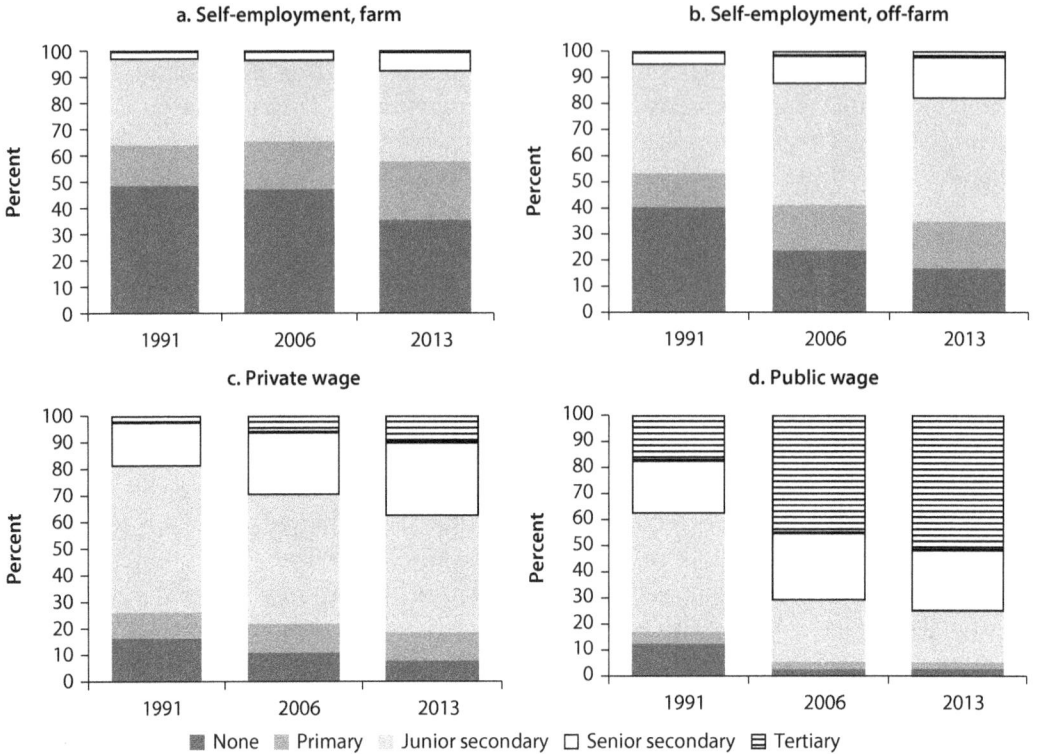

a. Self-employment, farm

b. Self-employment, off-farm

c. Private wage

d. Public wage

■ None   ▨ Primary   ▨ Junior secondary   ☐ Senior secondary   ▤ Tertiary

Source: Estimates based on GLSS3, GLSS5, and GLSS6.

Figure 2.20   Beneficiaries of Job Creation, by Sector of Work

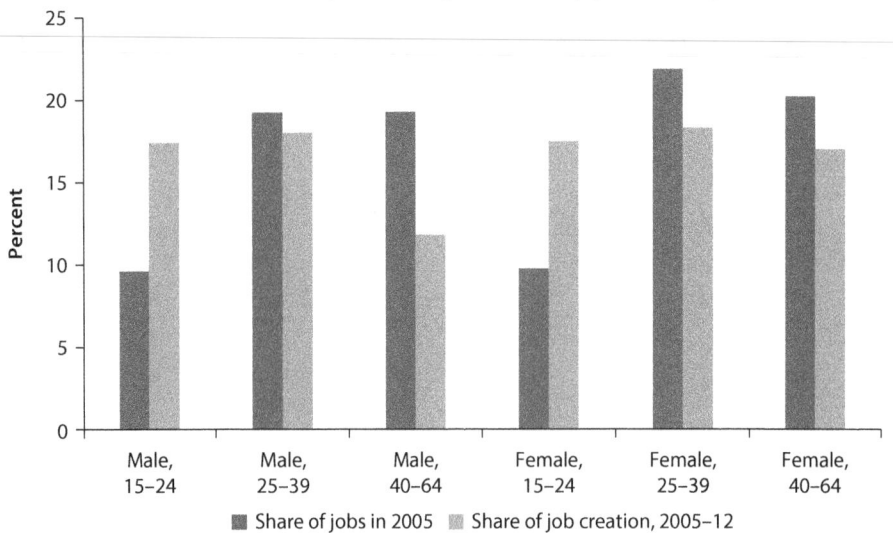

a. Share of jobs and net job creation, by gender and age

■ Share of jobs in 2005   ▨ Share of job creation, 2005–12

figure continues next page

Figure 2.20 Beneficiaries of Job Creation, by Sector of Work *(continued)*

b. Distribution of net job creation by sector and gender

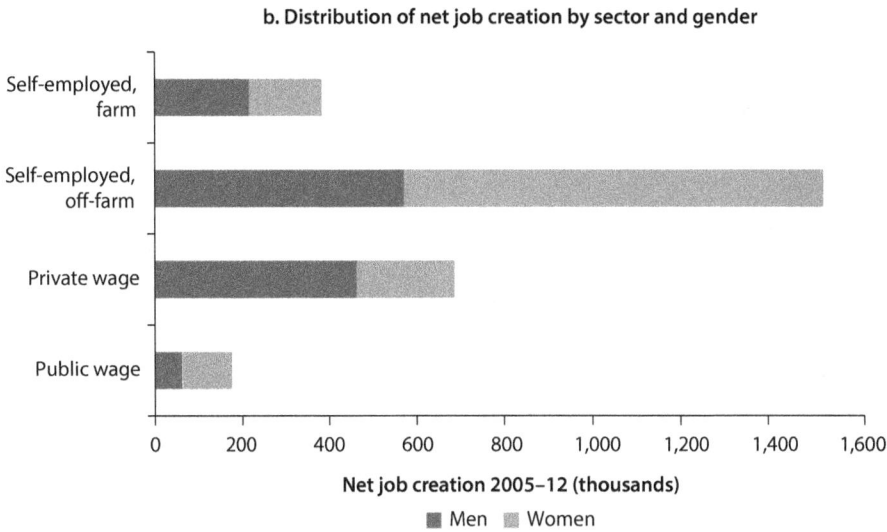

Source: Estimates based on GLSS3, GLSS5, and GLSS6.

Job opportunities are diverging by region, implying that the structural changes taking place in Ghana are not balanced by region, and that regional inequalities are worsening. First, while job creation was balanced between rural and urban areas from 1991 to 2012, from 2005 to 2012, the vast majority of jobs were created in urban areas—especially the two major cities, Greater Accra and Ashanti (figure 2.21). This reflected both the slowdown in agricultural job creation, higher job creation in self-employment and wage work in the urban services sector, and urban-rural population dynamics. Second, in terms of sectors, the regional patterns are very different. In Greater Accra, the only region where agriculture contributed less than half (and in fact very little) to employment already in 1991, private wage employment has increased significantly, and now accounts for 42 percent of all employment. The private wage sector has expanded at the expense of public employment, on the one hand, and self-employment, on the other. In Ghana's other southern regions (Ashanti, Western, Eastern, and Central regions), where the agricultural sector in 1991 accounted for a majority of employment, the share of workers involved in both off-farm self-employment and private wage employment has replaced some of the agricultural work. In the remaining northern regions (Volta, Brong Ahafo, Upper East, Northern, and Upper West), the private wage sector also increased, but remains much less important than off-farm self-employment.

While rural-to-urban migration has been significant in the past 10 years, especially to Accra, and there have been significant flows between rural areas and between urban areas, migration for the primary purpose of employment is low. The urban population increased by 4.7 million between 2005 and 2012, with

Figure 2.21 Job Opportunities, by Region

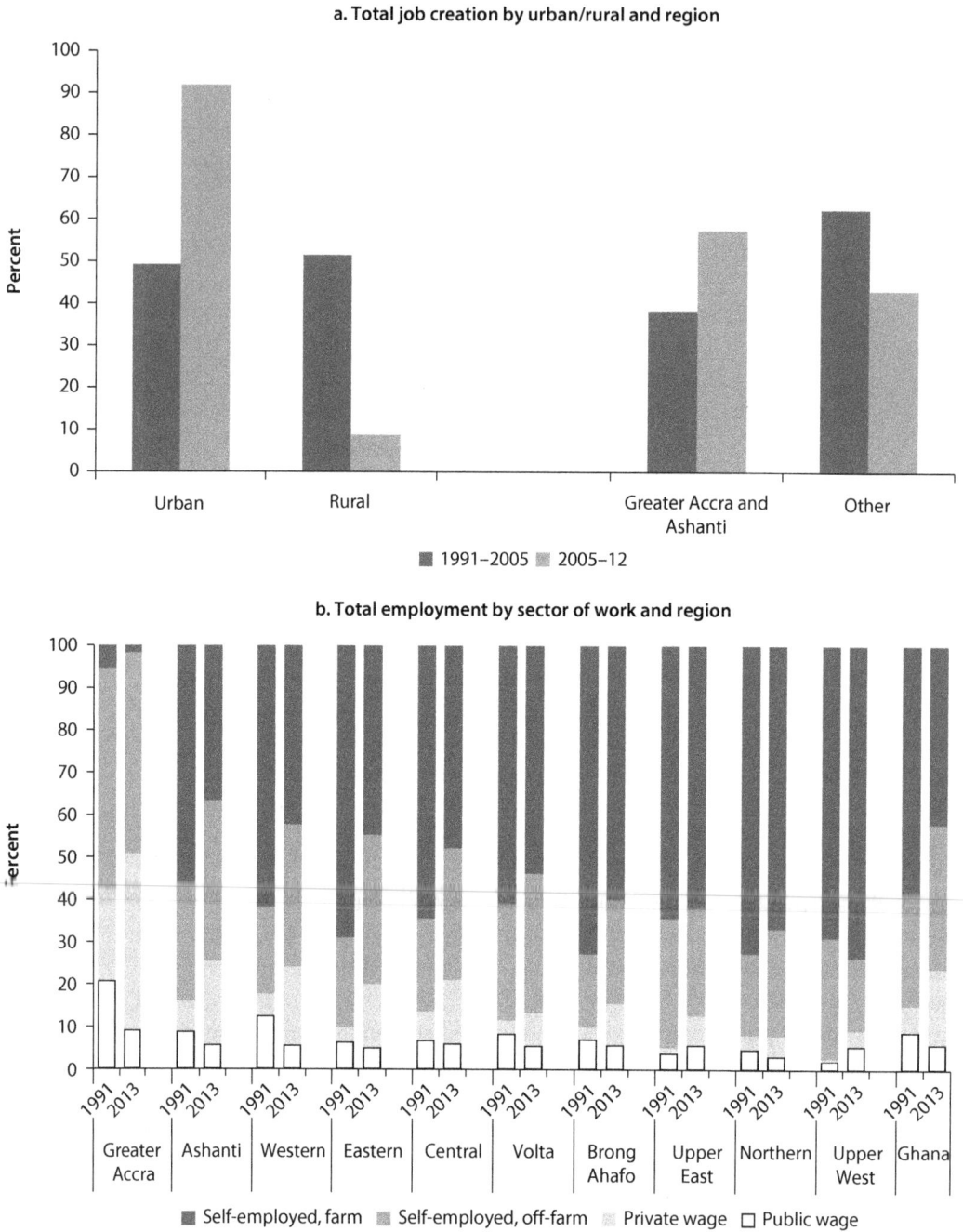

a. Total job creation by urban/rural and region

■ 1991–2005 ■ 2005–12

b. Total employment by sector of work and region

■ Self-employed, farm ■ Self-employed, off-farm ▨ Private wage ☐ Public wage

Source: Estimates based on GLSS3, GLSS5, and GLSS6.

more than 1 million new people in Accra and Ashanti alone. In 2012, some 57 percent of Greater Accra's population, and 42 percent in urban areas overall, had been born somewhere else (figure 2.22). However, the main reasons for internal migration are not directly related to employment or spouse's employment; rather, movements are motivated by marriage, in order to accompany a

Figure 2.22 Internal Migration, by Region and Motive

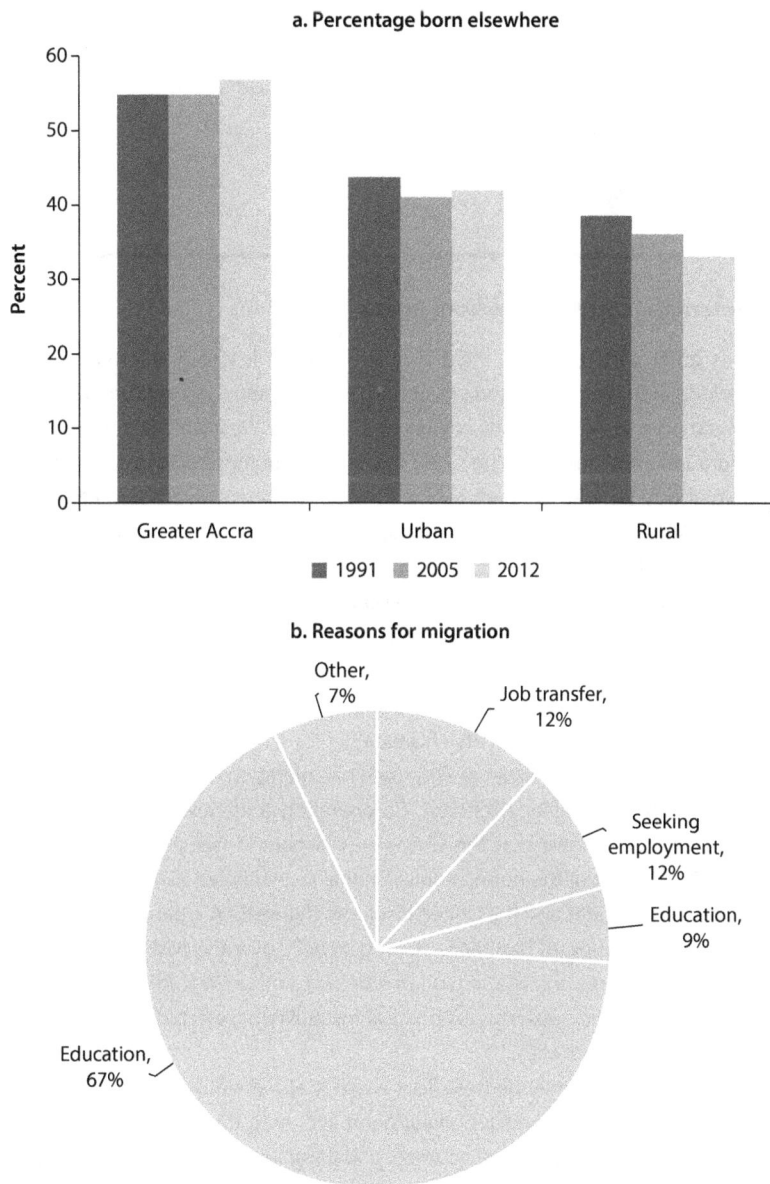

a. Percentage born elsewhere

b. Reasons for migration

Source: GLSS3, GLSS5, and GLSS6.
Note: Data refer to migrants, defined as all individuals aged 15 and over who are living in towns/villages where they were not born (this includes nonreturning migrants only).

parent, pursue education, or escape a natural disaster. Rural-to-rural migration in the form of temporary seasonal migration from northern rural regions to southern regions is also a long-standing feature of Ghana's farming and labor patterns, a response to food insecurity and/or lack of work during the agricultural low season (Rademacher-Schulz, Schraven, and Salifu Mahama 2014). According to the GLSS data, international migration has been very limited; only 5 percent of individuals had migrated from either other African countries or outside of Africa. Numbers on migrants abroad are notoriously difficult to come by. Census-based data from OECD countries suggest that, while Ghana's emigration to OECD countries is low, it is quite high in relation to African countries at similar levels of development, and much of the migration to the developed world is made up of highly educated persons (box 2.4).

Box 2.4 International Migration from Ghana

In Ghana, as other parts of Africa, international migration is largely informal and undocumented, making accurate data on the phenomenon extremely scanty (figure B2.4.1, panel a). Internal migration is very significant in Ghana, as in many West African countries. Flows of internal migration are estimated to be larger in volume than those of international migration. There are significant flows to other parts of the African continent, in particular North, Central, and Southern Africa. But the vast majority move within West Africa, where mobility across porous borders within the region is among the highest in the world (Olsen 2011). More recently, the discovery of oil in Ghana, as well as other pull factors, have attracted internal and international migrants. The discovery of valuable resources is often accompanied by a boom in services and other industries, leading to a boom in employment that attracts a diverse population of job seekers and stimulates entrepreneurship among the local population and migrants (Center for Migration Studies, University of Ghana).

The most comprehensive dataset on international migration from Ghana is based on census data from Organisation for Economic Co-operation and Development (OECD) countries. These estimates suggest that the Ghanaian Diaspora in OECD countries in 2010 was equivalent to 2.3 percent of the population in Ghana: an estimated 270,000 Ghanaians, most of them in the United States and the United Kingdom (figure B2.4.1, panels a and b). The emigration rate to OECD countries has been growing steadily over the past 20 years, and is high compared to African peers and is also high in relation to other West African countries. Wage differentials, demographic patterns, and political instability have acted as push factors spurring migration to OECD countries.

International migration may be beneficial when it allows efficient allocation of labor to both origin and destination countries. Major gains accrue to the migrants themselves, who access better job opportunities; to consumers and complementary factors of production in the recipient countries (capital, land, and labor, other than the mobile type); and to remittance recipients and labor in the sending country. While migration creates huge potential increases

box continues next page

Box 2.4 International Migration from Ghana *(continued)*

Figure B2.4.1 International Migration from Ghana to OECD

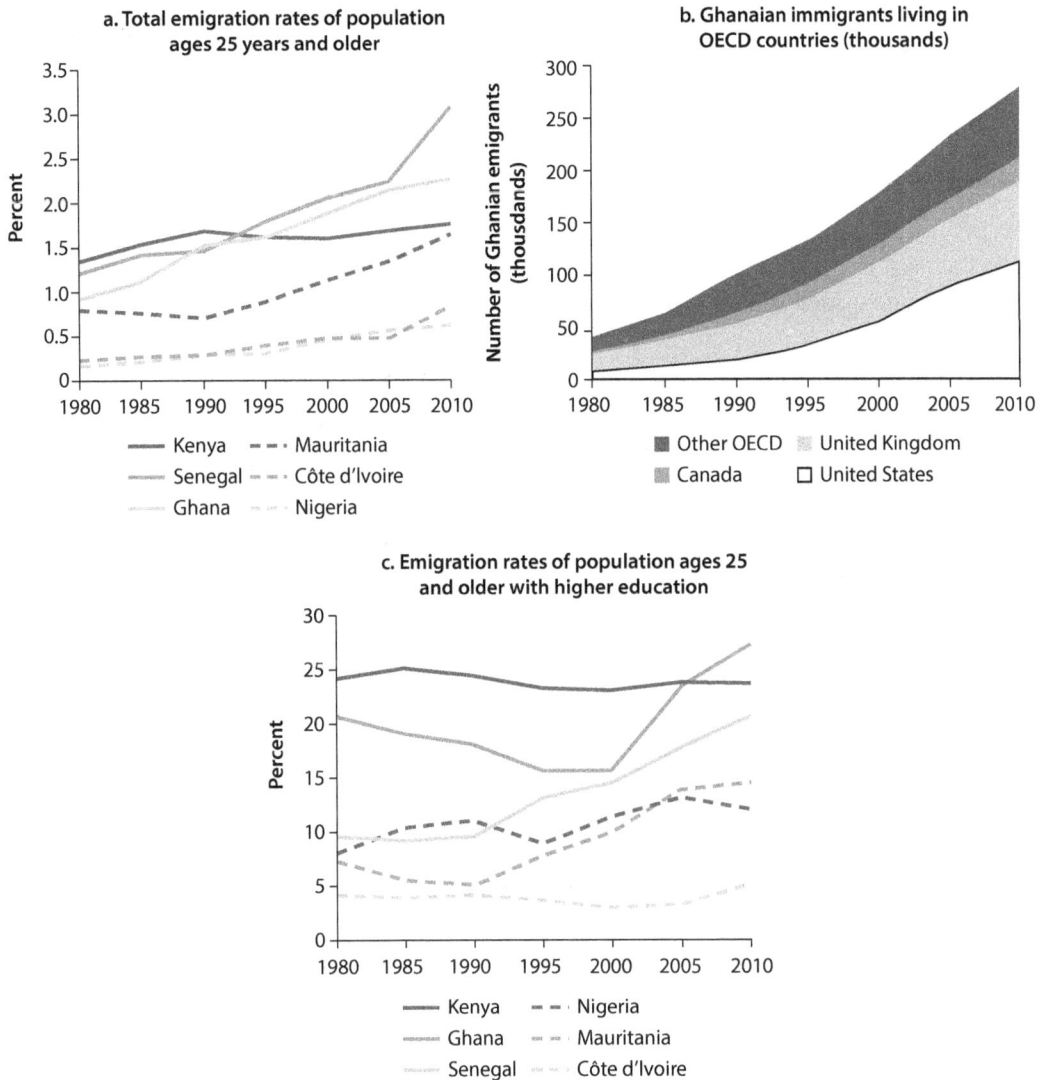

a. Total emigration rates of population ages 25 years and older

b. Ghanaian immigrants living in OECD countries (thousands)

Kenya — Mauritania — Senegal — Côte d'Ivoire — Ghana — Nigeria

Other OECD — United Kingdom — Canada — United States

c. Emigration rates of population ages 25 and older with higher education

Kenya — Nigeria — Ghana — Mauritania — Senegal — Côte d'Ivoire

in global economic development, realizing these gains requires careful management and facilitation of labor flows. Undesired consequences include the pressure on service delivery, housing, and planning in urban centers; segmented labor markets for low-skilled workers; and increased cross-border irregular migration.

The costs and benefits of high-skilled migration are much debated. While the benefits to migrants themselves are quite clear, sending countries may face a tradeoff. Risks include losing investments in education made by Ghana to countries abroad and a resulting skills gap in Ghana. Opportunities include remittances and networks, productive use of resources that

box continues next page

Box 2.4 International Migration from Ghana *(continued)*

would not have been employed in occupations and sectors relevant to their education at home, and more (private) investment in education because of opportunities abroad. High-skill migration rates—the number of highly skilled emigrants expressed as a proportion of highly skilled adults in the sending country—are highest from small island states and from low-income countries. Ghana is among the top sending countries in West Africa, with high emigration rates for the highly educated workers. This rate increased sharply between 2000 and 2010, from a steady 15 percent to 27 percent (figure B2.4.1, panel c).

Source: Estimates based on database prepared for Brücker, Capuano, and Marfouk 2013.

Table 2.3 Employment Mobility through Migration
Percent

		Sector of actual job				
		Agriculture	*Mining/gas/ construction*	*Manufacturing*	*Wholesale and retail trade*	*Other services*
Sector of job before migrating	Agriculture	**80.4**	2.8	3.8	7.4	5.5
	Mining/gas/construction	45.6	**31.8**	2.8	11.5	8.2
	Manufacturing	40.2	3.2	**32.2**	16.0	8.4
	Wholesale and retail trade	39.9	4.2	4.5	**36.5**	15.0
	Other services	35.3	1.6	6.0	17.0	**40.1**

Source: Estimates based on GLSS6.

Internal migration is characterized by little employment mobility in the industrial and service sectors, and high persistence of employment in agriculture, probably reflecting the rural-to-rural migration flows, where northern workers go to more fertile areas in search of land or job opportunities as laborers on larger farms (table 2.3). Unsurprisingly, there is mobility from inactivity and unemployment to employment; however, one out of three of those who were in school before migrating did not find a job and is inactive in the new town/city where they migrated (table 2.4). Sectoral mobility among (nonreturning) migrating workers is limited. The majority of migrating farmers continue being engaged in agriculture activities, while less than half of migrants who were working in industry and services persist in the respective sectors. The remaining workers engage in agriculture.

The spatial patterns of poverty reduction in recent years suggest that location of residence is a major correlate of the risk of poverty, and that geographical mobility may be an effective strategy among individuals to escape poverty (GSS 2014; Molini and Paci 2015). A recent study estimated the impact of internal migration on consumption level. Results show that migrant households have on average a consumption level about twice as high as the consumption of non-migrant households The estimated impact is larger for migrant households that come from northern Ghana than for those that were already in the south, when they are compared to their nonmigrant counterparts still residing in the same area of origin (Molini, Pavelesku, and Ranzani 2016).

Table 2.4 Labor Force Participation through Migration
Percent

		Actual labor force participation		
		Employed	Unemployed	Inactive
Labor force participation before migrating[a]	Full time in education	67	1	32
	Looking for a job	73	5	23
	Inactive	74	2	23

Source: Estimates based on GLSS6.
a. Jobless only

Notes

1. Casual workers and apprentices are excluded from this sectoral categorization because they cannot be assigned to any sector of work. (They are considered in chapter 4, which looks at household enterprises.)

2. The STEP (Skills Towards Employment and Productivity) household survey defines as informal the self-employed, unpaid family workers, and wage workers with no access to social security.

3. As there is often no separation between business revenues, profits, and personal earnings in off-farm household enterprises ("self-employment, off-farm") and small family farmers ("self-employment, farm"), this measure must be interpreted with caution and cannot be strictly compared with "wages" or work compensation. This report takes the earning measure captured by the GLSS as indicative of the general pattern and scale of labor income across different types of employment.

References

Brücker, H., S. Capuano, and A. Marfouk. 2013. *Education, Gender and International Migration: Insights from a Panel Dataset, 1980–2010.* Institute for Employment Research database.

Center for Migration Studies. n.d. "Dynamics of Migration in West Africa." Migration Factsheets Series 1, No. 1, University of Ghana.

Darvas, P., M. Favara, and T. Arnold. 2016. *Snapshot of the STEP Skills Measurement Survey.* Washington, DC: World Bank.

Falco, P., and L. Haywood. 2016. "Entrepreneurship versus Joblessness: Explaining the Rise in Self-employment." *Journal of Development Economics* 118: 245–65.

Falco, P., A. Kerr, P. Paci, and B. Rijkers. 2014. "Working toward Better Pay: Earning Dynamics in Ghana and Tanzania." World Bank Study 88483, World Bank, Washington, DC.

Falco, P., A. Kerr, N. Rankin, J. Sandefur, and F. Teal. 2011. "The Returns to Formality and Informality in Urban Africa." *Labour Economics* 18 (1): S23–31.

Filmer, D., and L. Fox. 2014. "Youth Employment in Sub-Saharan Africa." Africa Development Forum Series, World Bank and Agence Française de Développement.

Gatti, R., and M. Honorati. 2008. "Informality among Formal Firms: Firm-level, Cross-country Evidence on Tax Compliance and Access to Credit." Policy Research Working Paper 4476, World Bank, Washington, DC.

GSS (Ghana Statistical Service). 2012. *How Ghanaian Women and Men Spend their Time: Ghana Time Use Survey 2009*. Accra, Ghana: GSS.

———. 2013. *2010 Population and Housing Census: National Analytical Report*. Accra, Ghana: GSS.

———. 2014. *Poverty Profile in Ghana (2005–2013)*. Accra, Ghana: GSS.

Loayza, N., and J. Rigolini. 2006. "Informality Trends and Cycles." Policy Research Working Paper 4078, World Bank, Washington, DC.

Molini, V., and P. Paci. 2015. *Poverty Reduction in Ghana: Progress and Challenges*. Washington, DC: World Bank.

Molini, V., D. Pavelesku, and M. Ranzani. Forthcoming. "Should I Stay or Should I Go? Internal Migration and Household Welfare in Ghana."

OECD (Organisation for Economic Co-operation and Development). 2015. *Taxing Wages 2015*. Paris: OECD.

Olsen, A. S. W. 2011. "Reconsidering West African Migration." DIIS Working Paper 21, Danish Institute for International Studies (DIIS), Copenhagen.

Perry, G. E., O. Arias, P. Fajnzylber, W. F. Maloney, A. Mason, and J. Saavedra-Chanduvi. 2007. *Informality: Exit and Exclusion*. Washington, DC: World Bank.

Rademacher-Schulz, C., B. Schraven and E. Salifu Mahama. 2014. "Time Matters: Shifting Seasonal Migration in Northern Ghana in Response to Rainfall Variability and Food Insecurity." *Climate and Development* 6 (1): 46–52.

Rankin, N., J. Sandefur, and F. Teal. 2010. "Learning & Earning in Africa: Where Are the Returns to Education High?" CSAE Working Paper Series 2010-02, Centre for the Study of African Economies, University of Oxford.

Ranzani, M., and M. Tuccio. Forthcoming. *Is Government Employment Attractive? Public Wage Premiums and Job Queues*.

Schneider, F. 2014. "The Shadow Economy and Shadow Labor Force: A Survey of Recent Developments." IZA Discussion Paper 8278, Institute for the Study of Labor (IZA).

Twumasi-Baffour, P. 2015. "Determinants of Urban Worker Earnings in Ghana: The Role of Education." *Modern Economy* 6: 1240–52.

World Bank. 2012. *World Development Report 2013: Jobs*. Washington, DC: World Bank.

Transitions into Work and the Role of Skills

Main Messages

Skills and education play a role in increasing the number of productive jobs and the productivity of existing jobs. While access to formal education has increased in Ghana, gaps remain, and the transition from school into productive jobs is too slow, especially for girls. Moreover, the quality of education is a problem, as some of those who have passed through basic education still lack basic functional skills. Access to skills development outside of formal education (through training, apprenticeships, and the like) is modest, especially for the nonwage sectors.

Education, Skills, and Jobs

Rapid and successful school-to-work transition for youth is important for the individual as well as for society. A smooth transition from school to a reasonably good job is critical for Ghana's youth, who make up one-third of working-age adults and one-fifth of the total population. Better equipped with education than previous generations, and witnesses to a significant transformation of the Ghanaian economy from a farm-dependent to a more dynamic services-driven economy, they are looking for a first job experience that will set them on a good income path. Not being able to secure a job, or entering into low-productivity jobs, risks scarring workers for life: they never acquire the experience necessary to move ahead (and they perhaps never had the requisite skills or characteristics necessary to enter a higher-paid job in the first place). There is significant evidence of low earnings mobility for the low paid in developing countries (Fields 2011). Work on earnings dynamics in Ghana shows that a pattern of once low paid, always low paid (path dependence) is significant, and that women and youth are particularly vulnerable to such "scarring" in labor markets (Falco and others 2014). Even starting off in a low-paid activity is therefore a concern because there are few prospects of upward mobility over the working life and because lifelong employment and earning opportunities are determined early, and often by factors that are unrelated to talent or effort.

Education and labor market-related skills are significant factors in individuals' labor outcomes, firm productivity, and economic growth. From a macroeconomic perspective, it is not controversial to suggest that the level of skills in the population and the degree to which these skills can be put to use in the economy play an important role in sustainable development in any one country. The skill content of occupations is changing globally toward less routine and more nonroutine analytical skills, requiring a host of problem-solving and other competencies, not only in developed countries but also in developing countries like Nigeria (Acemoglu and Autor 2011; World Bank 2016). The extent to which formal and informal education systems can impart those skills to children and youth will matter for individual employment outcomes, as well as for economy-wide productivity. Moreover, the time lag involved in building a skilled work force (with basic education as a first building block) suggests attention needs to be given to the acquisition of job-relevant skills before it becomes a binding constraint to doing business.

Rapid technological change is generating new employment and earnings opportunities in urban areas, but also risks. These include the destruction of jobs linked to large-scale automation, nonstandard forms of work, and shorter job tenures, which are becoming more common, especially among youth. The challenge for labor market institutions is to adapt to these changes and to facilitate rather than impede transitions between jobs. The challenge for social protection systems is to support workers with shorter work tenures and interrupted career trajectories (World Bank 2015).

Transitions into Work

Slow or No Transition of Youth into Productive Work

The transition from school to work is different for girls and boys. Because of increasing enrollment in secondary school, the transition into work now happens later for youth. Access to school has increased significantly for girls, even since 2005. At age 15, the shares of girls and boys in work versus school are fairly similar, although boys are more likely to combine school and work than girls. However, by age 20, the rate of girls not in employment, education, or training is twice as high as that of boys (26 percent versus 13 percent) and the share of girls in employment (only) and school (only) is lower (figure 3.1, panels a and b). The transition into wage work is also slower or does not happen for girls. Girls leave school earlier than boys to begin to work, but the access to wage employment is very limited, even for adult women. Instead, girls enter—and stay within—the off-farm household enterprise sector (figure 3.1, panels c and d).

Young people's opportunities for education and better jobs are markedly different between rural and urban areas. Consider the cases of urban boys and men on the one hand, and rural girls and women on the other. At age 15, 62 percent of urban boys are in school and not working, compared to 39 percent of rural girls—and the gap widens to 45 versus 18 percent by age 20 (figure 3.2, panels a and b). These gaps are likely to reflect several interrelated differences: the tendency for girls to marry and get pregnant earlier in rural areas, which affects girls' access to labor markets (discussed later in this chapter); lower rural income levels, which compel rural inhabitants to work rather than study; and the concentration of secondary school institutions in urban areas. The lack of prospects for young people to enter wage work in rural areas is also evident. At age 25, 40 percent of urban men are employed in the private wage sector, but only 8 percent of rural women aged 25 have access to wage work. Instead, more than half of them are working in agriculture (figure 3.2, panels a and b).

Inequalities between young men and women have also been increasing over time. First, young men (15–23) are more likely to move into farm work or private

Figure 3.1 School-to-Work Transition, by Age Group and Gender

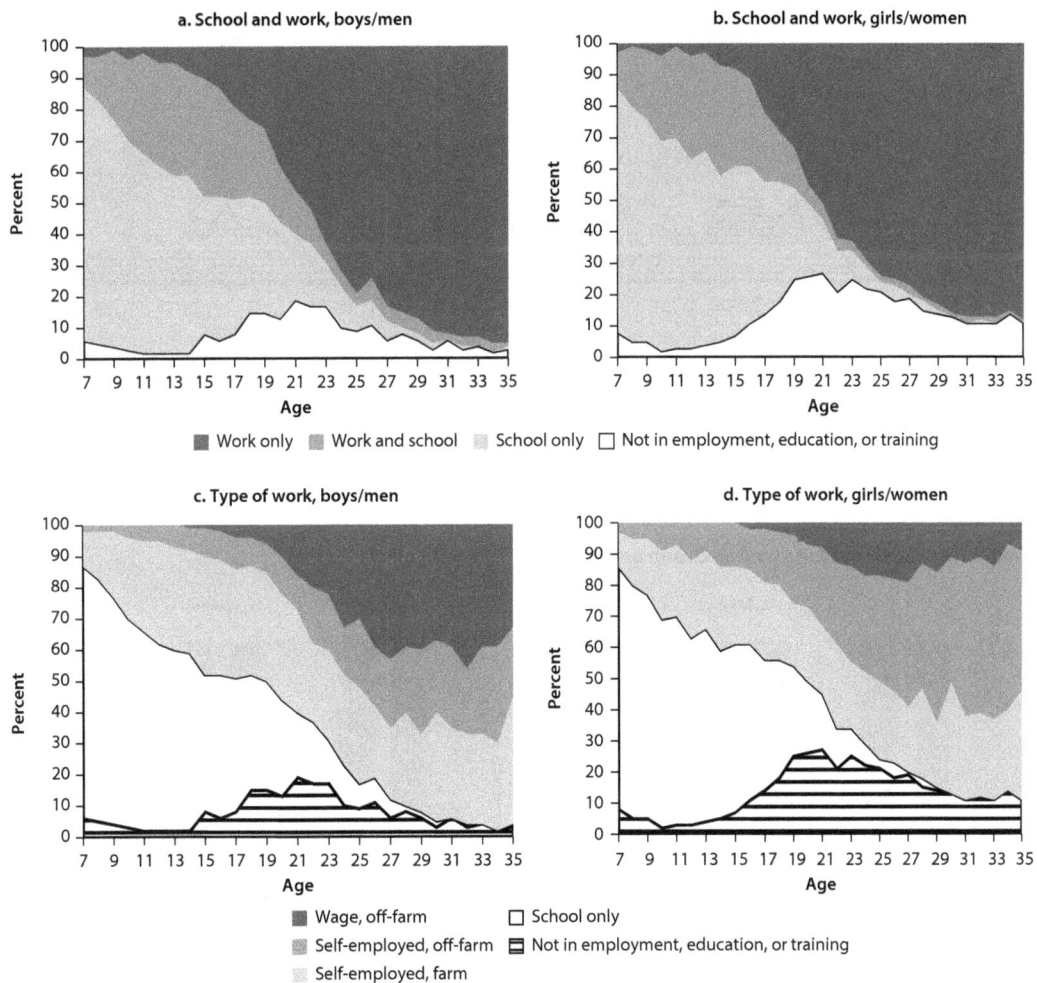

a. School and work, boys/men

b. School and work, girls/women

■ Work only ▨ Work and school ▨ School only □ Not in employment, education, or training

c. Type of work, boys/men

d. Type of work, girls/women

■ Wage, off-farm   □ School only
▨ Self-employed, off-farm   ▤ Not in employment, education, or training
▨ Self-employed, farm

Source: Estimates based on GLSS6.

sector work than young women of the same age group. Second, young men seem to experience more dynamic movement over age cohorts, as well as over time (figure 3.3, panels c and d). Most notably, 25- to 39-year-old males are much less likely to work in farming than the youngest males; instead, many of them have moved into private wage work. Women do not appear to escape their first job opportunity in a similar way, except that the importance of self-employment in the off-farm sector increases for the 25- to 39-year-olds compared to 15- to 24-year-olds. Corroborating this story, the distribution of employment has changed more significantly for young men than for young women since 1991.

Figure 3.2 School-to-Work Transition, Urban Boys and Rural Girls, by Age Group

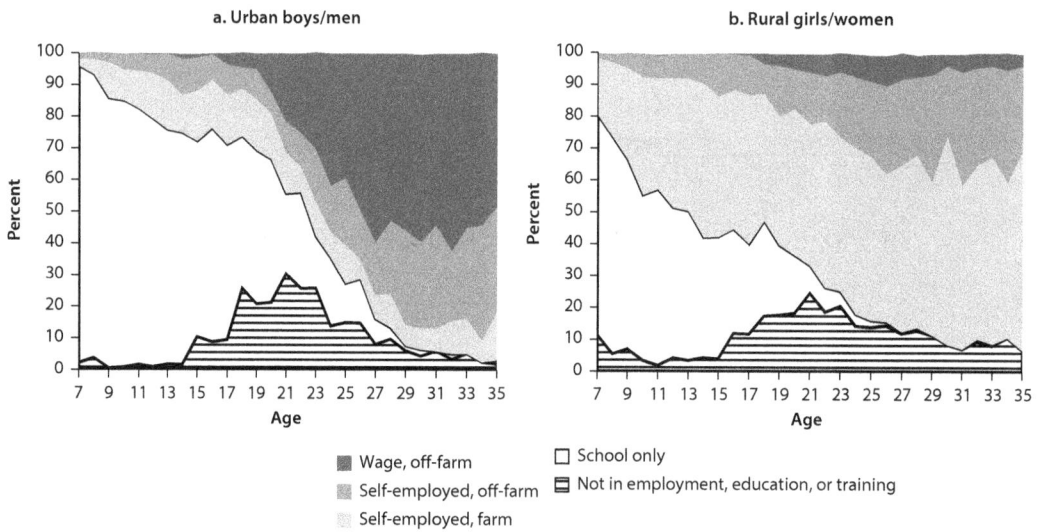

Source: Estimates based on GLSS6.

Figure 3.3 Sector of Work, by Age Group and Gender

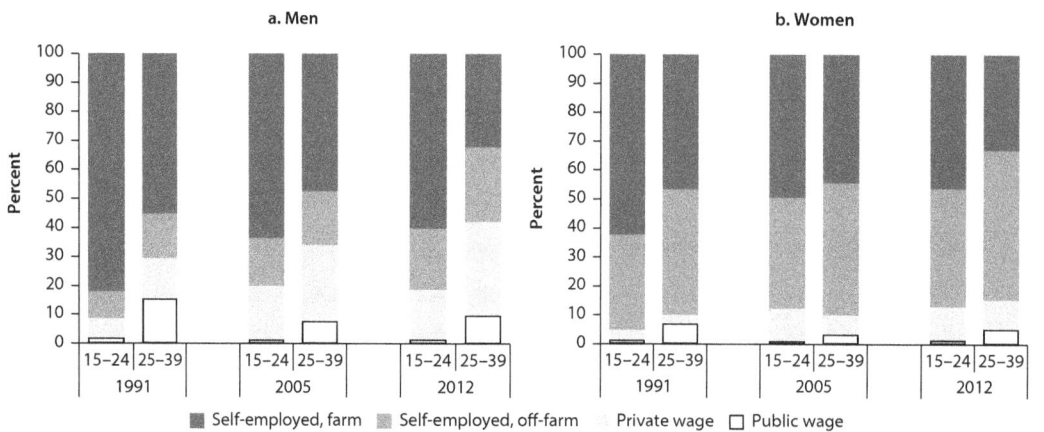

Source: Estimates based on GLSS6.

Early Marriage and Insufficient Schooling Both Matter for Transitions

The incomplete transition of girls into working life is related to early pregnancies and family formation, especially in rural areas, and particularly for girls from low-income families. Women tend to marry earlier than men, although the gaps have fallen somewhat (figure 3.4, panel a). At the age of 20, less than 5 percent of men are married, compared to over 30 percent of women; at the age of 25, only one-third of men are married, compared to two-thirds of women. The risk of being married before age 18 (which is the lawful age in Ghana) is higher among rural girls, among those with low levels of education, and among the poor (UNICEF 2015). Whether in or out of wedlock, women bear children early in Ghana: about half of women between ages 20 and 24 have had at least one birth (figure 3.4, panel b). Early marriage increases the chances of early pregnancies; more than 70 percent of girls aged 15–19 who are married have had a child,

Figure 3.4 Marriage and Family Formation in Ghana

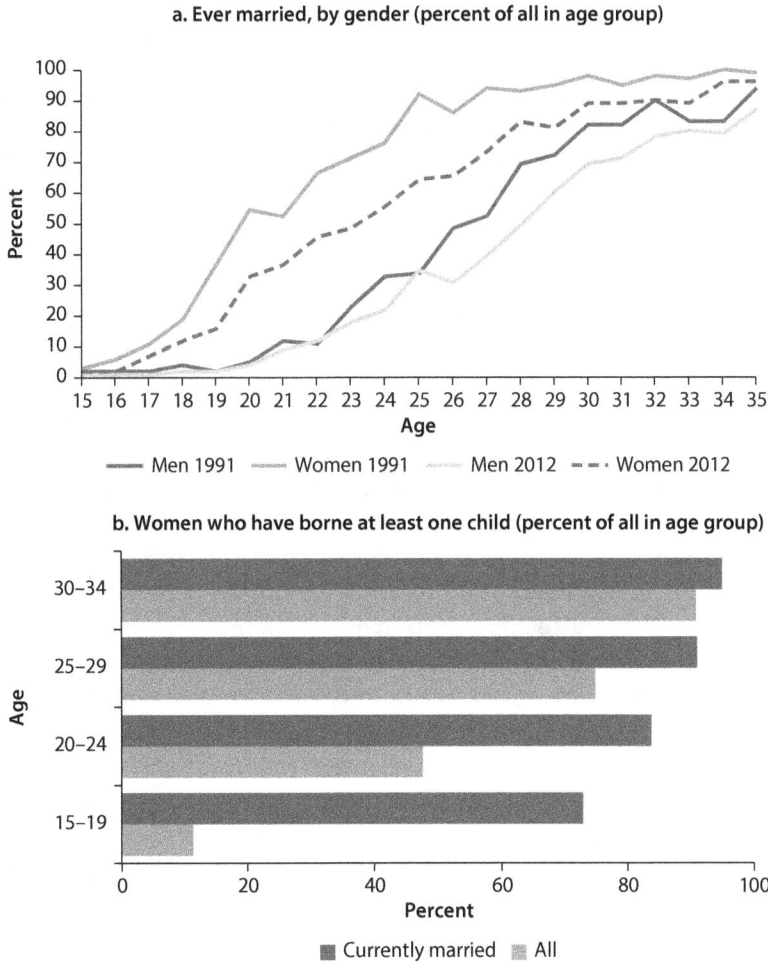

a. Ever married, by gender (percent of all in age group)

b. Women who have borne at least one child (percent of all in age group)

Sources: Estimates based on GLSS3 and GLSS6 (panel a), and GSS, GHS, and IFC International 2015 (panel b).

compared to 10 percent for the entire age group. As noted, women are more likely than men to be charged with household chores, including childcare, and so are less able to establish or join activities outside of their household's immediate needs.

Insufficient schooling is related to early entry into labor markets, but hinders transition into productive work. Those who drop out before completing secondary school, or youth who never enroll in school, tend to be confined to taking up low-productivity jobs, as evidenced by the importance of agricultural jobs for youth. Around 7 percent of children between ages 7 and 14 are not in school. Another 30 percent combine school and work. Light work may be considered a reasonable contribution to the household economy, but more heavy work schedules are known to take a toll on schooling outcomes. For 10- to 14-year-olds, the school attendance of child laborers is 10 percentage points lower than that for other children. For those who do attend, the quality of school attendance is negatively affected by absences, late arrivals, and exhaustion (box 3.1). Conversely, children who start school late and/or who repeat courses during their schooling take longer to enter working life.

Parents' education is an important determinant of choices about schooling and transition to work. In Sub-Saharan Africa, young children from households with a parent with more than secondary education are 20 percent more likely to be in school than children in households where the head has little or no education. The number of working adults in the household also increases the probability that the young will attend school, especially in countries

---

Box 3.1 Child Labor in Ghana

What is child labor? Child labor is defined in International Labour Organization (ILO) Conventions as work that children should not be doing because they are too young to work or—if they are old enough to work—because it is dangerous or otherwise unsuitable for them. Children's or adolescents' participation in work that does not affect their health and personal development or interfere with their education is generally regarded as being something positive. In the developing world, the majority of laborer children are unpaid workers employed in their household enterprise or farm, helping with household duties.

Why do we care? The cost of child labor for human development and economic growth is high and may persist across generations. There are different channels through which child labor affects economic development. Child labor can seriously endanger children's immediate health and safety, as well as their health status later in life. Child labor also compromises children's ability to enroll and stay in school, and to benefit from the time they do spend in the classroom. Finally, child labor may lower the wages of jobs children compete for (typically unskilled labor) (Edmonds 2015). The consequences of child labor are multifaceted, possibly leading to social vulnerability, marginalization, and to permanent lifetime patterns of education, employment choices, and marital status (Beegle, Dehejia, and Gatti 2009).

box continues next page

Box 3.1 Child Labor in Ghana *(continued)*

There is also compelling evidence of intergenerational persistence: child laborers become adults with children who are also child laborers.

Why does it happen? Child labor is a complex problem; numerous factors influence whether children work or not. Poverty and its correlates emerge as the most compelling reason why children work. Poor households need their children to work for survival and to cope with income shocks, such as natural disasters or economic or agricultural crises. Other factors include costly access to education, cultural norms, poor enforcement of regulations, and local labor market demand. Hence, unsurprisingly, Sub-Saharan Africa continues to be the region with the highest incidence of child labor (21.4 percent of 5- to 17-year-olds in 2012). This compares with 9 percent in Asia and the Pacific and Latin America and the Caribbean, and 8 percent in the Middle East and North Africa. The incidence of child labor is highest in poorer countries and, within countries, in poorer households. The highest share of child laborer is still in agriculture, but it is increasing in the service and manufacturing sector in the informal economy (ILO 2013).

How are children protected in Ghana? The legal framework for child labor in Ghana is contained in the Children's Act (Act. 560, 1998). The Act sets the minimum age for admission of a child to employment at 15 years (Sec. 89) and the minimum age of admission to light work at 13 years (Sec. 90.1), where light work is defined as work that is not likely to be harmful to the health or development of the child and does not affect the child's attendance at school or the capacity of the child to benefit from school work (Sec. 90.2). The Hazardous Child Labor Activity Framework for Ghana, while acknowledging this Act, recommends a minimum age of 12 years for light work. Based on national legislation, child labor is defined in Ghana as including all 5- to 11-year-old children in employment; 12- to 14-year-olds who are engaged in "non-light" work; and 15- to 17-year-olds engaged in "hazardous" work.[a]

What is the incidence of child labor in Ghana and why does it happen? In spite of the regulatory framework, 1.9 million children were in child labor in 2012 in Ghana, corresponding to 22 percent of the 5- to 17-year-old age group. Worse, the number of child laborers has increased since 2005 (UCW 2016). The incidence is high, even taking into account Ghana's income level (figure B3.1.1). Econometric analysis of the GLSS data shows that involvement in child labor increases with the age of the child, and decreases with household income or consumption and levels of education of the household head. Poor access to water and electricity is also strongly correlated with higher child labor, as core tasks need to be performed in the household economy, raising the opportunity costs of keeping children in school. Substantial regional disparities are present in Ghana: 36 percent of children are in child labor in the Upper West region, compared to 5 percent in Accra. Generally, child labor in rural areas is more than double that in urban areas. Aside from these "push factors," "pull factors" also affect the incidence of child labor. For example, there are no significant differences in the incidence of child labor in cocoa-growing communities and other communities, even though households in cocoa-growing communities are less poor than households in other communities, and the majority of child laborers in cocoa-growing communities come from nonpoor households (UCW 2016). This suggests that demand from the cocoa plantations is also driving the demand for labor.

box continues next page

Box 3.1 Child Labor in Ghana *(continued)*

Figure B3.1.1 Incidence of Child Labor in Ghana Compared with Other Countries and Regions

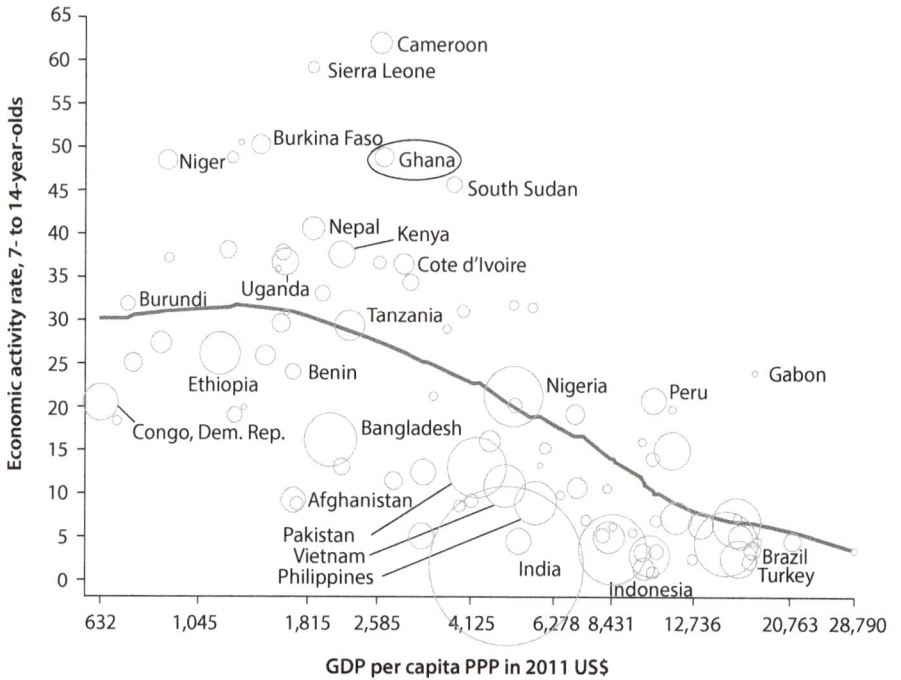

Source: Edmonds 2015.

Note: The figure plots the fraction of children who are economically active between the ages of 7 and 14, inclusive, against gross domestic product per person adjusted for purchasing power parity (PPP) and expressed in 2011 purchasing power adjusted dollars (WDI). The size of each circle reflects the population of children under 15 in the country (larger circle = more children). The curve is a local kernel smoother.

What are the policy options? While significant progress has been made globally, addressing the challenge of child labor in the future is going to require a substantial acceleration of efforts at all levels. There are still 168 million children involved in child labor worldwide (11 percent of the child population). Policy areas to address the child labor challenge include expanding social protection systems to provide poor households with a minimum income and protect against the risk of destitution and child labor as a coping strategy; making basic education and skill development programs accessible, relevant, and meaningful; and strengthening the legislation and enforcement mechanisms on minimum age and prohibited work for children (ILO 2013).

Sources: Beegle, Dehejia, and Gatti 2009; ILO and IPEC 2013; Edmonds 2015; UCW 2016.

a. Hazardous work includes going to sea; mining and quarrying; porterage of heavy loads; manufacturing industries where chemicals are produced or used; work in places where machines are used; and work in places such as bars, hotels, and places of entertainment where a person may be exposed to immoral behavior (Sec. 91.3).

with good schooling outcomes. Nonetheless, many youth drop out of school because formal education has, or is perceived to have, little payoff in contexts where there are no prospects for wage employment. Parents in rural Ghana, Kenya, Uganda, and Zambia often do not send their children to school because they think completing formal high school will not lead to a job (Inoue and others 2015).

Higher schooling is strongly linked with the type of jobs and the quality of jobs youth can access. As noted, youth with higher education attainment are more likely to work in wage jobs, while those with lower levels of education are more likely to work on the family farm or be self-employed in off-farm activities. More educated workers are also more likely to have a better quality job in terms of benefits and written contracts, which are largely found in the public sector. Evidence from experiments in some developing countries, including the Dominican Republic, Madagascar, Malawi, and Mexico, suggests that parents and youth often have misguided perceptions about the returns to schooling and that there are substantial benefits (in terms of guiding schooling decisions) to increasing the accuracy of information (Nguyen 2008; Jensen 2010; Dizon-Ross 2014; Avitabile and De Hoyos Navarro 2015).

The increase in education attainment needs to be accompanied by the accumulation of skills in terms of cognitive, socioemotional, and job-specific competencies. A wide set of skills are needed to do more advanced jobs well: cognitive skills (reading, writing, analysis); socioemotional skills (discipline, teamwork skills); and job-specific skills (technical skills, but also management, supervision, computer skills, and the like). There is evidence from advanced economies, as well as from Ghana, that the use of skills is an important determinant of earnings, even when education levels are taken into account. In Ghana, the best-paid jobs require intensive writing and job-specific skills, as well as conscientiousness (the ability to stay on task) (Darvas, Favara, and Arnold 2016).

Skills Development for Labor Markets

Skills formation begins in early childhood and is ideally developed in education systems that strengthen the development of both analytical and soft skills, such as discipline, proactiveness, flexibility, and teamwork skills. At the secondary and tertiary levels, more job-specific (vocational) skills should also be beginning to develop (Banerji and others 2010). After school, these skills should be maintained and upgraded throughout adult life, with on-the-job training and other training opportunities provided by employers or by other institutions.

Access to Formal Education Has Increased, but Has Not Translated Sufficiently into Learning

Education levels have increased in Ghana, and gender disparities are falling in the younger generation. By 2012, 61 percent of young women and 72 percent of young men had at least finished basic education. However, two out of five women still have no more than primary education. In all, there are over 3 million people in Ghana between ages 15 and 39 who have completed no more than primary education; nearly one out of five in this age group of women does not have any education at all (figure 3.5).

Educational achievements remain strongly correlated with socioeconomic status, in terms of entry into school, of highest level completed, and of dropping out. Household survey data show that the net primary enrollment rate for children from the poorest 20 percent of the population is more than 20 percentage points lower than that for the richest 20 percent of Ghana's population. These differences are accentuated only for higher levels of education; less than one in five children belonging to the poorest 20 percent is enrolled in lower secondary education. Children with low socioeconomic status are more likely to start school late, which in turn is strongly correlated with early dropout. Given the role of education for earnings opportunities, such inequities in access are bound to perpetuate income inequalities across generations (figure 3.6).

The quality of schooling also needs improvement, from primary to higher levels: in spite of higher enrollment, some basic cognitive skills such as numeracy and literacy are still lacking. Basic functional skills such as literacy and numeracy have increased in Ghana. The share of young men and women who can read and write is higher than in many comparator countries, although lower than in lower-middle-income countries in general (figure 3.7, panel a). These skills are not universally acquired, however, and there are still significant gender gaps (figure 3.7, panels b and c). According to household survey data, one in four young women (aged 15–24) cannot read and write, and less than half of women older than 25 are literate. A 2009–10 study of literacy in Ghana showed that one in five third graders could not read a single word, and one in five could also not perform simple subtraction (Cloutier, Reinstadtler, and Beltran 2011). Learning trajectories are also low in Ghana. For instance, while reading performance improves with more schooling, the increase is slow (Filmer and Fox 2014).

Figure 3.5 Highest Level of Education Completed, by Age Group and Gender

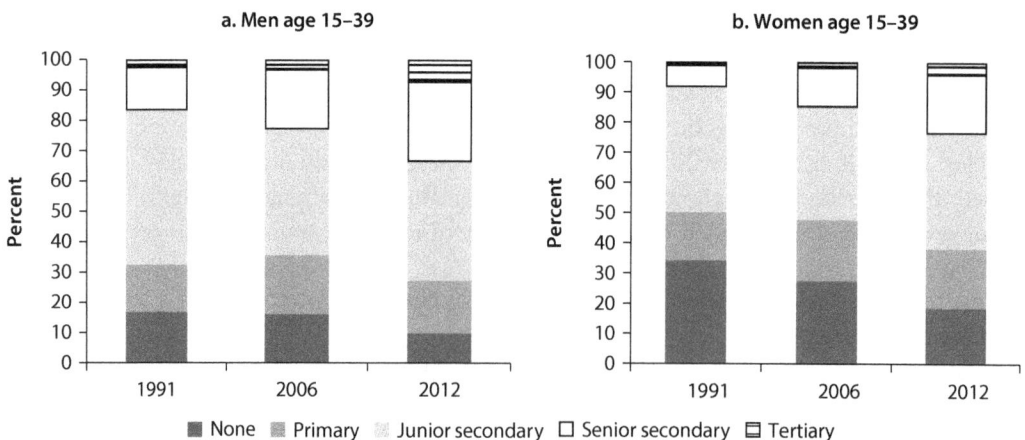

Source: Estimates based on GLSS3, GLSS5, and GLSS6.

Figure 3.6 Access to Education and Dropout Rate, by Poverty and Socioeconomic Status

a. Net enrollment rate, poorest and richest population quintile

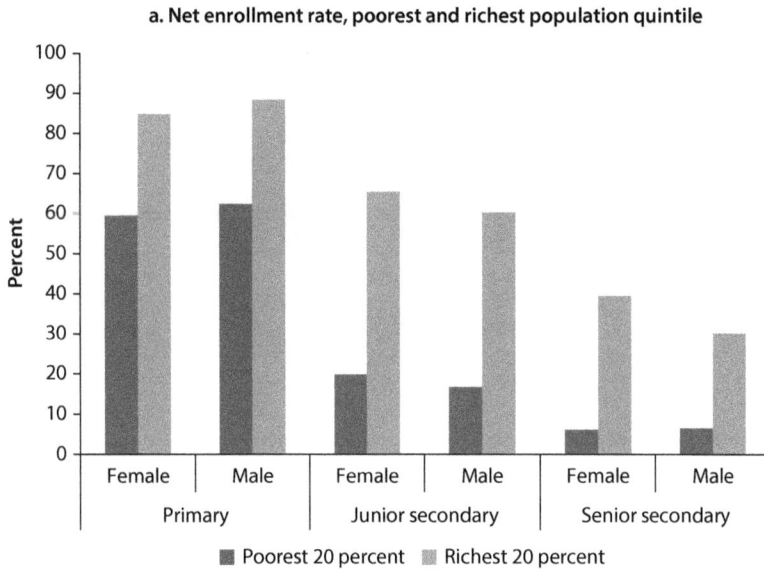

Source: GLSS6.

b. Percent of early dropouts, by socioeconomic status

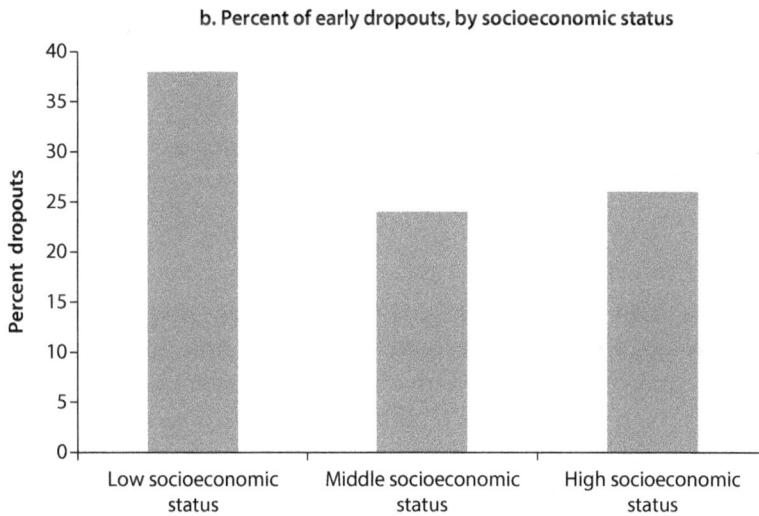

Source: Darvas, Favara, and Arnold 2016.

More in-depth studies of skills, by way of analysis based on the STEP skills measurement survey (box 3.2), also show that functional literacy is low among adults, and especially so for people from families with low socioeconomic status. When respondents took a more elaborate reading test in English, over half of those who elsewhere in the survey had reported that they did speak, read, and write English failed the test (Darvas, Favara, and Arnold 2016).

Figure 3.7 Literacy and Numeracy Rates in Youths and Adults

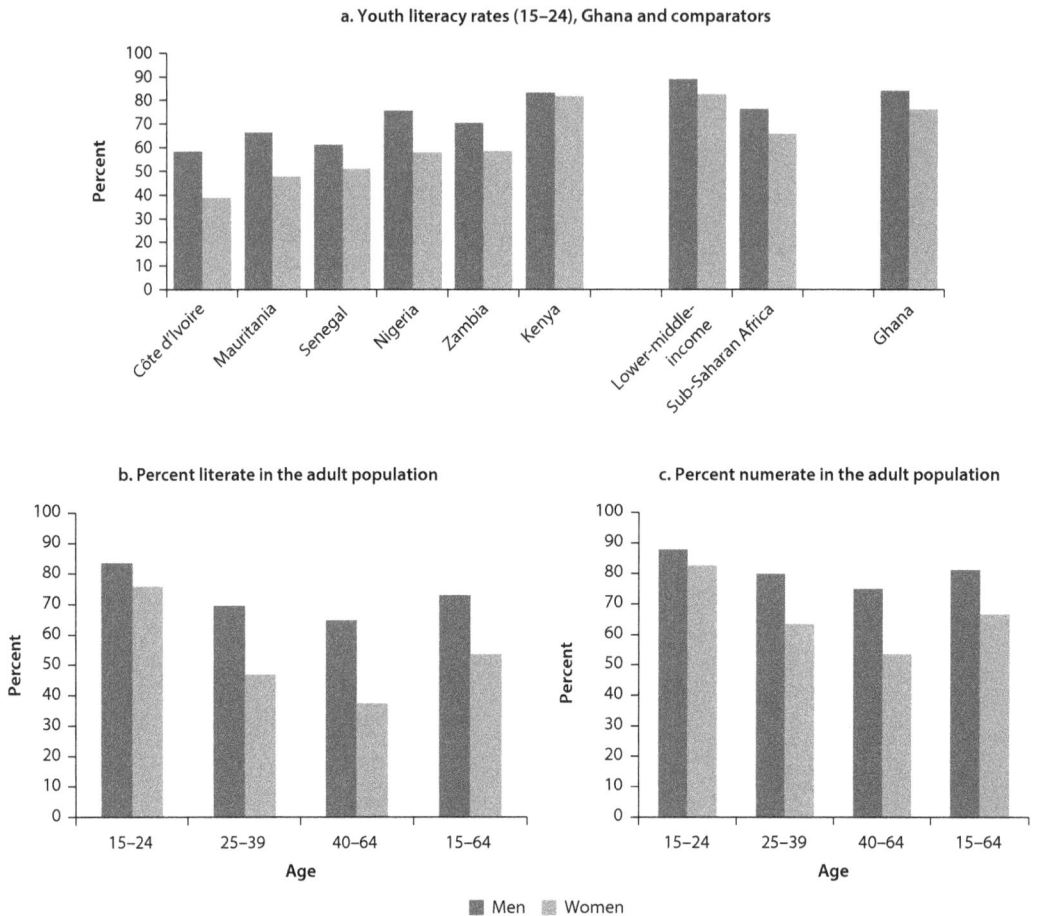

a. Youth literacy rates (15–24), Ghana and comparators

b. Percent literate in the adult population

c. Percent numerate in the adult population

■ Men ■ Women

Source: Estimates based on GLSS6 (Ghana) and WDI (comparators).

Almost one out of two workers is underqualified in terms of education mismatch. Another way to assess the availability of skills in Ghana is to consider qualification mismatch in terms of overeducation and undereducation (ILO 2015). Overeducation and undereducation are quantified following ILO (2014), according to the normative approach based on the International Classification of Occupations (ISCO).[1] More than half of workers were underqualified in 2005 (52 percent) and only 5 percent were overqualified; the remainder (43 percent) were correctly matched. By 2012, workers with skills matched to their jobs had become the single largest group (49 percent), and the proportion of underqualified workers had decreased to 45 percent. The gender gap between men and women remains high in terms of skills mismatch. Elementary occupations and clerks demonstrated the largest share of overqualified workers, both in 2005 and in 2012, while underqualification affected the majority of workers in the major groups skilled agricultural workers, technicians, and managers in 2012 (ILO 2015).

Box 3.2 Results from the STEP Household Survey on Education, Skills, Employment, and Productivity

The STEP (Skills Towards Employment and Productivity) household survey was carried out in Ghana as part of the first wave of surveys under the STEP Skills Measurement Program between September 2011 and December 2013. The Ghanaian sample was retrieved through a two-stage random sampling of households and individuals. It consists of 2,987 individuals aged 15–64, and covers urban areas, only.

The STEP focuses on measures of education and skills, including cognitive skills, social and behavioral skills, and technical skills, all of which are needed to function in different jobs. *Cognitive skills* include literacy and numerical ability, as well as the ability to understand complex ideas, learn from experience, and analyze problems using logical processes. *Social and behavioral skills* capture personality traits that are linked to labor market success, such as openness to new experiences, conscientiousness, extraversion, agreeability, and emotional stability. These "character-related" skills have been shown to have significant importance for social performance, including schooling choices, risky behavior, and wages (Heckman, Stixrud, and Urzua 2006). *Technical skills* range from manual dexterity for using complex tools and instruments to occupation-specific knowledge and skills in areas such as engineering and medicine.

Key Take-Aways Concerning Jobs

The STEP survey reveals that, while access to education has increased in Ghana, there are still important problems with the quality of education. This is reflected in early dropouts, high repetition, and delayed completion, as well as in low accumulation of basic functional skills like reading. Those who left school after primary levels took almost nine years to complete this level, four years more than expected. Almost one out of four adults had dropped out of school—almost half of them before completing primary levels of education. Most dropouts came from households with low socioeconomic status, and indeed, lack of funds was the most common reason for leaving school.

Literacy assessments suggest very low levels of functional literacy, raising questions about the quality of basic education. A vast majority of survey respondents are not able to read at a minimum "pass" level, even when they had finished junior secondary school.

Education is linked to skills. It is not really possible to determine whether those with high skills levels are better able to complete education, or whether education builds skills. But it is clear that the use of skills increases with level of education. Socioemotional skills are also closely related to educational attainment, in particular conscientiousness and (lack of) hostile bias (the tendency to perceive hostile intent in others, even when this is not the case).

Formal sector workers are much more likely to use skills intensively than other groups. The use of more nonroutine cognitive, socioemotional, and technical skills is much higher in the formal sector. For example, working in the formal sector is related to learning new things at work regularly, and more frequently involves supervising others' work and making presentations. Work in the informal sector demands fewer cognitive skills, and is more centered on repetitive and physically demanding tasks. However, self-employed workers reported having more autonomy at work and performing more repetitive tasks than wage workers.

box continues next page

Box 3.2 Results from the STEP Household Survey on Education, Skills, Employment, and Productivity *(continued)*

The impact of socioemotional skills on job opportunities is not clear. Although some correlations can be discerned, they disappear once education is accounted for. The only statistically significant results are that individuals scoring higher on socioemotional skills, and lower on hostile bias are less likely to be self-employed, and that emotional stability is positively related to work in mid- to high-skilled occupations.

Skills intensity is linked to earnings, independently of levels of education. The returns in terms of increased earnings of any additional year of education decrease by 2 percentage points after all skills have been controlled for (but do not disappear). The best-paid jobs are those that require intensive writing and job-specific skills such as the use of the computer, and these also involve cognitive challenges and supervision responsibilities. For socioemotional skills and traits, only conscientiousness (the ability to focus and stay on task until it is well done) is statistically significant.

Source: Darvas, Favara, and Arnold 2016.

The distribution of educated workers highlights the risk of a skills deficit in the private sector. Tertiary educated workers are concentrated in the public wage sector: More than half of the tertiary educated are in the public sector, with less than 30 percent in the private wage sector. As a result, only 10 percent of those in private wage sector have tertiary education, and over 60 percent have completed only the most basic education (figure 3.8). Educated workers are also concentrated in urban areas, where they have better opportunities. More than one-third of those working in agriculture have no education at all. Lack of schooling could make it significantly more challenging to introduce measures to enhance productivity, like new technology or methods and linking up smaller firms within larger agricultural value chains. Lack of enough skilled workers in the private wage sector is likely to hamper Ghana's potential for providing more sophisticated and technology-intensive goods.

Access to Vocational Training and Apprenticeships Is Limited

Less than 10 percent of the population between 15 and 35 years of age has been through either vocational training (school-based) or traditional apprenticeship. Opportunities for these forms of training are more urban than rural: 6 percent of urban women have been through vocational training, and 6 percent have had an apprenticeship; the corresponding numbers for urban men are 6 percent and 9 percent. Rural people are less likely to have had these forms of training. The options that result from vocational training and apprenticeships differ, however. Those in the wage sector (especially public) are more likely than those in other sectors to have been through vocational training. By contrast, apprenticeships appear to offer entry into self-employment in off-farm activities (figure 3.9).

Figure 3.8 Education Levels by Sector of Work

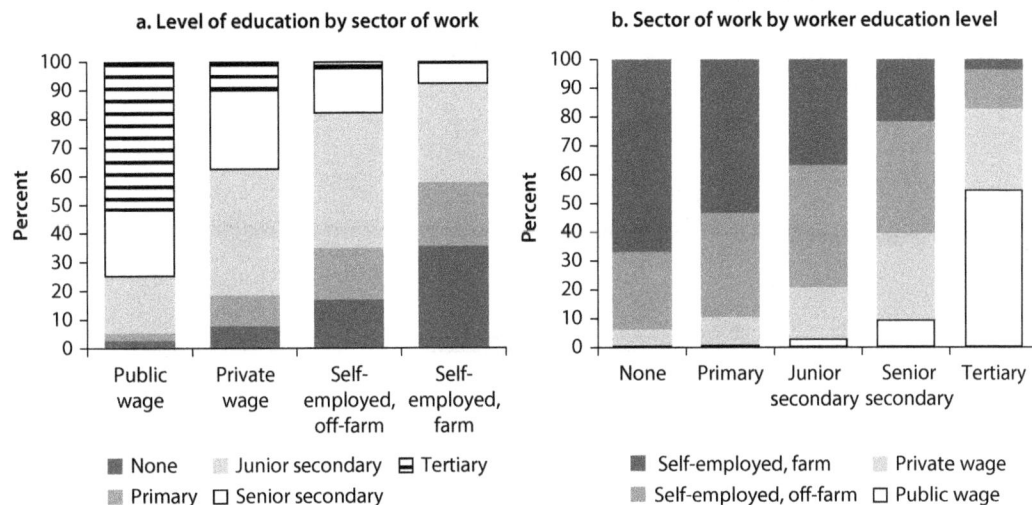

a. Level of education by sector of work

b. Sector of work by worker education level

Legend (a): ■ None ▨ Junior secondary ⊟ Tertiary ▨ Primary ☐ Senior secondary

Legend (b): ■ Self-employed, farm ▨ Private wage ▨ Self-employed, off-farm ☐ Public wage

Source: Estimates based on GLSS6.

Apprenticeships provide an alternative to more formal vocational or general education at the higher secondary level or above. Ghana's system of traditional apprenticeships is well established, as in many parts of Africa. According to the STEP survey, it is a significant provider of training in urban areas: nearly two out of five self-employed, and one out of four wage employees, had undertaken an apprenticeship. In the informal wage and self-employment sector, apprenticeships are the main form of jobs-related training. The GLSS household survey suggests a lower incidence of apprenticeships overall: in 2012, between 8 and 12 percent of the urban adult population had passed through an apprenticeship. Nationwide, 16 percent of workers report having gone through an apprenticeship and 5 percent of working youth aged 15–35 were engaged in apprenticeships in 2012. Apprenticeships are essentially a training tool for the self-employed in activities outside agriculture, and, to a smaller extent, private wage workers. Virtually no public wage workers and—at the other extreme—no farm workers have been through apprenticeships.

Apprenticeships are a complement to basic education, and thus not a substitute for formal schooling. Apprenticeships generally take place between ages 15 and 30, with the highest incidence in the early twenties. Apprenticeships are by far most common for those who have completed junior secondary school, but not more (figure 3.10). Generally, basic skills like literacy and numeracy rates are higher for those self-employed who completed an apprenticeship than for those who did not (World Bank 2009). Apprenticeships are much less common for the minority who had secondary levels of education or more, and who likely pursue more theoretical and academic subjects.

Figure 3.9 Vocational Training and Traditional Apprenticeships in Urban and Rural Areas, by Age Group, Gender, and Sector of Work

a. Vocational training (ages 15–35)

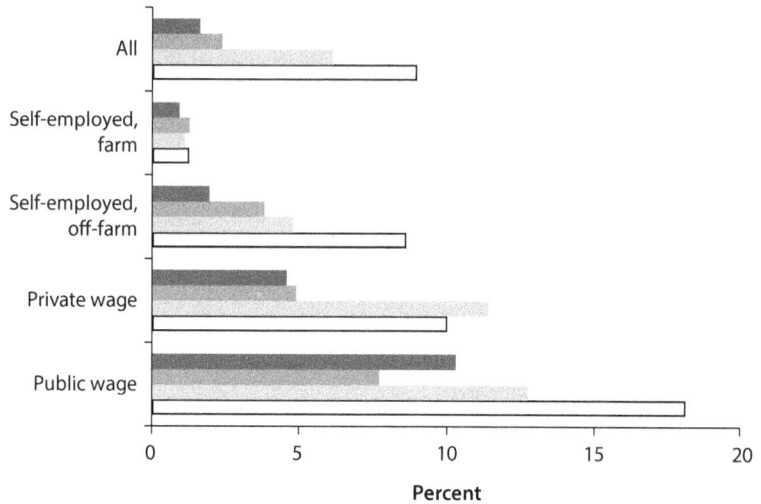

b. Traditional apprenticeship (ages 15–35)

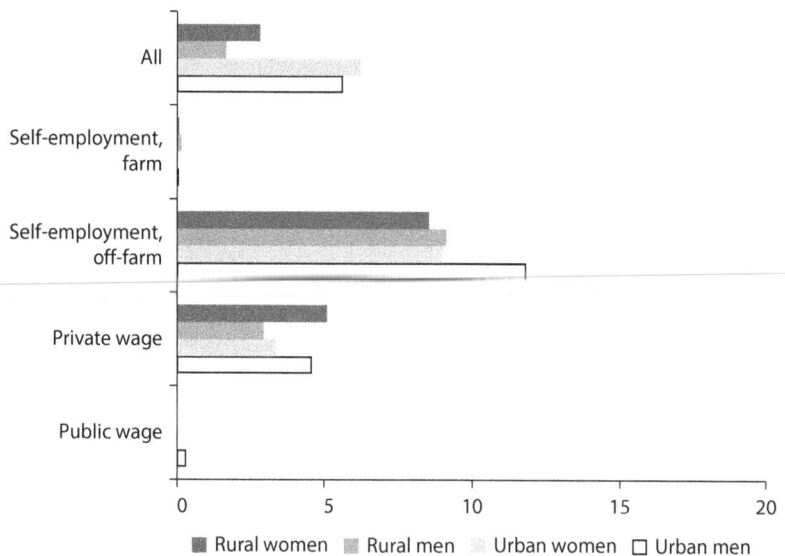

■ Rural women ▨ Rural men ░ Urban women □ Urban men

Source: Estimates based on GLSS6.

The apprentice system, while a traditional form of training, has both strengths and weaknesses. A young person works for around three years as an apprentice, often paying a fee up front to get the apprenticeship and sometimes getting paid very little. "Traditional" apprenticeships are not well regulated; often they are managed informally by firms and youth though family networks.

Figure 3.10 Participation in Apprenticeship in Relation to Education Levels

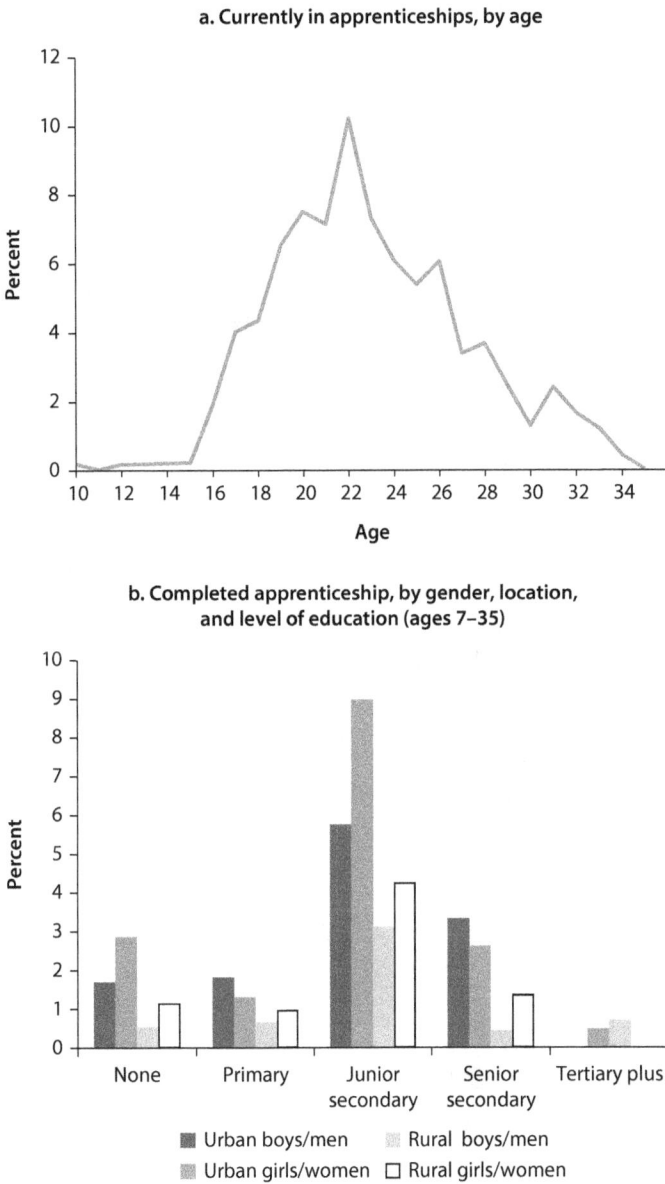

a. Currently in apprenticeships, by age

b. Completed apprenticeship, by gender, location, and level of education (ages 7–35)

Urban boys/men ■ Rural boys/men
Urban girls/women □ Rural girls/women

Source: GLSS6.

Apprentices usually do not receive official certificates after completing their apprenticeship, limiting the signaling power of training certificates for potential employers. In addition, the apprentice selection process may be costly for firms. A recent experiment in Ghana providing a novel worker screening technology found that firms that were offered apprentices by the program hired and retained them (Hardy and McCasland 2015), shedding light on potential search costs for firms in their hiring decisions. Overall, advantages include the fact that the system is self-financed and closely linked to the labor market in terms of needs and skills. However, significant support is needed to upgrade pedagogical and technical skills and approaches (Johanson and Adams 2004).

Medium and large firms engage in training to upgrade the skills of their workforce. The World Bank's Enterprise Survey for Ghana suggests that, at least in the formal sector, some firms do provide training to their employees and that, when they do, a majority of workers benefit. Larger firms are more likely than smaller ones to provide training to their staff. In the manufacturing sector, firms in the chemicals sector are more likely to train staff than other subsectors. In services, firms in the retail trade sector (where many of the urban low-income jobs are) are much less likely to offer training to their staff than other forms of services.

Skills are needed across sectors and jobs, but needs and training approaches differ between larger and formal firms and small businesses and microenterprises. Larger firms in Sub-Saharan Africa can have the resources to identify skills needs, to identify skilled workers, and to provide continuous skills upgrading on the job (figure 3.11). Smaller businesses are different: they often require multitasking, including both production and sales of products, and face more severe opportunity costs between training and production/work. This explains the popularity among smaller firms of firm-based training that combines work with training, such as traditional apprenticeships (World Bank 2009; Adams, Johansson de Silva, and Razmara 2013).

Figure 3.11 Firms Providing Training to Staff, by Size and Sector

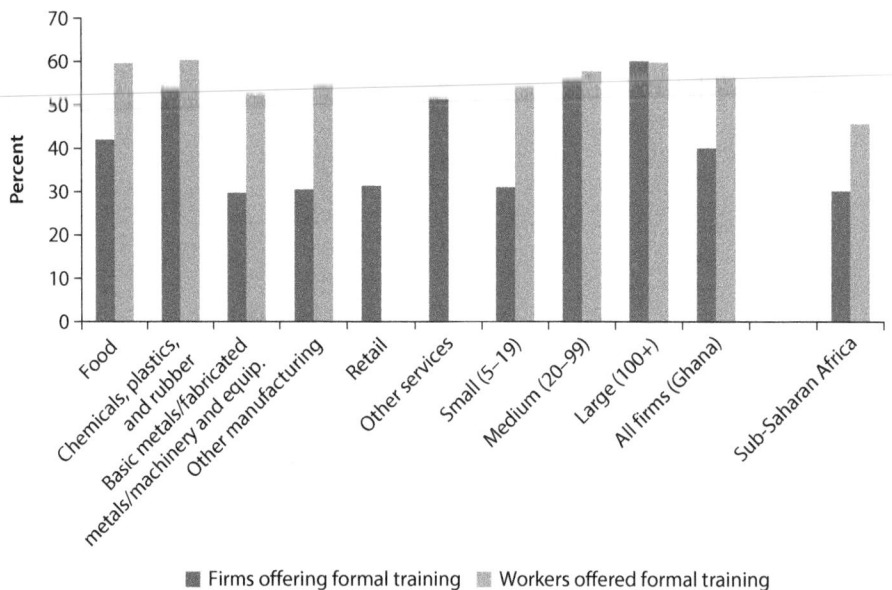

Source: World Bank Enterprise Surveys 2013.

Note

1. This normative approach starts from the division of major occupational groups (first-digit ISCO levels) into three groups and assigns a level of education to each group. The first three major occupational groups are assigned tertiary education; major groups 4 to 8 are assigned secondary education (lower or higher); and major group 9 is assigned primary education. Workers in a particular group who have the assigned level of education are considered well matched. Those who have a higher (lower) level of education are considered overeducated (undereducated) (ILO 2015).

References

Acemoglu, D., and D. Autor. 2011. "Skills, Tasks and Technologies: Implications for Employment and Earnings." In *Handbook of Labor Economics*, vol. 4, Part B, edited by D. Card and O. Ashenfelter, 773–1823. Elsevier.

Adams, A. V., S. Johansson de Silva, and S. Razmara. 2013. *Improving Skills Development in the Informal Sector: Strategies for Sub-Saharan Africa*. Directions in Development: Human Development. Washington, DC: World Bank.

Avitabile, C., and R. De Hoyos Navarro. 2015. "The Heterogeneous Effects of Information on Student Performance: Evidence from a Randomized Control Trial in Mexico." Policy Research Working Paper 7422, World Bank, Washington, DC.

Banerji, A., W. Cunningham, A. Fiszbein, E. King, H. Patrinos, D. Robalino, and J-P Tan. 2010. *Stepping Up Skills for More Jobs and Higher Productivity*. Washington, DC: World Bank.

Beegle, K., R. Dehejia, and R. Gatti. 2009. "Why Should We Care About Child Labor? The Education, Labor Market, and Health Consequences of Child Labor." *Journal of Human Resources* 44 (4): 871–89.

Cloutier, M. H., C. Reinstadtler, and I. Beltran. 2011. "*Making the Grade*: Assessing Literacy and Numeracy in African Countries." DIME Brief, Washington, DC: World Bank.

Darvas, P., M. Favara, and T. Arnold. 2016. *Snapshot of the STEP Skills Measurement Survey*. Washington, DC: World Bank.

Dizon-Ross, R. 2014. "Parents' Perceptions and Children's Education: Experimental Evidence from Malawi." Unpublished Manuscript. Massachusetts Institute of Technology. http://economics.yale.edu/sites/default/files/dizon-ross_jmp.pdf.

Edmonds, E. 2015. "Economic Growth and Child Labor in Low-income Economies." IZA Synthesis Paper, August, Forschungsinstitut zur Zukunft der Arbeit (IZA, Institute for the Study of Labor), Bonn.

Falco, P., A. Kerr, P. Paci, and B. Rijkers. 2014. *Working toward Better Pay: Earning Dynamics in Ghana and Tanzania*. World Bank Study 88483. Washington, DC: World Bank.

Fields, G. S. 2011. "What We Know (and Want to Know) about Earnings Mobility in Developing Countries." International Labor Relations School, Cornell University (accessed September 9, 2015), http://digitalcommons.ilr.cornell.edu/workingpapers/154.

Filmer, D., and L. Fox. 2014. *Youth Employment in Sub-Saharan Africa*. Africa Development Forum Series. World Bank and Agence Française de Développement.

GSS, GHS, and IFC International (Ghana Statistical Service, Ghana Health Service, and IFC International). 2015. *Ghana Demographic and Health Survey 2014*. Rockville, MD: GSS, GHS, and IFC International.

Hardy, M., and J. McCasland. 2015. "Are Small Firms Labor Constrained? Experimental Evidence from Ghana." Unpublished.

Heckman, J., J. Stixrud, and S. Urzua. 2006. "The Effects of Cognitive and Noncognitive Abilities on Labor Market Outcomes and Social Behaviour." *Journal of Labor Economics* 24: 411–482.

ILO (International Labour Office). 2013. *Measuring Informality: A Statistical Manual on the Informal Sector and Informal Employment*. Geneva: ILO.

———. 2014. *Skills Mismatch in Europe. Statistics Brief*. Geneva: ILO.

———. 2015. *Structural Change, Employment and Education in Ghana*. Geneva: ILO.

ILO and IPEC (International Labour Office and International Programme on the Elimination of Child Labour). 2013. *Marking Progress against Child Labour—Global Estimates and Trends 2000–2012*. Geneva: ILO.

Inoue, K., E. di Gropello, Y. Sayin Taylor, and J. Gresham. 2015. *Out-of-School Youth in Sub-Saharan Africa. A Policy Perspective*. Directions in Development Series. Washington, DC: World Bank.

Jensen, R. 2010. "The (Perceived) Returns to Education and the Demand for Schooling." *Quarterly Journal of Economics* 125 (2): 515–48.

Johanson, R., and A. V. Adams. 2004. *Skills Development in Sub-Saharan Africa*. World Bank Regional and Sectoral Studies. Washington, DC: World Bank.

Nguyen, T. 2008. "Information, Role Models and Perceived Returns to Education: Experimental Evidence from Madagascar." MIT Working Paper, Massachusetts Institute of Technology.

UCW (Understanding Children Work). 2016. *Child Labor and the Youth Decent Work Deficit in Ghana*. Inter-Agency Report.

UNICEF (United Nations Children Fund). 2015. "Child Marriage. Really Simple Stats." *The UNICEF Ghana Internal Statistical Bulletin* Issue 4, July.

World Bank. 2009. *Ghana: Job Creation and Skills Development*. Washington, DC: World Bank.

———. 2013. Enterprise Surveys (database). www.enterprisesurveys.org. Accessed October 2015–May 2016.

———. 2015. *World Development Report 2016: The Digital Dividend*. Washington, DC: World Bank.

———. 2016. *More, and More Productive, Jobs for Nigeria: A Profile of Work and Workers*. Washington, DC: World Bank.

———. WDI (World Development Indicators) 2016 (database). World Bank, Washington, DC, http://data.worldbank.org/data-catalog/world-development-indicators. Accessed October 2015-May 2016.

CHAPTER 4

Where Are Jobs Created?

Main Messages

In the search for more productive jobs, it is important to discern whether the investment climate in Ghana encourages or discourages entry and expansion of particular firms, and whether the recent pattern of hiring in terms of demand for skills matches the improvement in education among the new entrants to the workforce.

Informal firms and household enterprises (HHEs) are the major source of employment, engaging about 6 million people (54 percent of total employment). Microenterprises and small firms (representing 91 percent of registered firms) are also an important segment of employment creation, though only a few grow to sustain increased demand for work.

Private sector formal employment is a tiny share of total employment (about 2 percent). The bulk of the formal employment stock in 2012 is in large and old firms. Large firms also provide higher wages, are more productive, and accounted for most of the aggregate net formal job creation between 2010 and 2012.

Only 3 percent of HHEs are job-creating. Services dominate the HHEs, especially in urban areas. Female workers are concentrated in HHEs. They represent only 32 percent of the workforce in formal firms.

While the formal sector has grown in terms of employment and labor productivity, it favors large firms over small and medium ones. Large firms may be operating in more competitive markets, while small and medium face higher distortions and constraints.

Jobs and the Private Sector

This chapter looks at the distribution of jobs among formal and informal private enterprises operating in industry and services. The analysis combines different firm-level data to look at important aspects of jobs as viewed from the firm side: where the off-farm jobs are located in Ghana, the characteristics of the formal and informal firms that create them, the education and gender of the workers employed, and—importantly—what firms, if any, grow and create more employment (box 4.1).

Box 4.1 Firm-Level Data Used

The Formal Economy

The main sources of data used in the analysis of labor demand are the World Bank 2013 Enterprise Survey (henceforth ES) and Micro Surveys (1–4). The World Bank ES and Micro Surveys collect information from a representative sample of nonagricultural formal private firms in the industry and services sectors. The surveys interviewed a representative sample of microenterprises, small and medium enterprises (SMEs), and large private sector firms in four of the most active economic cities in Ghana: Accra Metropolitan Area and Tema (Accra), Kumasi (Ashanti), Tamale (Northern) and Takoradi (Western). The Ghana ES includes two sectors within industries according to the group classification of ISIC Revision 3.1: all manufacturing sectors (group D) and the construction sector (group F). The ES does not represent firms operating in the mining and quarrying and electricity sectors (groups C and E). Within the services sector, the ES includes wholesale and retail trade, hotels and restaurant (groups G and H); transport, storage, and communications sector (group I); and computer and related activities (group K, subsector 72, IT [information technology]). It does not represent financial intermediation (group J), real estate and renting activities (group K, except subsector 72, IT, which was added to the population under study), and all public or utilities sectors.

The sample consisted of 720 SMEs and large business establishments and 604 microenterprises surveyed from December 2012 through July 2014. Formality here means being registered with the Ghana Registrar's General Department. These establishments were located from lists compiled from the following: firm registry, list of firms paying value added tax (VAT), list of large taxpayers, Ghana Chamber of Commerce and Industry, business associations, General Department of Cooperatives, District Assembly registries, and block enumeration conducted by the fieldwork team. The ES includes rich information about the business environment and firms' characteristics for 604 microenterprises and 720 small, medium, and large formal firms, respectively. Further analysis is based on two cross-sections of the ES from 2007 and 2013 to provide insights into the main changes in the distribution and characteristics of firms and jobs between 2007 and 2013. This means that the analysis cannot address the dynamics of firm or job survival and destruction or growth of firms over the two periods. As the 2007 data do not cover the region of Tema and the 2007 Micro Survey data are not weighted, comparisons will be made only on two comparable samples (excluding microenterprises and Tema).

A number of caveats about the data should be kept in mind. First, the sample of the ES survey, while designed to be nationally representative of the universe of formal private sector firms working in manufacturing and services, is subject to the quality of sampling frames, and information on aggregate figures are subject to issues of nonresponse. The ES relied on several sources to build a sampling frame: the firm registry, the list of firms paying VAT, and the list of large taxpayers maintained by GSS were complemented with additional lists of firms from the Ghana Chamber of Commerce and Industry and Business Associations. Nonetheless, the sampling frame proved to be incomplete and was not sufficient to draw the target sample. A block enumeration was also undertaken in order to build an additional list. The block enumeration allowed a list of establishments to be physically created, from which the sample was drawn.

box continues next page

Box 4.1 Firm-Level Data Used *(continued)*

Based on the ES and Micro Surveys, the employment stock in 2012 is about 170,000, including permanent and temporary employees, equivalent to about 15 percent of the employment stock estimated in 2012 from GLSS6 for private workers in the same sectors (about 1.24 million). Considering that not all the private wage workers in those sectors are working in formal firms, and that only about 30 percent of private wage workers report having either a written contract or any type of social insurance benefits (to proxy formal workers), the employment stock captured in the ES formal firms represents about half of the "formal" employment stock estimated through the GLSS6 in the same sectors.

The Informal Economy

To analyze the informal economy, the analysis used the GLSS6 (2012) special module on off-farm household enterprises (87 percent are nonregistered enterprises) administered to about 9,000 off-farm household enterprises. The chapter also draws on the 2013 World Bank informal survey administered to about 700 firms. Although not representative, the informal survey provides complementary evidence to the GLSS6.

Note: Both the Enterprise Survey and GLSS6 collect industry data using the ISIC Rev 3.1 classification.

The Ghanaian economy has been characterized by important changes over the past few decades. In the mid-1980s, Ghana launched one of the most ambitious structural adjustment programs in Africa, abolishing price controls, opening capital markets, and eventually privatizing the majority of state-owned enterprises. These reforms contributed to a period of sustained economic growth, increases in consumption expenditure, the discovery and production of oil, and a rise of the service industry (see chapter 1). Over the past two decades, the relative size of the informal sector has increased rapidly, and the average size of manufacturing activity has declined.

Mapping Jobs to Formal Nonagricultural Firms

Formal private sector (nonagricultural) firms captured in the Enterprise Survey (ES) account for only about 2 percent of all jobs in Ghana. The formal private sector is developing, but does not offer enough opportunities for formal off-farm wage employment. Private wage workers who are "formal" (measured as either having a contract or any form of social security benefit) account for about 5 percent of all jobs in Ghana (about 30 percent of private wage employment), according to GLSS6. This suggests that the formal sector (both public and private) is not generating jobs in sufficient numbers and people are pushed into the informal sector.

Microenterprises and small firms represent the vast majority of the formal private sector firms, but employ only 33 percent of the workforce. The ES estimates that registered firms in Ghana are composed of microenterprises with 0–4 workers (63 percent); small firms with 5–19 workers (28 percent);

medium firms with 20–99 workers (7 percent); and large firms employing more than 100 workers (2 percent).[1] However, the minority of large firms in Ghana account for nearly half the entire workforce in the formal private sector. The employment stock distribution is concentrated in larger firms (47 percent), and roughly equally shared between microenterprises (14 percent) and small (17 percent) and medium firms (21 percent). Females participate in the ownership structure in less than one-third of these firms. These formal private firms are generally domestically owned firms, and only 4 percent of firms export their production (figure 4.1).

Over one-third of firms are "young" (operating for 5 years or less), indicating relatively low barriers to firm entry. On average, most firms (43 percent) are "mature," having been in business for more than 11 years, while 25 percent of firms have been operating between 6 and 10 years on average ("mid-age"). Young firms operating between 3 and 5 years represent 19 percent of firms, while start-ups (2 years) and new entrants (one year or less) represent 6 percent and 7 percent, respectively (figure 4.2). The share of entrants and start-ups is higher in the services sector than in industry (14 percent and 9 percent, respectively), indicating lower entry costs in the services sector. This structure is similar to that of more advanced economies: in Organisation for Economic Co-operation and Development (OECD) countries, young firms account for less than 30 percent of total firms in the manufacturing sector and 40 percent in the services sector. The presence of young firms is important: there is evidence from OECD countries that young firms have a stronger role in job creation than older firms (Criscuolo, Gal, and Menon 2014; Calvino, Criscuolo, and Menon 2015). Unsurprisingly, very few large firms are young.

However, the majority of workers are employed in older firms. In Ghana, the average 40-year-old firm employs 100 workers, 10 times the number employed

Figure 4.1 The Formal Private Sector, by Size of Firm

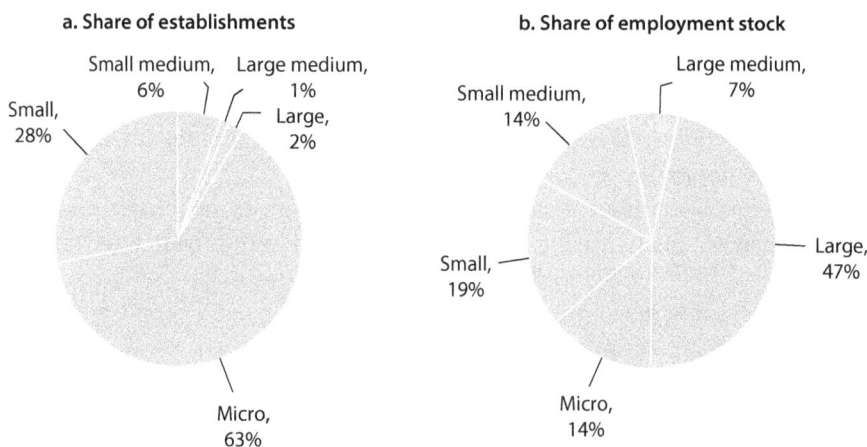

a. Share of establishments

Small medium, 6% Large medium, 1%
Small, 28%   Large, 2%
Micro, 63%

b. Share of employment stock

Small medium, 14%   Large medium, 7%
Small, 19%   Large, 47%
Micro, 14%

Source: Estimates based on Enterprise Survey 2013.

Figure 4.2 The Formal Private Sector, by Age of Firm

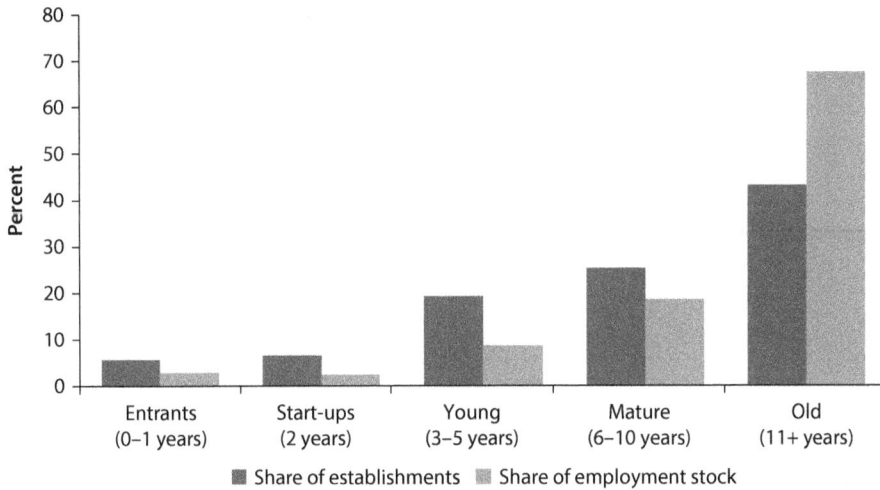

Source: Estimates based on Enterprise Survey 2013.

by a firm 5 years old or younger. The majority of workers are accounted for by old firms that are large, located in Accra, and operating in the construction or chemical industries.

The majority of formal jobs are in the industry sector.[2] The formal private sector is quite broadly spread across the industry and services sectors, which each constitute nearly 50 percent of formal establishments. Yet while industry makes up to nearly 50 percent of establishments, the same sector accounts for more than 70 percent of employment, an indication of much higher relative size in the sector (table 4.1). This scale of establishments is particularly remarkable in the areas of chemicals, rubber, plastics manufacturing, and construction. By contrast, while nearly one in four formal private sector establishments in Ghana is in wholesale trade, these establishments are disproportionately small, accounting for only 5 percent of employment.

More than half of the workers in formal firms are concentrated in Accra and other urban areas. The distribution of jobs reflects the geographical distribution of formal firms: 54 percent of firms are in the Accra Metropolitan Area, and they employ 60 percent of the formal private sector workforce; 14 percent of firms are in Tema; 22 percent are in Tamale (Northern region); and 10 percent are in Takoradi (Western region). The location of establishments is related to agglomeration effects (urban centers). Thus the employment density is highest in Accra and decreases with the size of the firm locality.

Medium and large firms are more likely to offer full-time contracts to workers, while microenterprises and small firms rely more on temporary jobs. Job stability is high among medium and large firms, where full-time permanent workers represent 90 percent of the workforce. By contrast, one out of every four workers engaged in microenterprises and small firms has a temporary contract (figure 4.3).

Table 4.1 The Formal Private Sector, by Economic Sector
Percent

		Share of employment stock	Share of establishments
Industry	Food	8	5
	Metals, machinery & equip.	7	7
	Chemicals, rubber & plastics	20	5
	Garments	1	2
	Construction	20	6
	Other manufacturing	17	21
Services	Wholesale	5	26
	Retail	10	21
	Other services	12	7
		100	100

Source: Estimates based on Enterprise Survey 2013.

Female employment is generally low, except in the garments, food, and retail industries. Females represent only about 30 percent of the formal workforce overall; the share of female workers is higher in firms where females participate in the ownership (30 percent of establishments). Participation varies by sector; the percentage of full-time female employees in the garments, food, and retail sectors is 69 percent, 48 percent, and 42 percent, respectively.

Firms in Ghana grow over time during their life cycle, especially firms that start out large. Models of firm growth predict higher growth rates (employment growth) for young and smaller firms if they invest resources efficiently and there are not major distortions in the business climate. Once firms grow larger and older, and reach a high level of productivity, the scope for further growth is limited. However, international evidence shows that this is not always the case, as for example in India and other developing countries compared to U.S. and European patterns (Hsieh and Klenow 2014). Table 4.2 shows that there is within-firm growth in Ghana between the respective firm size at inception and its size as of 2012. Conditional on survival, growth rates are higher for micro-enterprises and firms that start already large, indicating that starting size may play a key role in firm's dynamics. The table also shows that, as firms get older, they get larger, consistent with the theory that surviving and more productive firms scale up. There is not much difference in firm dynamics between manu-facturing and services.

By contrast, firm expansion among a panel of manufacturing firms in Ghana was limited between 1987 and 2003 (Sandefur 2010).[3] Similarly, focusing only on a panel of surviving manufacturing firms between 2003 and 2013, only 35 percent of firms grew in employment; but, consistent with the results of the ES, the smallest and largest firms were more likely to grow. Over this last period, the overall exit rate of manufacturing firms[4] was about 21 percent (another 22 percent could not be traced). Small and young firms were also more likely to exit than large firms. Higher exit rates were found in the food and textile and garments industries (Davies and Kerr 2015).

Figure 4.3 Formal Employment, by Contract Type and Firm Size

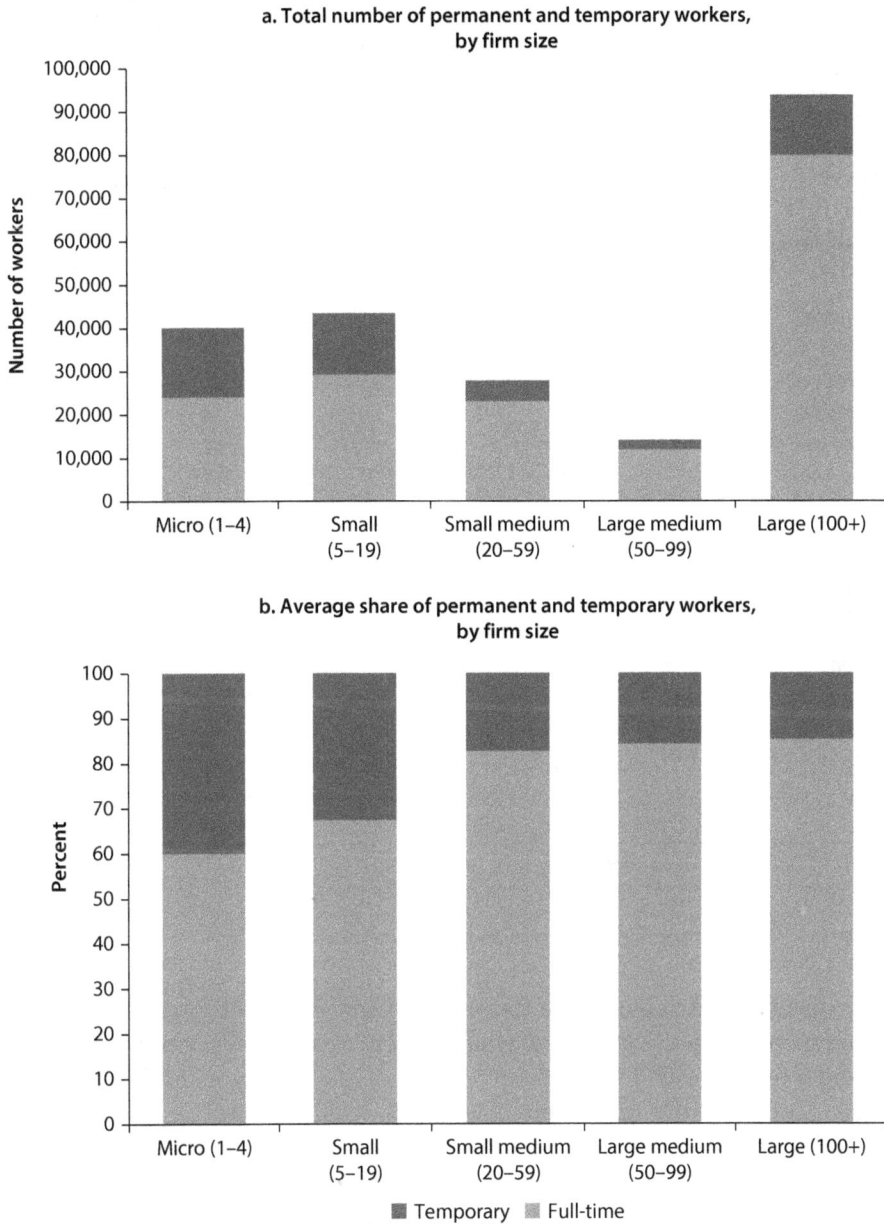

a. Total number of permanent and temporary workers, by firm size

b. Average share of permanent and temporary workers, by firm size

■ Temporary ■ Full-time

Source: Estimates based on Enterprise Survey 2013.

Small and medium firms have a harder time growing and adding jobs than large firms. Together, the figures above suggest some firm dynamics in Ghana conditional on survival, especially among microenterprises and large establishments. Table 4.2 indicates that it is easier to expand from 1 to 5 workers and from 100 to 150 workers than for small and medium firms to increase their size.

Table 4.2 Firm Dynamics during Their Life Cycle

	Size change since inception			
	Shrunk (change <5%)	*Same size (change ≤ ±5%)*	*Grew (change >5%)*	*Total*
Age group				
Entrants (0–1)	2	62	36	100
Start-up (2)	13	38	49	100
Young (3–5)	14	28	58	100
Mature (6–10)	9	23	67	100
Old (11+)	15	15	70	100
Size (initial)				
Micro (1–4)	3	29	68	100
Small (5–19)	44	13	43	100
Sm. Medium (20–59)	38	7	54	100
Lg. Medium (50–99)	53	6	42	100
Large (100+)	19	0	81	100
Sector				
Manufacturing	17	19	64	100
Construction	8	35	57	100
Services	10	27	63	100
Region				
Accra	10	20	70	100
North	21	30	48	100
Takoradi	15	27	58	100
Tema	7	25	69	100
Total	13	24	64	100

Source: Estimates based on Enterprise Survey 2013.
Note: Current firm size is measured as number of full-time employees. The employment growth is the percentage size change with respect to the number of full-time employees when the firm started operations (based on recall data). Numbers refer to the percentage of firms that shrunk, remained the same size, or grew with respect to their size at inception

One possible explanation is that the sector is segmented, with large firms operating in more competitive markets, while distortions and constraints hit small and medium firms harder. This has been referred as "the missing middle" in developing countries, or the underrepresentation of small and medium firms in the overall size distribution because of higher constraints to growth. It should be noted that the high growth rate for microenterprises is also in part explained by selection; only the ones that started as own-account and survived, as they were eventually more productive, were observed (those that closed were not part of the 2013 sampling frame).

Aggregate formal net employment grew between 2010 and 2012, mostly in large firms. In terms of overall job growth, between 2010 and 2012, private sector wage employment in aggregate grew at a rate of 8 percent per year on net (a 12 percent rate of job creation and a 4 percent rate of job contraction over the same period).[5] The 8 percent net job creation is an upper bound, as it does not take into account the jobs destroyed by firms that closed between 2010 and 2012 (figure 4.4).

Figure 4.4 Aggregate Formal Employment Creation and Contraction between 2010 and 2012

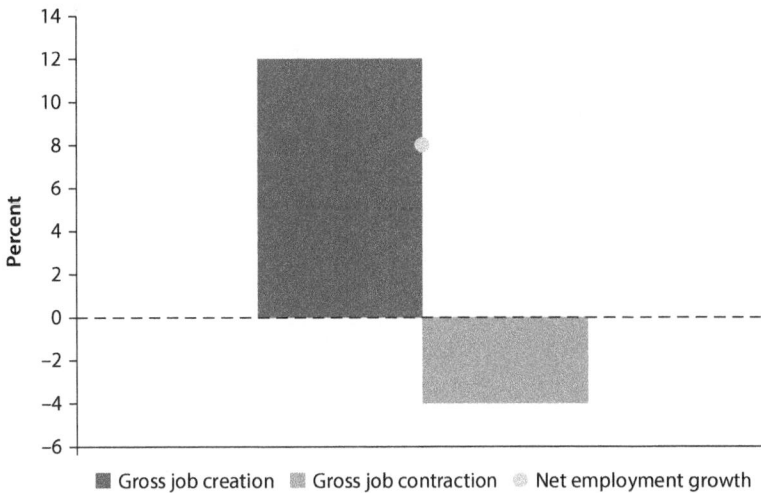

Source: Estimates based on Enterprise Survey 2013, annualized growth rates.

Consistent with within-firm dynamics, and in contrast to recent findings in the literature elsewhere from the developing world, large firms accounted for the majority of aggregate formal workforce growth (nearly 60 percent). Young firms accounted for about half of the net employment growth (table 4.3).

Along with positive net employment growth, formal firms in Ghana also experienced robust labor productivity growth between 2010 and 2012. Ideally, growth is based on both higher productivity and rising employment, as more resources are put to work productively. In Ghana, employment and productivity growth moved in the same positive direction, with the average productivity growth rate higher than the employment growth rate (meaning that sales grew more than employment) (figure 4.5). This is not the case across the board, however. In large and micro industrial firms, jobs were positively added on net, while labor productivity showed marginal (or even slightly negative) growth (both signs of somewhat job-intensive growth). For small and medium industrial firms, however, labor productivity grew at substantially higher rates than jobs, a sign of growth biased against labor. The positive relationship between firm productivity and employment growth is particularly strong in the industrial sector. Multivariate analysis indicates that more productive firms are also creating more jobs, controlling for firm age, exporting status, ownership structure, location, industry, and manager and worker characteristics (Francis and Honorati 2016). Formal microenterprises are growing faster, experiencing higher employment growth given the low starting size. However, the bulk of net employment growth is accounted for by large firms that are growing, by virtue of their size.

Larger firms are more productive and dynamic and provide higher wages. Controlling for firm age, exporting status, ownership structure, location, industry, and manager and worker characteristics, large incumbent firms in Ghana

Table 4.3 Job Creation and Contraction Rates, by Firm Size and Age, 2010–12
Percent

	Gross job creation	*Job contraction*	*Net employment growth*
Micro (1–5)	2.2	−0.4	1.8
Small (5–19)	1.8	−1.8	−0.1
Small medium (20–49)	1.7	−0.9	0.8
Large medium (50–99)	0.8	−0.1	0.7
Large (100+)	5.3	−0.5	4.7
Young	4.8	−0.5	4.3
Mid-age	2.1	−0.9	1.1
Mature	4.8	−2.2	2.6
Total	11.7	−3.7	8.0

Source: Estimates based on Enterprise Survey 2013.
Note: Annual job creation and contraction rates between 2012 and 2010. Rates for gross job creation (job contraction) are taken for only positive-growth (negative-growth) establishments.

Figure 4.5 Employment and Labor Productivity Growth, by Firm Size and Sector, 2010–2012

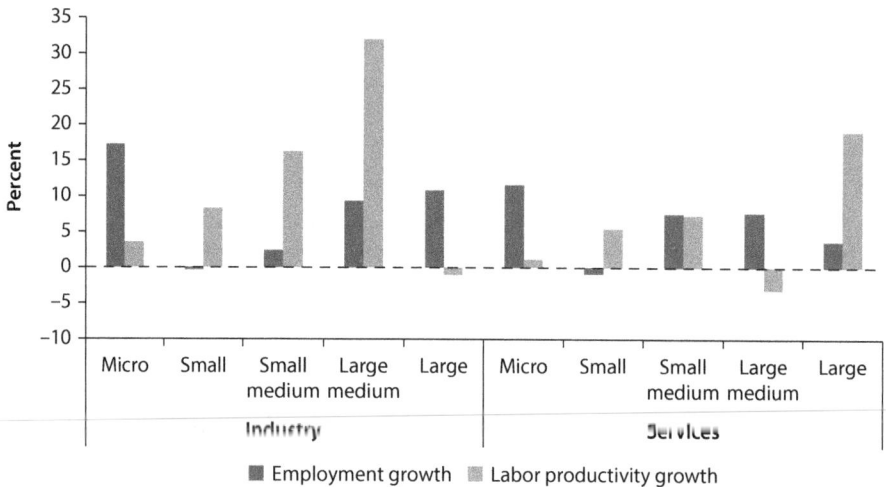

Source: Estimates based on Enterprise Survey 2013.
Note: Both measures are expressed as annualized growth rates and take into account only full-time permanent workers.

significantly outperform small and medium firms and microenterprises (Francis and Honorati 2016). Large firms in 2012 were more productive, paid higher wages per worker, and experienced higher sales and productivity growth. This indicates that resources (in terms of sales and workers) efficiently flow to more productive firms. The more productive firms are large, mostly start large, further expand, and gain the most over the life cycle. Microenterprises are dynamic, although they experience lower productivity growth. Small and medium firms are more constrained, especially in the service sector.

The skills content of jobs in formal establishments is positively associated with higher wage per workers and firm productivity. The share of full-time workers who completed secondary school varies by sector and region. Sectors that demand higher shares of educated workers are information technology (IT), transport, and plastics and rubber manufacturing, while the least educated workers are in manufacturing of woods, furniture, and fabricated metal products. The formal workforce is better educated in Takoradi (76 percent of full-time workers have completed high secondary school), while the least educated workers are in the North, consistent with overall population education patterns. Controlling for firm, location, and sector characteristics, firms with higher shares of better educated workforce pay a significantly higher wage per worker and are more productive (Francis and Honorati 2016).

Aggregate firms' performance improved between 2007 and 2013. Overall, annual labor productivity growth (the annual rate of growth of real sales per worker) was 5.2 percent per year between 2010 and 2012, compared to 4.5 percent between 2005 and 2007.[6] Ghanaian firms perform better than their lower-middle-income comparators in terms of labor productivity, which averaged 2 percent for lower-middle-income countries and negative 4.5 percent for Sub-Saharan Africa between 2010 and 2015.

While only a few firms were exporting in 2013, the aggregate exposure to international goods and capital markets has increased in the past five years. The majority of firms in 2013 produced and sold in the domestic market, with only 8 percent of firms exporting. Exporting firms are large, accounting for more jobs than nonexporting firms. Between 2007 and 2013, the share of exporting firms increased only among larger firms. Similarly, larger firms are more likely to be owned partially (more than 10 percent) or totally by foreign owners (figure 4.6). Foreign ownership increased over the same period among all firm sizes (except large medium firms).

Figure 4.6 Exporting Status and Foreign Ownership, by Firm Size

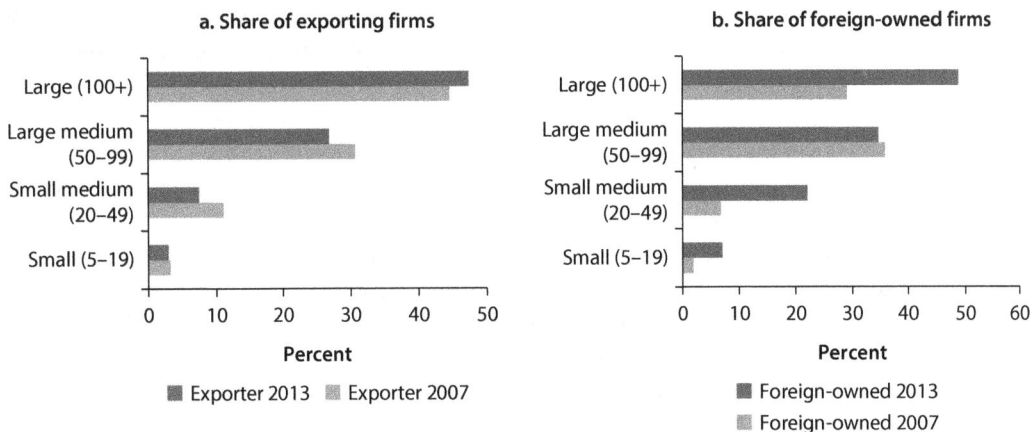

Source: Estimates based on Enterprise Survey 2013.
Note: Exporting firms are defined as those where more than 10 percent of their sales go to foreign markets. Firms with foreign ownership are defined as those where at least 10 percent of shares are owned by foreign owners.

Expanding Job Opportunities in Ghana • http://dx.doi.org/10.1596/978-1-4648-0941-5

The Profile of Informal Off-Farm Household Enterprises and Jobs

Informal firms account for the majority of off-farm jobs in Ghana through own-account microenterprises, contributing family members, and informal wage employment. Among informal firms, HHEs are sizable and play an important role, compared to nonregistered firms. The GLSS6 is the main source of data to analyze informal microenterprises. While not nationally representative, the informal ES complements the analysis by providing some insights to better understand the rationale for and characteristics of informal firms.

HHEs are the major source of employment in Ghana, engaging about 6 million people: 3.6 million households—43 percent of all households in the country—run a microenterprise.[7] Typically, HHEs are small, are not registered with public authorities, and lack a physical establishment separated from the household (box 4.2). They are owned and run by a family member, and the income produced often accrues to the person responsible for the business. Household members usually contribute to the enterprise without wage compensation. Sometimes they receive a cash payment, and in a few cases, HHEs hire people external to the household. They are usually operating in the household location or are mobile, as in the case of retail trade services and street vendors (box 4.3), and are engaged in nonagricultural activities, such as manufacturing activities, wholesale and retail trade, and other services that take place during agricultural off-seasons.

The majority of HHEs in the sample are owned and run by a single household member. Seventy-two percent of enterprises are own-account economic activities, with one household member as the sole proprietor and responsible for the enterprise; 13 percent are enterprises engaging 2 people; another 13 percent

---

Box 4.2 What Is an Off-Farm Household Enterprise?

Household enterprises (HHEs) in this report are defined as microenterprises that are owned and run by one or more family members. They may engage family members without paying them (unpaid family members) or hire workers within or outside the household (wage workers). From the employment perspective, the owner of the HHEs falls under the "nonagriculture self-employment" category described in chapter 2, while workers engaged and receiving a cash payment from the HHEs are counted among the "private wage workers."

Unlike establishments, HHEs do not have a physical location or establishment; they operate in the same place where the household members live, or are mobile (often in the case of retail trade services). Most HHEs are located on farms, even though they are defined as "off-farm." Often business and household finances are combined, and the HHE constitutes a second job or a seasonal activity to diversify income sources.

Sometimes households are pushed into operating an off-farm enterprise when they have difficulty coping with shocks or dealing with agricultural seasonality, or when

box continues next page

Box 4.2 What Is an Off-Farm Household Enterprise? *(continued)*

Figure B4.2.1 Household Enterprises Play a Greater Role in Absorbing Off-Farm Employment in Africa than in Asia and Latin America

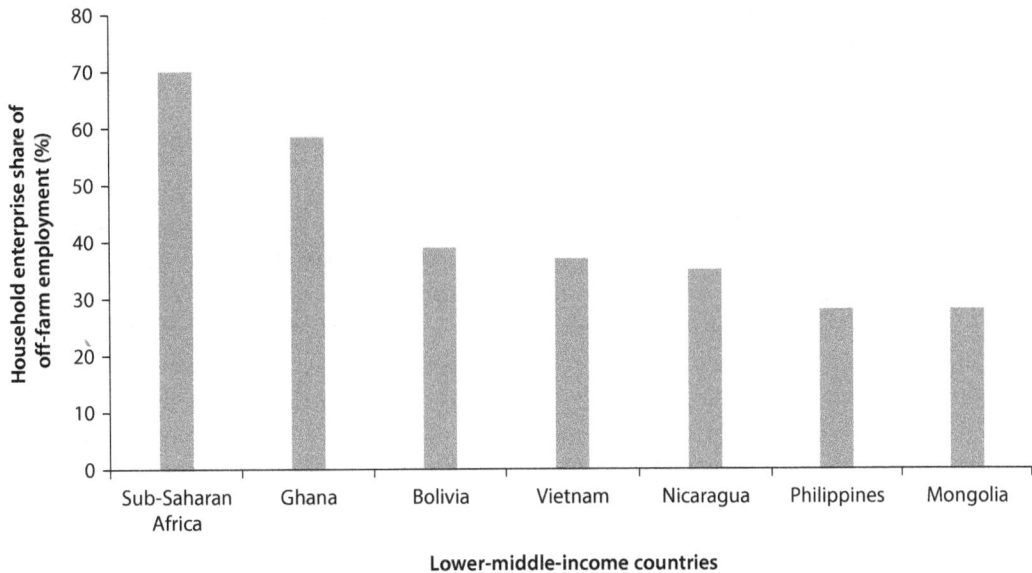

Source: Filmer and Fox 2014; GLSS6 for Ghana.

household members need employment. Rural households often launch these enterprises to pursue positive business opportunities—particularly households living closer to denser markets. The extent and frequency of these determinants vary widely, and many enterprises do not operate throughout the year. Rural and female-headed enterprises and enterprises with young owners are less productive than urban and male-owned enterprises and enterprises with older owners, a sample of HHEs in six other African countries (Ethiopia, Malawi, Niger, Nigeria, Tanzania, and Uganda) indicates (Naugler and Naudé 2014).

The growth of off-farm HHEs has played a key role in the developing world in the structural transformation of shifting workers out of agriculture to manufacturing and services. For example, in Asia and Latin America, HHEs provided an important pathway to move out of agriculture as farm productivity improved. In Africa's low- and middle-income countries, employment in HHEs is even larger than in comparator countries (Filmer and Fox 2014; Fox 2015) (figure B4.2.1).

The rapid expansion of household enterprises or off-farm self-employment in Ghana between 2005 and 2012 (see chapter 2) and Africa more generally is consistent with the lack of a fast-growing wage sector. A recent report from the UN Economic Commission for Africa (UN 2015) shows that the manufacturing sector in Africa, including the more labor-intensive industries, contributed declining shares to economic growth in the past 20 years and that it provides only 6 percent of all jobs, compared to 16 percent in Asia.

Box 4.3 The Challenges of Street Vending in Ghana

Street vending, like many informal sector activities, has long been undertaken in both rural and urban Ghana. Recently, however, the activity has increased significantly in urban areas. With no social assistance in place to support the unemployed, engagement in informal activity becomes a survival strategy for most economically active persons.

Street vendors are predominantly women of all ages. They tend to have no or low education, and come from poor households. The majority of street vendors are own-account workers or self-employed without employees. In the major cities, street vendors are often migrants from other parts of the country. In Ghana, informal workers are organized in associations to facilitate their involvement in policy making. The Petty Traders Association counted about 30,000 members in 2011, most of whom were street vendors.

The rise in the activity has been met by antagonism from local assemblies and agencies, including town and city planning and law enforcement. The legal framework includes bylaws passed by the Accra Metropolitan Assembly on activities that are prohibited on streets and lists a series of places where street vending is prohibited. As are other workers in Ghana, street vendors are affected by laws regulating the relationship between employers and employees, taxation laws, and copyright laws prohibiting piracy of original products and sale of pirated products. Informal workers' entitlement to social security benefits is provided by the voluntary third pillar of the Social Security National Insurance Trust (SSNIT), though its coverage is very low. Coverage for informal workers is higher in the National Health Insurance Scheme (NHIS), the other public social protection instrument. Street vendors and petty traders are levied a daily fixed rate tax (referred to as a ticket); it was GH¢0.20 per day in 2011.

Qualitative evidence collected through focus groups and interviews from street vendors in Accra in 2011 yields the following findings:

- Child labor is common.
- Though many had regarded their street activities as temporary, lack of opportunity for transition has made the activities permanent.
- Informal workers with higher levels of education tend to belong to the SSNIT pension scheme and NHIS.
- The occupational health and safety conditions are very poor. Street vendors are commonly found in open public places, sometimes in very deplorable working environments with poor sanitary conditions.
- Shoplifting and burglary are challenges to vendors.
- The high cost of market stalls is one reason vendors sell on the streets.
- Town and city planning and development have often disrupted the activities of the street vendors without relocating vendors appropriately. Dialogue between policy makers and street vendors needs to be enhanced.
- Involving street vendors in city planning would not only facilitate ownership of policies but also ensure that the needs of traders are taken into account, which would foster harmony.

Source: Osei-Boateng 2012.

---

are microenterprises engaging between 3 and 5 people; and 3 percent employ more than 5 workers (figure 4.7). These one- or two-person enterprises are self-financed. The main source of capital comes from household savings, proceeds from family farms, and informal support from relatives and friends.

The majority of own-account enterprises are run by females; however, as the HHE grows, men are more likely to run and own the business. In Ghana, HHEs are female-dominated businesses (figure 4.8). Overall, 70 percent of HHEs are run by females, reflecting cultural and social norms in household dynamics, but also other constraints to growth (including skills, capital, information, and proximity to markets). By contrast, only one-third of firms in the formal private sector have some female participation in ownership. The gender of the owner is associated with the role that the enterprise plays in the household portfolio of job activities. Females are more likely to run own-account businesses that may represent seasonal jobs during the off-season, in the case of farming smallholders, or a secondary activity to diversify household income sources. The share of female-owned enterprises decreases as size increases and the enterprise becomes the main activity: most of the enterprises employing more than 5 workers are owned by males.

More than half of the enterprises have been operating for more than 10 years, without experiencing much growth or expansion during that time. They have kept producing at the same scale and at very low productivity levels, without experiencing dynamic growth or changes in the production function, despite their longevity. They may have been launched to remain subsistence enterprises, with no ambitions to grow into a "proper" business. However, entry is considerable: 20 percent of the HHEs are start-ups having been operating for one year or less. Eventually, not all start-ups will survive (figure 4.9).

Figure 4.7 Household Enterprises Distribution, by Number of Workers

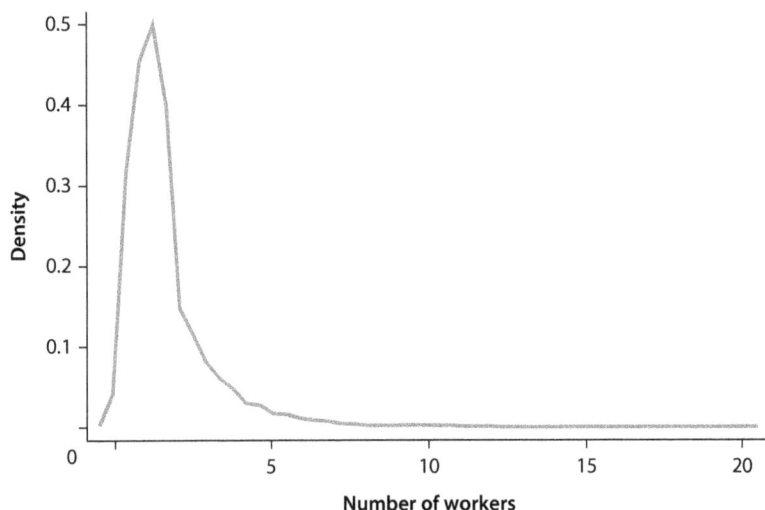

Source: Kernel density estimates based on GLSS6.

Figure 4.8 Owners of Household Enterprises, by Age and Gender

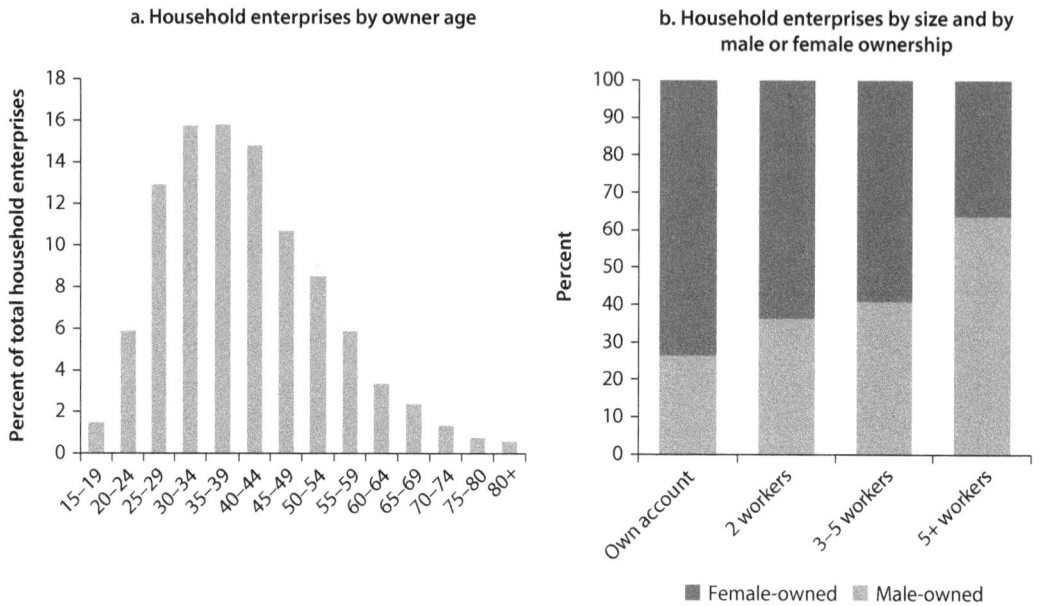

a. Household enterprises by owner age

b. Household enterprises by size and by male or female ownership

Source: Estimates based on GLSS6.

Figure 4.9 Household Enterprises Distribution, by Years of Operation

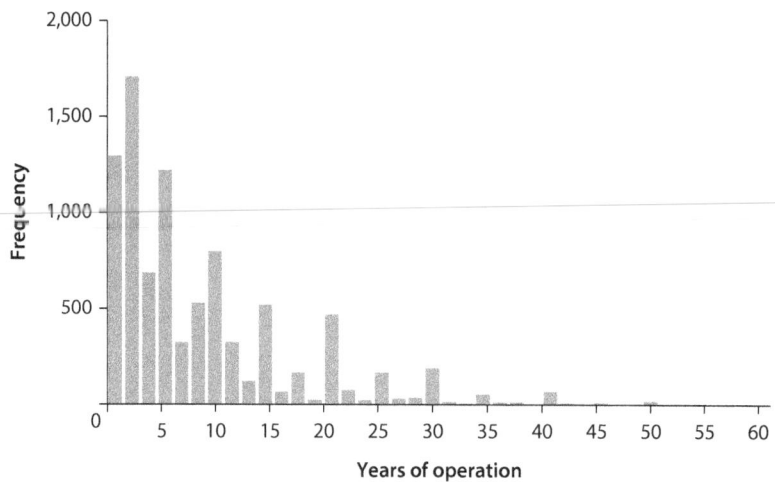

Source: Estimates based on GLSS6.

Services dominate the activities of HHEs, especially in urban areas. The majority of HHEs engage in wholesale and retail trading activities (54 percent of HHEs), but also catering and lodging, food services (making and selling snacks or meals), transport, and personal services such as barbering and hairdressing. Manufacturing activities are also common (21 percent of the HHEs), such as artisanal activities (producing custom furniture and ironwork, dressmaking, and tailoring) and transforming agricultural goods or natural resources into products such as charcoal, flour, roof thatching, or bricks. Manufacturing activities are more common in rural areas than in urban areas. Although most of the population lives in rural areas, most HHEs in Ghana are located in urban areas, where the positive agglomeration effects create higher demand for the services and low-quality goods mobile retail traders offer (figure 4.10).

However, the manufacturing and construction sectors may offer good opportunities to expand. While half of the larger HHEs are operating in services, local markets for manufacturing goods and construction offer better opportunities to expand and hire more labor, mostly in Accra and Ashanti regions. An analysis (multinomial logit) of factors that influence entry into various economic sectors in the off-farm economy finds that, while men are more likely to enter the manufacturing sector, women appear to dominate the wholesale/retail sectors, indicating the possibility of some gender discrimination in the off-farm economy. Marriage also reduces the likelihood of participation in the services sector, especially among women, but increases likelihood of participation in the wholesale sector, where activities are perceived to be more flexible and women are better able to balance work and domestic responsibilities (Owoo 2015).

The majority of HHEs are not registered, operate "by necessity," and are not considering formalizing. On average, only 13 percent of HHEs are registered with any government agency, either with the District Assembly or the Registrar General Department. The share of registered HHEs is higher among larger enterprises (35 percent of the HHEs with more than 5 workers) and among owners with higher education a (senior secondary school and beyond) (23 percent). The 2013 World Bank informal ES, while not representative, offers some insights to

Figure 4.10 Household Enterprises, by Sector and Location

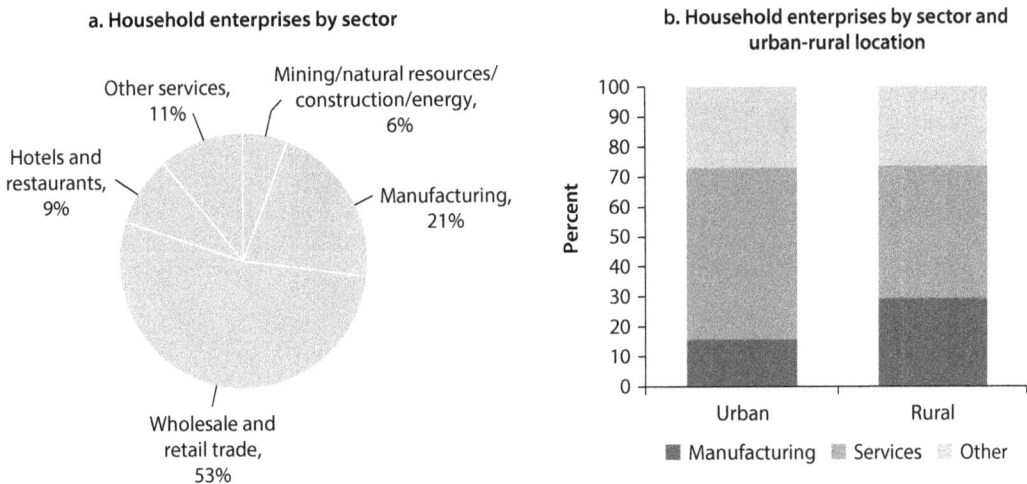

a. Household enterprises by sector

Other services, 11%
Mining/natural resources/construction/energy, 6%
Hotels and restaurants, 9%
Manufacturing, 21%
Wholesale and retail trade, 53%

b. Household enterprises by sector and urban-rural location

■ Manufacturing ■ Services Other

Source: Estimates based on GLSS6.

better understand the constraints and willingness to formalize and sheds light on the potential segmentation between the formal and informal labor market. Data indicate that only 50 percent of informal enterprises want to formalize; even among more educated owners, on average only 60 percent respond that they want to formalize.

Lack of knowledge about the potential benefits (and costs) of formalization, rather than monetary and time costs, seem to keep microenterprises in the informal sector. Most informal (and household) enterprises do not know how much registration costs are, and whether the expected benefits from formalization would exceed the costs. When all respondents were asked to estimate the time it would take them to register, nearly 80 percent report that they do not know; 13 percent estimate that this process would take less than 14 days (which is closest to the Doing Business estimate of 14 days to start a business). Among those firms who want to formalize, high costs (time, fees, paperwork) are cited as the main reason not to formalize.

Almost half the owners of HHEs have not completed secondary school, while better-educated owners are more likely to run job-creating enterprises. Typically, HHEs provide employment opportunities for lower-educated workers (those who have not completed secondary education). These are people who lack the education for a wage job but can pursue the economic opportunities that HHEs offer—as a full-time activity or together with agriculture. Indeed, the median owner of an own-account HHE or two-person enterprise has not completed secondary junior school (figure 4.11). This contrasts starkly with the two-thirds of workers in the formal private sector who have completed senior secondary school.

Figure 4.11 Household Enterprises, by Size, Sector, and Education of the Owner

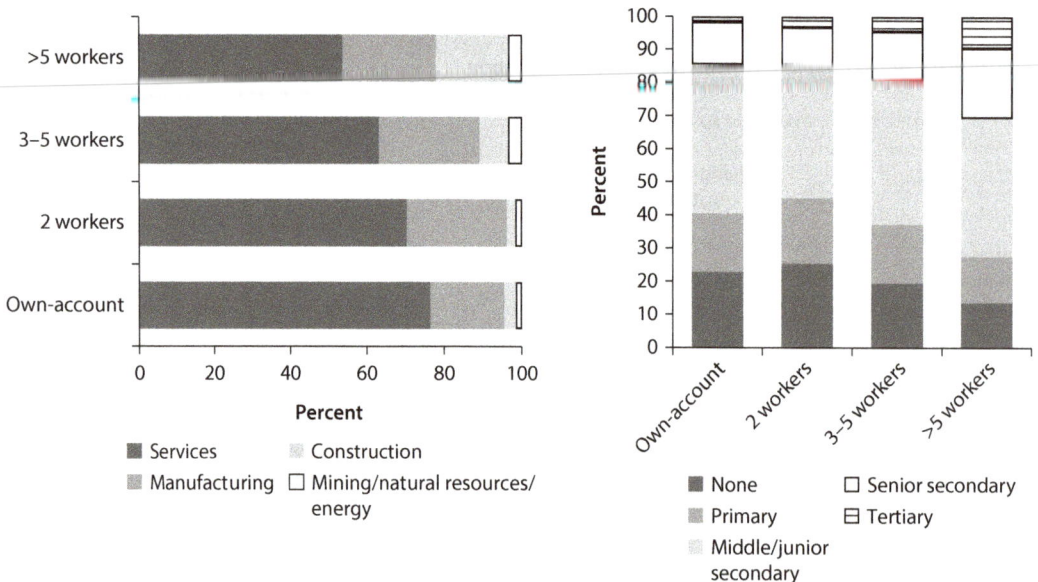

Services   Construction
Manufacturing   Mining/natural resources/energy

None   Senior secondary
Primary   Tertiary
Middle/junior secondary

Source: Estimates based on GLSS6.

The share of higher-educated owners increases with the size of the enterprise, pointing to the lack of basic education and skills as one constraint to expand own-account activities into enterprises that engage more people and produce at larger scale. There is no correlation between larger HHEs and years of operations. It is rather the education of the owner, the industry of operation, and local demand that explain the potential of the enterprise to grow.

Overall, 6 million people are engaged in HHEs; 60 percent are the owners (mostly female), who work full-time on the business, while the other 40 percent are either family members also working full-time (5 percent mostly female), or contributing family helpers (17 percent). About 1 million people (20 percent of people engaged), mostly not family members, are hired in the HHEs as casual workers (9 percent) or apprentices (8 percent). As the number of people engaged in the HHEs increases, the composition of the workforce changes, relying more on workers external to the household. The median two-person enterprise includes a full-time owner and a contributing family member. The median enterprise with three employees includes a casual or apprentice worker, a contributing family member, and the owner. In a five-person enterprise, two are either casual workers or apprentices (figure 4.12). The median five-person enterprise has three full-time

Figure 4.12 Household Enterprises Workforce Composition, by Type of Worker and Firm Size

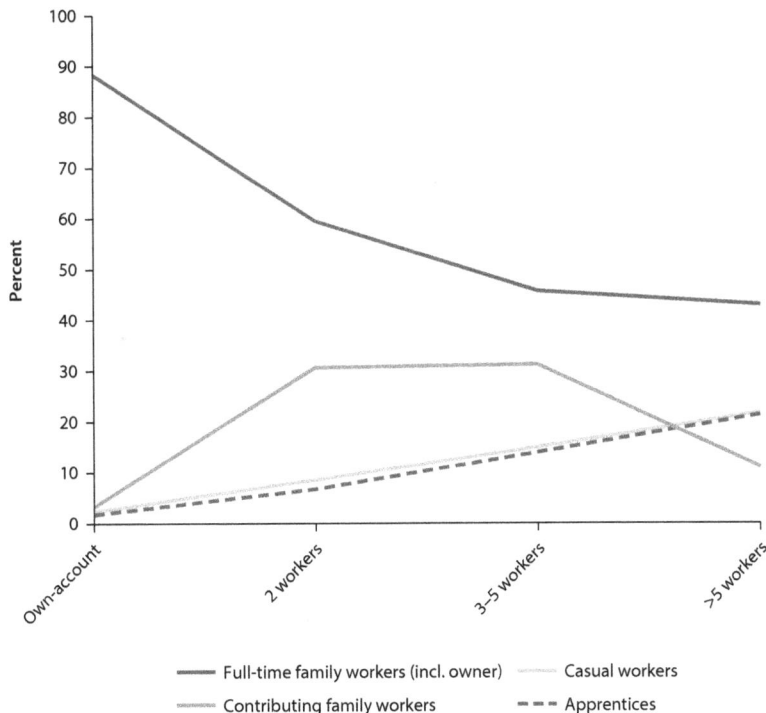

Legend: Full-time family workers (incl. owner); Casual workers; Contributing family workers; Apprentices

Source: Estimates based on GLSS6.
Note: Own-account enterprises account for 73 percent of household enterprises.

household members engaged (including the owner), one casual worker, and one apprentice. Among the job-creating HHEs, more than two-fifths of workers are nonhousehold members hired to work casually or as apprentices.

Most own-account entrepreneurs do not report personal income from the HHE. Forty percent of owners report zero earnings for themselves (in the case of sole proprietors) and for workers engaged in the HHE. While data on the personal earnings reported by HHEs owners are very noisy (as they may reflect the business income, rather than a "wage" paid against a certain amount of hours worked, as in the case of "wage workers"),[8] the measure captured in the GLSS6 is still indicative of the general pattern and scale of those businesses. The median HHE pays 80 cedis a month in salaries. Looking only at HHEs paying positive "salaries" to proprietors and workers, the median own-account entrepreneurs earn 200 cedis a month, while owners of larger HHEs earn double that amount (table 4.4).

HHEs operating in construction and services generate higher sales and income and pay higher "salaries" than those operating in manufacturing. The services sector appears to be the highest performing sector as measured by asset valuations of enterprises, while the manufacturing sector is the lowest performing sector (Owoo 2015). The median monthly income after deducting enterprise expenses also increases with firm size and age, and varies by gender. Enterprises in urban areas have higher asset valuations than those in rural areas (table 4.4).

Table 4.4 Median Monthly Salaries Paid by Household Enterprises
Ghana cedis

	Median monthly salary	*Median monthly revenues*	*Median monthly income*
Size			
Own-account	200	1,369	468
2 workers	200	1,587	546
3–5 workers	300	2,889	1,461
More than 5 workers	332	3,751	2,538
Sector			
Manufacturing	200	1,842	721
Wholesale retail	200	1,101	295
Other services	208	3,236	1,752
Mining/natural resources/ construction/energy	360	10,942	8,736
Years in Operation			
Less than 1 year	160	634	204
1–4 years	168	1,057	350
4–10 years	200	1,881	681
More than 10 years	240	2,206	959
Total	200	1,608	585

Source: Estimates based on GLSS6.
Note: Median monthly salary, income, and sales are calculated excluding zeros. Median monthly revenues are calculated using values of production and sale of products. Median monthly income equals total revenues minus expenditures of the enterprise. Outliers are defined as values greater or less than three standard deviations from the median value when checking for extreme values by some relevant subgroup.

Figure 4.13 Median Monthly Salaries, by Education of Owner

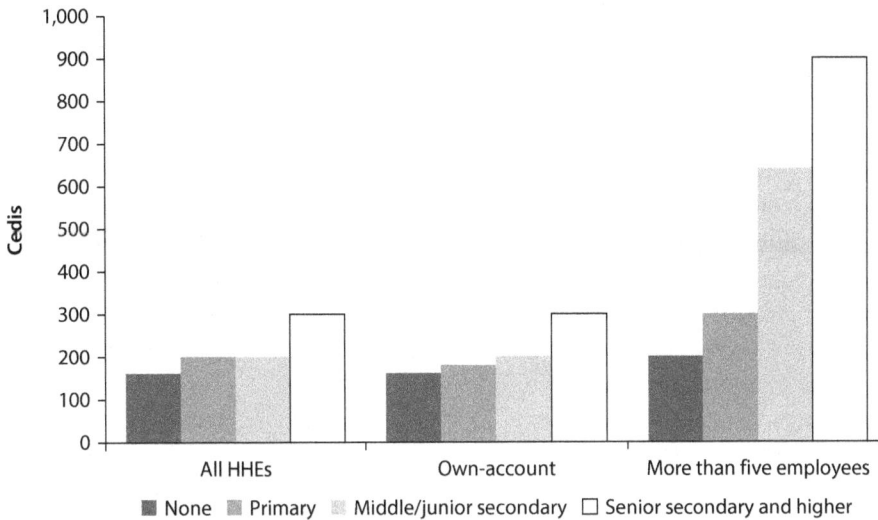

Source: Estimates based on GLSS6.

Women-owned HHEs have lower asset valuations, compared to men-owned enterprises. This has negative implications for business growth among these women-owned enterprises and further exacerbates constraints for women's access to credit, as the absence of assets (such as land) and absence of adequate collateral reduces their chances of obtaining regular loans. Gender-targeted policies should be developed to ease access to finance.

Most HHE income is allocated to household expenditures. An own-account business allocates on average about 45 percent of the income generated through the HHE after deducting for business expenditure to household expenditures. About 30 percent goes to the owner; 20 percent is allotted to savings for the enterprise; and 5 percent is allocated for other uses. The allocation to household expenditures varies slightly for HHEs engaging more workers: a HHE with more than 5 employees allocates on average 36 percent to household expenditures; 29 percent to the owner; 6 percent to workers; and 24 percent to savings and reinvestment in the HHEs.

While better-educated owners have higher income and sales, higher earnings also reflect the greater ability of these entrepreneurs to expand their business and engage more people (figure 4.13).

What Prevents Microenterprises from Transforming to Job-Creating Firms?

Females face higher constraints than men to join the formal workforce and to expand their HHEs. Females are more likely to operate and remain operating one- or two-person enterprises—sometimes for years, with no prospect (and intention) to grow. The reasons may be complex and linked to social and cultural norms, family-management practices, and intrahousehold dynamics,[9] among other constraints that are more severe for women, such as education, skills, and access to credit. Unlike men, female entrepreneurs have little mobility, which may be a binding constraint in the services sector and in urban areas, where mobile vendors have the flexibility to access more job opportunities. Female entrepreneurs run their business in the household also to fulfill their domestic obligations, housekeeping work, and child and elderly care. In Ghana, female microentrepreneurs rank the incapacity to work the desired number of hours as the major challenge. They rank the inability to travel in search of stock and difficulty of taking up new challenges and maintaining a work-life balance as other severe constraints to expanding a business. These factors are not reported as major constraints by men (ISSER 2015).

Women often lack the title to property, a further constraint to access to finance and entrepreneurial opportunities. One of the challenges for women is that titling has too often been done under the male head of household. In many countries, marriage changes the legal status and rights of women, conferring legal capacities and responsibilities on husbands and removing them from wives. The lack of property right affects women's economic and entrepreneurial opportunities in Sub-Saharan Africa. A recent study—the Women's Legal and Economic Empowerment Database for Africa (Women LEED Africa)—documents how gender gaps in economic rights reduce women's ability to grow a business and employ workers in 47 countries in Sub-Saharan Africa. It shows that the share of female employers is larger where women's economic rights are stronger (Hallward-Driemeier and Hasan 2012; Hallward-Driemeier and others 2013).

While access to finance is rated as the major business constraint by firms of all sizes, formal and informal, its severity is highest for microenterprises and HHEs. The high interest rate environment in the financial sector is a deterrent for borrowing by firms of all types, particularly small ones. More than half of microenterprises and small registered firms report access to finance as the top obstacle to grow their business. About half of the HHEs report lack of capital and credit as a serious difficulty to starting up a firm,[10] while the other half report not having any difficulty jump-starting their business. However, the majority of HHEs operate without access to external finance (91 percent of HHEs are clearly capital constrained); only 6 percent have tried and successfully gotten credit from banks or other financial institutions; and another 3 percent have tried to get credit, but unsuccessfully (table 4.5). They do not even rely on informal credit from money lenders, relatives, and proceeds from other household activities (farming, gardening, fishing); household savings are the main source of capital. Microenterprises and small and medium formal firms also mostly rely on internal funds to finance their operation and on informal sources of finance; only about one-quarter of formal firms (larger firms) rely on bank financial services and equity.

Lack of access to appropriate financing translates into insufficient levels of investment in innovation and firm growth. Ghanaian firms operate in an extremely high interest rate environment, face severe foreign exchange restrictions,

Table 4.5 The Majority of Firms Operate without Access to External Finance

Source	Household enterprises		Micro (0–5)	Small (5–19)	Medium small (20–49)	Medium large (50–99)	Large (100+)
	Male	Female					
Capital							
Household savings	75.4	72					
Proceeds from HHEs/ internal funds	8.3	5.4	75	76	67	63	64
Bank	2.0	1.8	6	8	16	17	20
Relative/friends, moneylenders	11.4	18.4	5	4	2	3	3
Other (suppliers and other)	2.9	2.4	14	12	15	17	13
Credit							
No credit	93.2	92.0	59.0	57.0	37.0	26.0	32.0
Proceeds from HHE/ internal funds	0.2	0.1	34.9	34.4	44.1	49.6	47.6
Bank	3.6	3.9	1.6	3.4	10.7	14.8	14.3
Equity			1.2	2.2	2.5	8.1	2.0
Relative/friends, moneylenders	2.0	3.6	2.1	1.7	1.3	0.0	0.0
Other (suppliers and other)	1.0	0.4	1.2	0.9	4.4	1.5	3.4

Source: Estimates based on GLSS6 and the Ghana Enterprise Survey 2013.
Note: HHEs = household enterprises.

and have very limited access to capital. Even liquidity credit in Ghana is prohibitively expensive and not accessible for most firms, particularly SMEs. As the risk-free rate has ballooned to more than 26 percent (January 2016), current real interest rate levels of around 10 percent are an impediment for both firm growth and debt stabilization. The lack of access to external finance also affects the ability of firms to manage liquidity, making them vulnerable to even small financial shocks and unable to invest in innovative activities. Competitiveness in export markets also suffers because of higher costs associated with trade logistics (World Bank 2015).

Inadequate electricity supply is the second most commonly cited major constraint mentioned by firms of all sizes, implying higher costs to firms and also leading to sporadic use of information and communications technology (ICT) systems. Lack of regular power supplies creates major problems for firms of all sizes, especially for microentrepreneurs in rural areas, where access to electricity is very limited. The average registered firm in urban areas faces more than seven power outages in a typical month, compared to an average of five outages in lower-middle-income countries (Enterprise Surveys). The implications for firms' profitability and competition are huge, preventing them from producing during dark hours; reducing the development of modern capital-intense technologies; and most important preventing firms from exploiting the potential of ICT (figure 4.14). Among formal firms, on average,

Figure 4.14 Internet Use among Microenterprises and SMEs

a. Firms using emails to communicate with clients and suppliers

b. Firms using their own websites

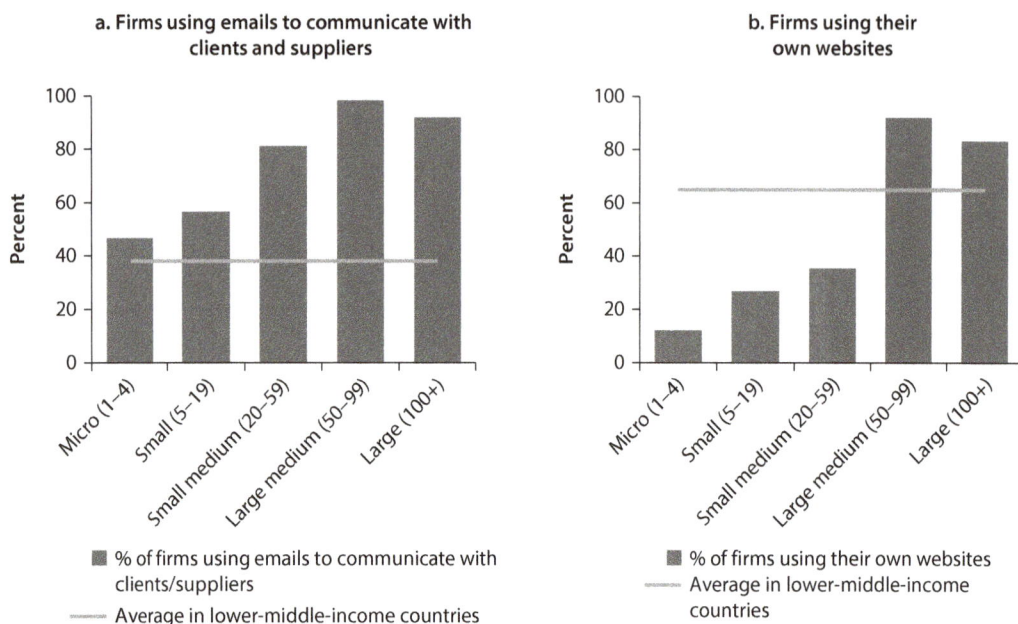

■ % of firms using emails to communicate with clients/suppliers
—— Average in lower-middle-income countries

■ % of firms using their own websites
—— Average in lower-middle-income countries

Source: Estimates based on the Enterprise Survey 2013.
Note: SME = small and medium enterprise.

about 9 percent of sales are lost because of power outages,[11] more than twice the amount lost by the average Sub-Saharan African country. Ghana performs poorly in terms of delays in obtaining electricity connection compared to other African countries and comparator low-income countries; the average firm experiences 37 days of delay to connect to electricity, discouraging firm entry and investment. The innovative use of mobile phones is at the forefront of the African technological progress in several domains, including business development. ICT and the use of Internet are important tools to reach out to local and international markets at low cost. Nonetheless, there is room to expand the use of computers, which is still quite low among microenterprises, but also among SMEs.

The worsening power situation emerged as the first challenge for the majority of businesses, according to the Association of Ghana Industries 2015 barometer (AGI 2015). To keep their business running, many companies have relied on generators as an alternative to electricity from the grid, incurring higher costs. Snap surveys by AGI on the effect of the power crisis revealed that some industries have laid off some of their staff as an interim measure to contain the situation. Other firms have rearranged the working schedule to ensure that production meets market demand. Manufacturing is the most affected sector, with 27 percent of chief executive officers (CEOs) planning to cut jobs in the next six months if the power crisis persists (AGI 2015). SMEs and large enterprises cited the depreciation of the cedi and exchange rate volatility as the second binding constraint to their businesses, while microenterprises cited unfair competition as their second challenge.

Although the firm tax wedge is low compared to international standards, tax-related issues feature highly among the key constraints. The tax wedge[12] in Ghana is about 18.5 percent of wages, well below the world average of 35 percent (Ghana SSNIT; Ribe, Robalino, and Walker 2012; OECD 2015). The average tax wedge measures the extent to which tax on labor income discourages formal employment. However, both the high tax rates and the time and other resources involved in dealing with tax administration are considered problematic in Ghana (figure 4.15), and their importance has increased significantly since 2007, when the previous ES was undertaken (figure 4.18).

Importantly, processes reflecting poor governance are also emerging as an obstacle: in 2007, only 10 percent of firms considered corruption an obstacle to doing business; by 2013, over 40 percent of firms were troubled by corrupt practices (figure 4.18). Weak governance also emerges as an issue from the Doing Business Indicators: the judiciary system is the area where Ghana is furthest from the best performers internationally (figure 4.16). Ghana is ranked 114th among 189 countries in the aggregate Ease of Doing Business 2016. While better than the regional average for Sub-Saharan Africa, Ghana's performance is below its country average in five out of the ten criteria considered: trading across borders, resolving insolvency, dealing with construction permits, getting electricity, and enforcing contracts.

Figure 4.15 Obstacles to Investment and Business in Ghana

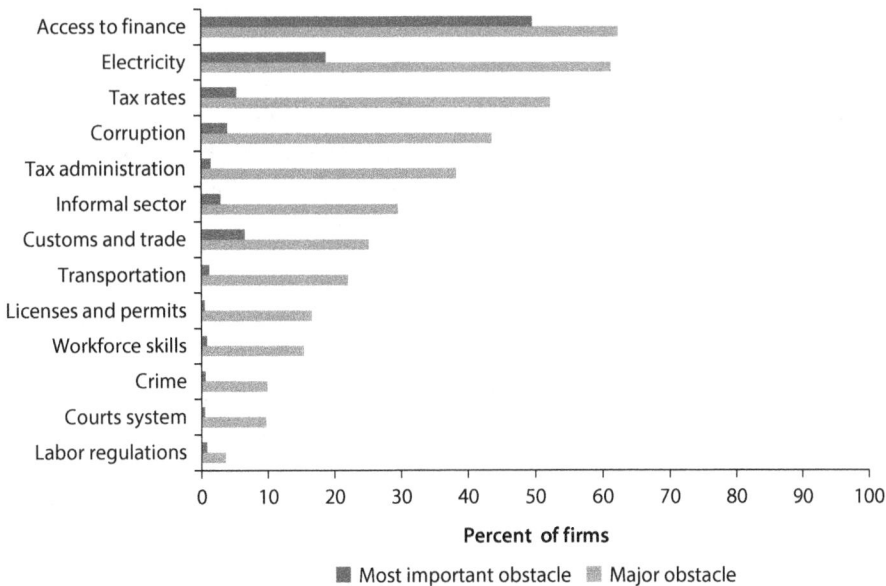

Source: Estimates based on the Enterprise Survey 2013.
Note: The percentage of firms perceiving respective problem as the top obstacle or as a major obstacle.

Figure 4.16 Ghana's Distance to Doing Business Frontier

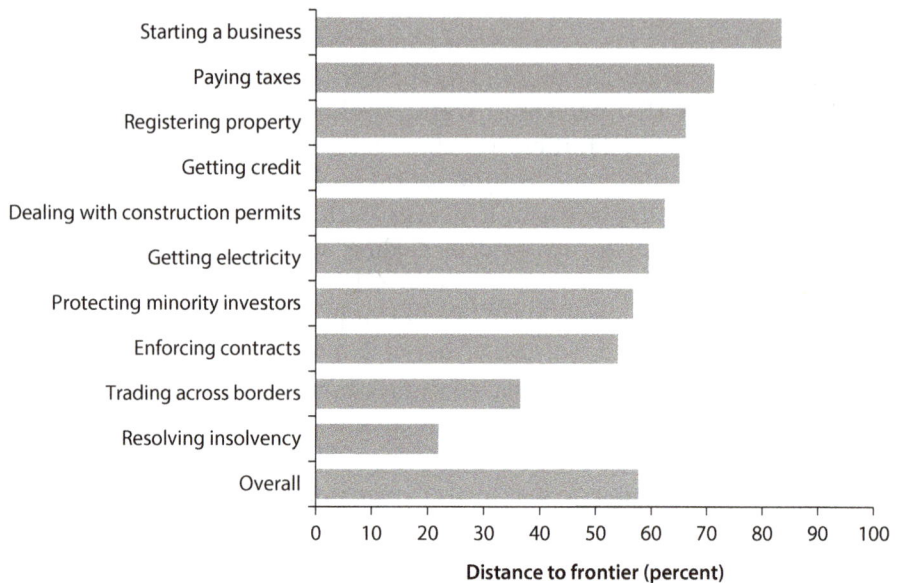

Source: World Bank Enterprise Surveys and Doing Business Indicators, www.enterprisesurveys.org and www.doingbusiness.org (2016 data).
Note: The "Distance to frontier" shows the distance of each economy to the best performance observed on each of the indicators across all economies and between 2005 and 2016. Ghana's distance to frontier is reflected on a scale from 0 to 100, where 100 represents the frontier: the lower the score, the further away is Ghana from the best performing economy over time. (For more information, visit http://www.doingbusiness.org/data/distance-to-frontier.)

Lack of basic education and entrepreneurial skills are binding constraints, especially for informal microentrepreneurs. Most microenterprise owners, especially female owners, lack the basic literacy and numeracy skills necessary to acquire further cognitive skills, adding greater challenges. In addition, most of those microentrepreneurs lack the management skills required to run a business that are not taught in the formal education system, such as how to keep records and manage accounts; deal with customers, banks, suppliers, and employees; and understand the difference between business profits and personal earnings from the business. These are skills that are not easily acquired, but are fundamental to separate the life of the enterprise from the household economy and make it grow independently. Evidence shows that better business practices lead to increase business profitability (McKenzie and Woodruff 2015).

However, entrepreneurial talent is heterogeneous and not perfectly observed. There is mixed evidence on the impact of skills training and capital on the transformation from microenterprises to small or medium businesses.[13] Recent experiments in Ghana suggest that either cash or in-kind capital grants help increase firm performance only among male and better-performing female microentrepreneurs. No gain was found among subsistence female entrepreneurs (Fafchamps and others 2014). Even providing individual consultative services (training on business practices, technical skills) to tailors in Accra did not help them improve their enterprise's profitability (Karlan, Knight, and Udry 2015). Part of the problem is that the entrepreneurs are a heterogeneous group: some are ambitious and innovative entrepreneurs with growth potential, whereas others are there by necessity (Schoar 2010). This suggests that the impacts may depend on characteristics or attitudes of the entrepreneur, and that the targeting of such interventions may be improved. While policies that ease the access to finance, to information, and to relevant skills (entrepreneurial, management, financial, vocational, and life skills) are needed, identifying the "high potential" entrepreneurs is the challenge.[14]

An inadequately educated workforce is reported as becoming an obstacle among formal firms, but not a major one, as firm size increases. Only formal firms with more than 50 employees perceive the lack of job-relevant skills as a major constraint. Indeed, on average, larger firms invest more in their workforce by offering them formal training. Firms operating in the service sector are more likely to offer training to increase the competitiveness of their firms (figure 4.17). Microenterprises and small firms provide mostly on-the-job training through apprenticeships.

The business climate deteriorated between 2007 and 2013, firms report. Employers' perceptions of the business climate worsened along several dimensions. Access to finance, trade regulation, education of the workforce, and corruption were reported as major constraints to business growth by more firms in 2013 than in 2007 (figure 4.18). Access to electricity, while still reported as the second most severe obstacle by all firms, has improved since 2007. Firms of different sizes also face different constraints. Credit and electricity are more binding for small firms, while trade regulation, tax rates, unskilled labor force, and corruption are perceived as more binding for large firms.

Figure 4.17 Formal Firms Offering Training to Workers, by Size and Economic Sector

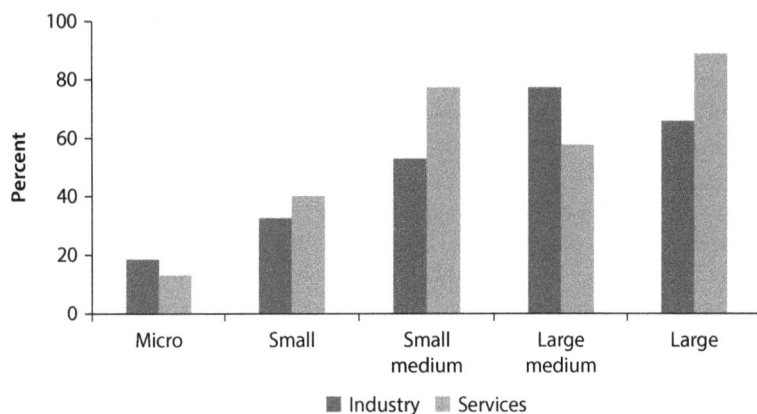

Source: Estimates based on the Enterprise Survey 2013.

Figure 4.18 Major Obstacles to Doing Business, by Firm Size

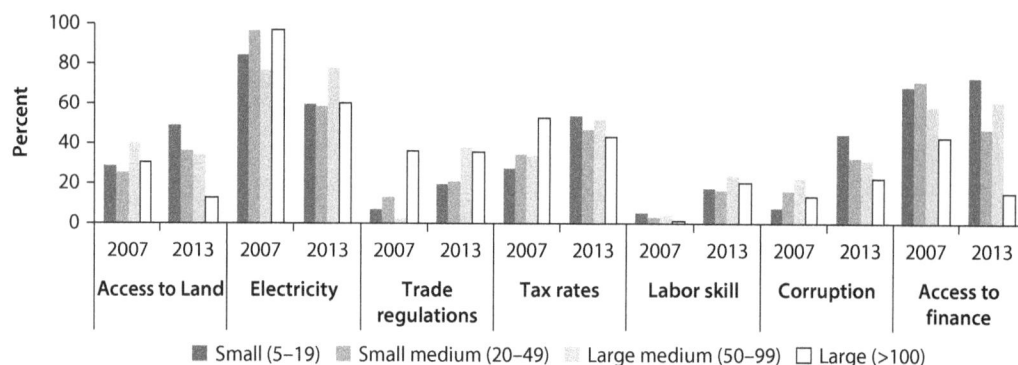

Source: Enterprise Surveys 2007 and 2013.
Note: Percentage of formal firms identifying the problem as a major obstacle.

Notes

1. The size categorization refers to the average number of permanent and temporary employees, based on reported and recall data.

2. Bear in mind that the ES does not represent some service subsectors. Within the industry sector, the mining and utilities sectors are not surveyed (see box 4.1).

3. Using panel data on manufacturing firms between 1987 and 2003 in Ghana, Sandefur (2010) showed that there was actually little evidence for within-firm growth: firms that were small in 1988 remained small in 2003, and the big firms operating in 2003 were already big in 1988.

4. They sampled about 1,000 manufacturing firms from the Ghana National Industrial Census (2003) and surveyed them in 2013; new entrants in 2013 are not captured— only those firms operating in 2003. Results reported here refer to the exit measured as those firms that closed and that could not be found/tracked in 2013.

5. These measures are based on the difference in survey-weighted employment for each establishment between FY2012 and FY2010 divided by the two-period average, annualized by the number of years elapsing between the two periods. Contraction and creation rates aggregated by taking the establishment rate multiplied by its relative share of overall employment. Rates for gross job creation (job contraction) are taken for only positive-growth (negative-growth) establishments. These measures are widely used and are explained fully in Haltiwanger Jarmin, and Miranda (2013).

6. The estimates refer to comparable samples in 2007 and 2013 (see box 4.1). Real growth rates are based on U.S. dollar deflators. Aggregate figures are based on latest Enterprise Survey data between 2010 and 2014 for about 37 countries in Sub-Saharan Africa and 31 lower-middle-income countries, including Ghana.

7. Some households also run two enterprises.

8. Module 10 of the GLSS6 asks about wage earnings of sole proprietors and people engaged in the HHEs. As there is often no separation between business revenues, profits, and personal earnings in household enterprises, this measure must be interpreted with caution and cannot be strictly compared with "wages" or work compensation.

9. There is suggestive evidence of hard choices in the face of poverty among female microentrepreneurs in Ghana; only in-kind grants—physical capital that remains in the business—had an impact on profits among females; providing cash grants of the same value did not have impact (Fafchamps and others 2014).

10. The GLSS6 does not ask which are the perceived obstacles to businesses expanding their business—just the difficulties in launching their businesses.

11. Enterprise Survey, Ghana Overview Report 2013.

12. The tax wedge is defined as the ratio between the amount of taxes paid by an average single worker (a single person at 100 percent of average earnings) without children and the corresponding total labor cost for the employer (OECD).

13. The impact of microcredit shows modest but not transformative results, and the impact of entrepreneurial training programs is mixed. For systematic reviews of impact evaluation literature, see McKenzie and Woodruff 2013; Cho and Honorati 2014; Card, Kluve, and Weber 2015; and Grimm and Paffhausen 2015.

14. Some work has been undertaken to identify the characteristics of the potential high-growth entrepreneurs (or "gazelles") with the ability to expand their firm size over time (Calderon, Cunha, and de Giorgi 2013; Fafchamps and Woodruff 2014) and to identify which aspects of business management and practice affect firm performance in the developing world (McKenzie and Woodruff 2015).

References

AGI (Association of Ghana Industries). 2015. *Business Barometer, 1st quarter 2015.* http://www.agighana.org.

Calderon, G., J. Cunha, and G. de Giorgi. 2013. "Business Literacy and Development: Evidence from a Randomized Controlled Trial in Rural Mexico." NBER Working Paper 19740, National Bureau of Economic Research, Cambridge, MA.

Calvino, F., C. Criscuolo, and C. Menon. 2015. "Cross-country Evidence on Start-up Dynamics." OECD Science, Technology and Industry Working Paper 2015/6, OECD, Paris.

Card, D., J. Kluve, and A. Weber. 2015. *What Works? A Meta Analysis of Recent Active Labor Market Program Evaluations.* Cambridge, MA: National Bureau of Economic Research.

Cho, Y., and M. Honorati. 2014. "Entrepreneurship Programs in Developing Countries: A Meta Regression Analysis." *Labour Economics* 28: 110–30.

Criscuolo, C., P. N. Gal, and C. Menon. 2014. "The Dynamics of Employment Growth: New Evidence from 18 Countries." CEP Discussion Paper dp1274, Centre for Economic Performance, London School of Economics.

Davies, E., and A. Kerr. 2015. "Firm Survival and Change in Ghana, 2003–2013." CSAE Working Paper 2015–06, Centre for the Study of African Economies, University of Oxford.

Fafchamps, M., D. McKenzie, S. R. Quinn, and C. Woodruff. 2014. "When Is Capital Enough to Get Female Microenterprises Growing? Evidence from a Randomized Experiment in Ghana." *Journal of Development Economics* 106: 211–26.

Fafchamps, M., and C. Woodruff. 2014. "Identifying Gazelles: Expert Panels vs. Surveys as a Means to Identify Firms with Rapid Growth Potential." CAGE Online Working Paper Series 213, Competitive Advantage in the Global Economy (CAGE).

Filmer, D., and L. Fox. 2014. *Youth Employment in Sub-Saharan Africa*. Africa Development Forum Series. World Bank and Agence Française de Développement.

Fox, L. 2015. "Are African Households Heterogeneous Agents? Stylized Facts on Patterns of Consumption, Employment, Income, and Earnings for Macroeconomic Modelers." Working Paper WP/15/102, International Monetary Fund, Washington, DC.

Francis, D., and M. Honorati. 2016. "Jobs in Ghana's Private Sector: Deepening without Broadening?" Policy Research Working Paper Series, World Bank, Washington, DC.

Grimm, M., and A. L. Paffhausen. 2015. "Do Interventions Targeted at Micro-Entrepreneurs and Small and Medium-Sized Firms Create Jobs? A Systematic Review of the Evidence for Low and Middle Income Countries." *Labour Economics* 32: 67–85.

Hallward-Driemeier, M., and T. Hasan. 2012. *Empowering Women: Legal Rights and Economic Opportunities in Africa*. Africa Development Forum Series. Washington, DC: World Bank.

Hallward-Driemeier, M., T. Hasan, J. Kamangu, E. Lobti, and M. Blackden. 2013. *Women's Legal and Economic Empowerment Database for Africa (Women LEED Africa)*. Development Economics. Washington, DC: World Bank.

Haltiwanger, J., R. S. Jarmin, and J. Miranda. 2013. "Who Creates Jobs? Small versus Large versus Young." *Review of Economics and Statistics* 95 (2): 347–61.

Hsieh, C.-T., and P. J. Klenow. 2014. "The Life Cycle of Plants in India and Mexico." *Quarterly Journal of Economics* 129 (3): 1035–84. doi:10.1093/qje/qju014.

ISSER (Institute of Statistical, Social and Economic Research). 2015. "Public Policy and Enterprise Development in Ghana." ISSER Policy Brief 2, University of Ghana (August).

Karlan, D., R. Knight, and C. Udry. 2015. "Consulting and Capital Experiments with Microenterprise Tailors in Ghana." *Journal of Economic Behavior & Organization* 118 (2015): 281–302.

McKenzie, D., and C. Woodruff. 2013. "What Are We Learning from Business Training and Entrepreneurship Evaluations around the Developing World?" *The World Bank Research Observer* 29 (1): 48–82.

———. 2015. "Business Practice in Small Firms in Developing Countries" Policy Research Working Paper 7405, World Bank, Washington, DC.

Naugler, P., and W. Naudé. 2014. "Non-Farm Enterprises in Rural Africa: New Empirical Evidence." Policy Research Working Paper 7066, World Bank, Washington, DC.

OECD (Organisation for Economic Co-operation and Development). 2015. *Taxing Wages 2015*. Paris: OECD.

Osei-Boateng, C. 2012. *Women in Informal Economy Law Project. A Report on Street Vending in Ghana*. Labor Research and Policy Institute, Ghana Trades Union Congress.

Owoo, N. S. 2015. *Determinants of Choice of Economic Sector in the Non-Farm Economy in Ghana*. University of Ghana, Unpublished.

Ribe, H., D. Robalino, and I. Walker. 2012. "From Right to Reality: Incentives, Labor Markets, and the Challenge of Universal Social Protection in Latin America and the Caribbean." World Bank, Washington, DC.

Sandefur, J. 2010. "On the Evolution of the Firm Size Distribution in an African Economy." CSAE Working Paper Series 2010-05, Centre for the Study of African Economies, University of Oxford.

Schoar, A. 2010. "The Divide between Subsistence and Transformational Entrepreneurship." *Innovation Policy and the Economy* 10 (1): 57–81.

UN (United Nations). 2015. *Industrializing through Trade*. United Nations Economic Commission for Africa.

World Bank. 2015. *Ghana Manufacturing Competitiveness*. Washington, DC: World Bank.

———. Enterprise Surveys (database). www.enterprisesurveys.org.

———. Doing Business 2016 (database). www.doingbusiness.org.

CHAPTER 5

Jobs for Development in Ghana: What Can Policy Do?

Ghana's progress in reducing poverty will continue to be closely linked to the quality of jobs generated by the economy and the equality of opportunities. In the past 20 years, transitions of jobs out of agriculture and into self-employment in the off-farm sector and, to a lesser extent, into wage employment have helped significantly raise income and consumption levels for Ghana's population. Going forward, Ghana will need not just more jobs but better jobs, and more jobs for those in the population who so far have not partaken in the development process to the same extent as others.

Ghana faces many jobs challenges that require policy action in order to reduce poverty and increase overall living standards. A majority of the population is still involved in low-productivity activities, especially in the agricultural and informal services sectors, despite rapid job creation in recent years. There are still significant inequities in terms of job opportunities, and these have become more entrenched over time. In particular, gaps have increased between northern and southern regions and between rural and urban areas; and women, youth, and the poor have not sufficiently reaped the benefits of recent economic growth. Two out of five workers in Ghana are still working in agriculture—most of them in subsistence farming, with little potential to generate household income beyond covering basic food and other needs. Jobs in the wage sector, although generally more promising in terms of earnings opportunities, are still a minority, and pay poorly. Women have much less access to wage jobs than men. Self-employment is concentrated in low-productivity sectors such as wholesale and retail trade. Skills levels, in terms of jobs content and workers' functional skills and education levels, are comparatively low, pointing to the low technology content and limited competitiveness of Ghana's production.

These challenges correspond to the four priorities expressed in Ghana's 2015 National Employment Policy (NEP): (a) to create more decent jobs to meet the growing demand for employment; (b) to improve the quality of jobs for those who are employed; (c) to increase labor productivity; and (d) to strengthen governance and labor administration (Ghana Ministry of Employment and Labor Relations 2014).

This chapter discusses general policy recommendations and identifies areas that would require a more in-depth policy approach. The chapter first looks at the demographic transition and projected population growth to predict how many new jobs need to be created in the near future and what type of jobs will need to be created. Next, it discusses general policy recommendations to foster the creation of formal wage jobs (by increasing the productivity of incumbent firms, the exit of firms that perform less well, and the entry of potential entrepreneurs); increase the productivity of existing jobs, including informal on-farm and off-farm jobs; and facilitate workers' transition from less productive jobs into more productive jobs.

How Many Jobs and What Kind of Jobs?

The demographic transition in Ghana will continue to influence the evolution of the working-age population and ultimately the labor force. The Ghana age structure has been changing over the last few decades, with fertility rates declining quickly and life expectancy improving—although slowly, and still at lower levels than other middle-income countries (figure 5.1). These demographic trends have led to an increase in the share of those of working age in the total population and to a decrease in dependency rates of the elderly and young. The working-age population is projected to continue to increase in the near future, going from 58 percent of the total population as of now to 65 percent in 2040, while the dependency ratio is projected to decrease from 71 percent to 54 percent.

Ghana will need to create about 1.5 million jobs to absorb the new labor force entrants by 2020. Like other countries in Sub-Saharan Africa, Ghana is facing the

Figure 5.1 Fertility Rates and Life Expectancy

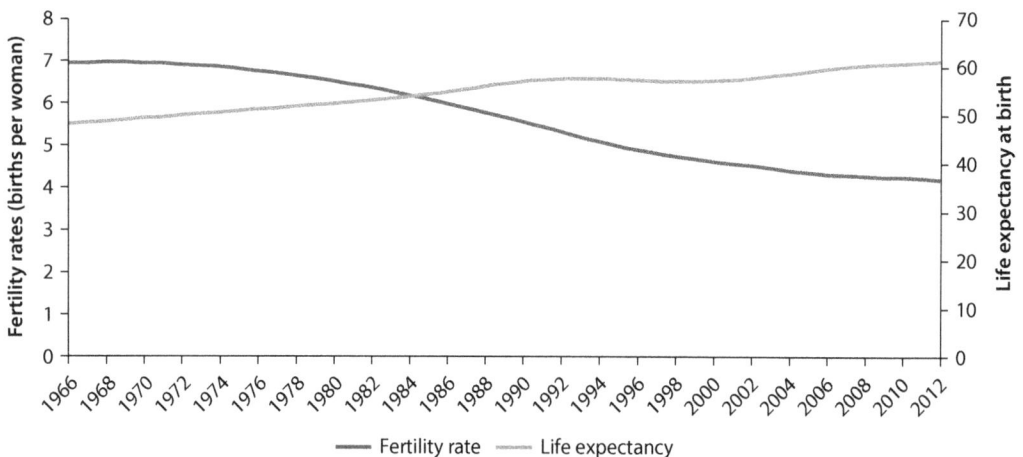

Source: WDI.

challenge of creating enough jobs for a growing adult population. As discussed in chapter 1, the job creation challenge was more than met in terms of numbers between 2005 and 2012. Total population growth will fall through 2040, projections from the United Nations suggest (UN 2015) (figure 5.2). Between 2015 and 2020, the growth of the working-age population will remain constant, at 3.1 percent, but will then recede. These numbers translate into about 300,000 additional labor market entrants *per year* who will need to find not only work but productive employment (assuming that labor force participation rates and employment-to-population ratios remain at their current, high levels: 80 percent and 78 percent, respectively).

Youth employment will present an even bigger challenge, given the bulge in young labor market entrants expected in the next five years. The growth in the youth population (15- to 24-year-olds) will be peaking in the coming decade, adding pressures on both education systems and job creation for less-educated youth (UN 2015). At the same time, urban population growth will remain significantly higher than rural population growth (UN 2014). On the one hand, the demand for jobs in urban areas will increase more rapidly than in rural areas; on the other, poverty is now by and large a rural phenomenon and is expected to remain so. There will hence be a strong need for balance between job opportunities in urban and rural areas in Ghana.

From job quantity to job quality: there needs to be a stronger focus on increasing the productivity of jobs. Good and better job opportunities would be those that involve higher productivity and more modern activities, reduce regional and gender equalities, and make migration more worthwhile (whether rural-to-urban or urban-to-urban migration domestically, or international migration). Good jobs for development are those that provide value added for people who hold them but also have positive spillovers for others in society. Such jobs would help reduce poverty in Ghana, connect people to global opportunities irrespective of location and gender, and foster a stronger sense of trust and fairness (box 5.1).

In the case of Ghana, good jobs imply more job creation in the formal wage sector and more productive jobs in agriculture and the off-farm informal sector. Until now, Ghana's population has found "better" jobs mostly by moving from farm into off-farm self-employment. This sector absorbed 2.6 million workers between 1991 and 2012, compared to 1.5 million for wage work. Job creation in off-farm self-employment accelerated from 2005 to 2012, creating about 200,000 jobs per year, compared to 100,000 for wage jobs and 60,000 for agricultural jobs. The process of structural transformation now needs to be deepened, increasing the productivity of off-farm self-employment (mostly informal jobs) and creating more wage job opportunities.

Fostering more productive jobs in the wage sector and facilitating formalization remains a development priority. More developed economies have higher shares of wage jobs, higher rates of formality of firms, and more employment in larger firms than less developed economies. Currently, however, the private wage sector in Ghana is small and pays relatively low wages compared to public employment. Women have very limited access to wage jobs, and wage jobs are also concentrated

**Figure 5.2 Projected Annual Growth Rates in Population in Ghana, by Age
Group and Geographical Area, 2015–40**

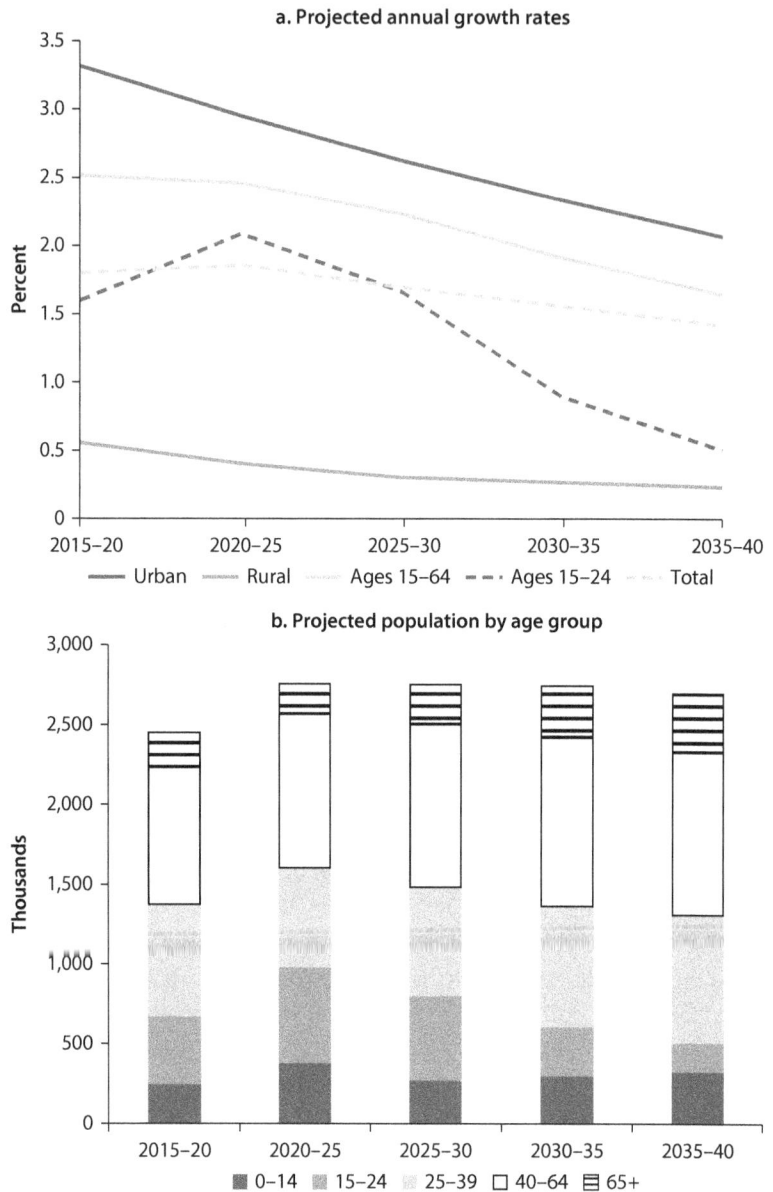

a. Projected annual growth rates

| | Urban | Rural | Ages 15–64 | Ages 15–24 | Total |

b. Projected population by age group

| | 0–14 | 15–24 | 25–39 | 40–64 | 65+ |

Source: Estimates based on United Nations population data (UN 2014, 2015).

in the southern regions (especially Accra). Although public wage jobs are the best
paid in Ghana, expanding public sector employment is not a viable long-term
vehicle for job creation. The level of public expenditures on the wage bill is unsustainable; it has grown rapidly since 2010, and was still around 10 percent of gross
domestic product (GDP) in 2015. Ghana needs to limit average public wage

Box 5.1 Jobs for Development: Some Messages from the *World Development Report* on Jobs

Some jobs do more for development than others (figure B5.1.1). Good jobs for the poor are the most important vehicle for reducing poverty. Jobs for women not only would empower half the workforce but could also change the way households invest in the education and health of children. Jobs in cities can take advantage of agglomeration economies (economies of scale, such as network effects), support greater specialization and the exchange of ideas, and thus make other jobs more productive. For policy makers, therefore, it is not only the number of jobs that matter but their quality and contribution to a country's development.

Good jobs for development are those with the highest value for society as a whole. Jobs with high pay and benefits may be attractive to individuals but may be less valuable to society if they are supported through government transfers or restrictive regulations, undermining the earnings or job opportunities of others. Jobs that reduce poverty, connect the economy to global markets, and/or foster trust and civic engagement can do more for development than others. Which jobs are good for development varies with a country's level of development, demography, endowments, and institutions.

What jobs are good for Ghana? Using the *World Development Report* typology, Ghana can be characterized as having elements of an agrarian economy (many people still work in agriculture and live in rural areas), but it is also rapidly urbanizing. It enjoys the mixed blessing of newfound wealth based on natural resources, which may undermine the competitiveness of other activities and encourage the creation of jobs supported through transfers. From this perspective,

Figure B5.1.1 How Jobs Drive Development

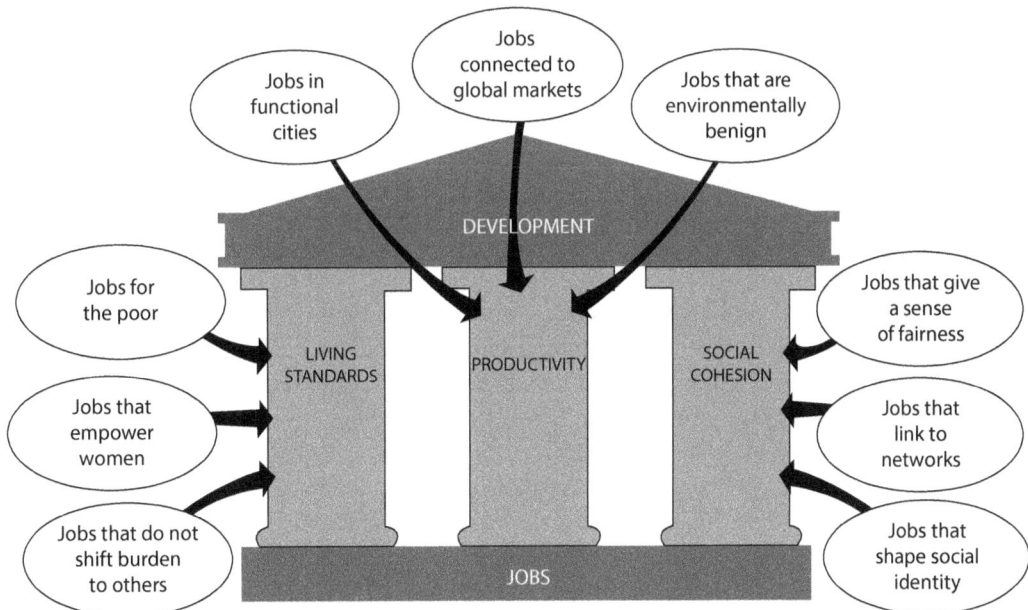

Source: World Bank 2012.

box continues next page

Box 5.1 Jobs for Development: Some Messages from the *World Development Report* on Jobs *(continued)*

Ghana's policy priorities should focus on making agriculture productive, avoiding urban congestion, and helping Ghana climb the value added chain, as well as identifying options for pulling women into productive jobs off the farm. In addition, jobs that lead to a diversification of exports can have large development payoffs.

Source: World Bank 2012.

---

increments, limit cash payments of allowances, and maintain the hiring freeze on public employees in order to reduce the size of wage bill to sustainable levels (World Bank 2016a).

Even with exceptionally high growth, the wage sector can absorb only some of the new entrants to the labor market. Given the small size of the wage sector, it will not be able to account for all of job creation, even in the most favorable circumstances. It would need to grow nearly 20 percent each year just to keep up with additional labor market entrants due to population growth—not including those that would come from transformation of self-employment on and off the farm. Moreover, not everybody will be able to find a job in the wage sector, given their skills and personal circumstances.

Hence, key policy priorities are protecting and increasing the productivity of household enterprises and informal off-farm jobs, which represent 32 percent of total workers and the majority of workers in urban areas. A considerable share of poverty reduction is likely to continue to come from diversification out of sole dependence on subsistence agriculture. In Ghana, diversification across farm and off-farm sectors is related to lower poverty; in countries such as Uganda, growth in rural off-farm economies has been central to poverty reduction (Filmer and Fox 2014). Hence, there is also a need to promote productivity in self-employment (small household enterprises) and agriculture. Self-employment is also the most likely option in areas struggling with a lack of agglomeration economies, including the availability of skills, which is holding back formal business development and wage employment.

While urbanization is part of Ghana's development path, accelerated poverty reduction will hinge on attacking the core poverty in rural areas, by offering better opportunities there. Rural households would benefit from higher agricultural productivity, commercialization of agriculture, and ventures into agribusiness, including wage job opportunities in the sector. Higher productivity in agriculture also tends to foster local demand for services and goods provided by off-farm household enterprises and free up labor resources to diversify into off-farm activities. Similarly, youth who enter labor markets early (and many will continue to do so, even with expanded vocational and general secondary education) enter in agriculture and off-farm self-employment. They need the necessary skills and inputs to be successful—especially women, who tend to run most of the off-farm household enterprises but are locked into low earnings activities.

Policy Options to Foster More Productive Jobs

This chapter aims to define policy priorities and identify elements of a jobs strategy in Ghana. A "jobs strategy" is a multisectoral policy agenda that goes far beyond traditional labor market measures and regulations. Economic diversification, productivity gains among all types of workers, and investment in secondary towns are the key priorities in the Ghana jobs agenda to promote inclusive and spatially balanced structural transformation going forward. Ghana's jobs strategy hence should encompass macroeconomic policies to preserve and diversify sources of economic growth, to boost internal demand and exports, and to limit the current deficit due to the public wage bill; investment climate reforms, including trade policies, skills, and education; and sectoral policies to improve the productivity of all types of firms, jobs, and workers.

Ghana also faces the challenge of creating more and better jobs in an economic slowdown. At present, Ghana is living through a significant fiscal and economic crisis, including an energy crisis, which is directly curtailing private sector activity through high inflation, a depreciated cedi, and lack of energy supply, providing very poor circumstances for job-creating investments. Macroeconomic uncertainty has taken a significant toll on both commercial agriculture and manufacturing (IMF 2016). The crisis is simultaneously heightening the need for urgent reforms while also limiting the room to maneuver and raising pressure for a careful prioritization of policy actions.

At the macroeconomic level, a more inclusive growth model is needed to generate more and productive jobs and boost shared prosperity. Economic growth is a necessary but not a sufficient condition to generate more jobs that are also more productive and more inclusive. Recent growth driven by natural resources helped create more jobs, especially in the retail and wholesale trade sector in urban areas, but has not generated enough productive jobs for all. Improvements in average labor productivity have been driven by sectors (mining, construction, services) with lower employment intensity. Meanwhile, labor productivity has remained lowest in agriculture and trade services, where the majority of Ghanaians, and almost all individuals in the bottom 40 percent of the income distribution, work. The manufacturing sector, traditionally more labor-intensive, has not reaped the benefits of growth and has become even less competitive given the recent high inflation, depreciation of the cedi, and high interest rates. Channeling resources from high value added sectors to sectors with high potential to create jobs should be considered as a policy priority to achieve inclusive growth. Industries such as agribusiness may have positive spillovers even on nonmanufacturing jobs up and down the supply chain, supporting the creation of jobs in the financial, transport, and logistical services sectors.

Table 5.1 provides an overview of policies that are paramount to help increase growth and productivity *within* each sector of work (agriculture, off-farm self-employment, wage sector); that can help workers move *between* sectors; and that *cut across sectors* and apply to all categories of workers. Some of these policies can be expected to have effects over the *short term*, making workers more productive within their current jobs and sector of work. Others work over time. *Medium- and long-term policies* aim to increase the overall productivity of jobs and accelerate the structural transformation into a modern and industrial economy, including the mobility of workers into better jobs.

Some policy priority areas require further research, and better firm-level data would help support sound empirical analysis of the demand for jobs. Areas requiring further research include understanding the drivers of agricultural productivity, the determinants of firms' formalization, and what holds firms back from formalizing; the internal dynamics of migration dynamics and their effects

Table 5.1 Sector Policies and Cross-Cutting Policies

	Agriculture	*Off-farm self-employment*	*Private wage employment*	*Cross-cutting*
Shorter-term	• Input subsidies • Technology innovation and advisory services for smallholders and family farms • Extension services	• Skills upgrading • Apprenticeships • Business start-up help, advisory services • Urban sector policies: improve infrastructure, reduce harassment from local authorities and the possibility of forced eviction, improve facilities	• Skills upgrading, vocational training • Link traditional apprenticeships system to NAP • Extensions and increased access to markets • Raise private firms' awareness of existing government policies (tax exemptions, subsidies)	• Macroeconomic stability • Access to finance • Provide information on the value of completing basic schooling, especially for girls, in rural areas • Information on returns to different occupations • Migration/remittances: mobile technology to facilitate savings, transfers • Women's property rights • Intermediation (ICT), jobs search assistance • Public works (safety nets) • Evaluate existing programs
Medium- to long-term	• Resilience to climate change • Development of irrigation schemes • Commercialization, measures to improve access to markets and connection to value chains • Land rights • Basic skills, literacy	• Expand coverage of SSNIT to informal workers	• Development of value chains • Tax policy and processes	• Continued macroeconomic stability • Infrastructure, urban planning • Access and quality of formal education • Economic governance • Land rights • Safety nets systems • More flexible labor regulation

Note: ICT = information and communications technology; NAP = National Apprenticeship Program; SSNIT = Social Security National Insurance Trust.

on labor markets; and urbanization trends to secondary towns other than Accra and Kumasi and their agglomeration effects. In addition, robust analysis at the firm level is hampered by data limitations: the World Bank Enterprise Survey data are useful, but have their own limitations (see box 4.1 in chapter 4).

Policies for Private Sector Development, Agriculture, and Self-Employment Off the Farm

Foster More and Better Jobs in the Private Wage Sector

Ghana needs to diversify its economy through productivity gains in sectors like the agribusiness industry, transport, construction, energy, and information and communications technology (ICT) services. Rapid urbanization has generated increased demand for processed food products both in terms of quantity and quality (certified products). The agroprocessing sector, which processes raw materials into market-ready products, is underdeveloped to meet local (and global) demand. It offers opportunities to create productive jobs, capture more value locally (instead of having raw products processed abroad), increase exports, and reduce the tremendous post-harvest losses affecting farmers and traders. Besides manufacturing of processed food, trade and the logistics of moving these products to meet market demand will be important to consider when thinking about job creation, given that the majority of off-farm jobs are actually in trade services. Importantly, "post-processing" (packaging, logistics, and marketing services) sectors offer opportunities for youth employment, more attractive than farming (for the many young Africans who do not want to be the farmers their grandparents were).

Encouraging the competitiveness of its exports would help Ghana tap into markets abroad. Given the economic slowdown since 2013 and overall decreasing internal demand, it is important for Ghana to find alternative sources of demand for its products on global markets. Whereas foreign markets could be a source of demand for Ghana's products and services, exports (free on board, f.o.b.) accounted for only 35 percent of GDP in 2013. By contrast, natural resources (cocoa, gold, and oil) accounted for 87 percent of exports. The depreciated cedi might help mitigate the effects of the "Resource Curse": a slowdown in tradable sectors beyond natural resources because of a real exchange rate appreciation, barring economic diversification. However, it must be recognized that building export competitiveness will be challenging, given the international environment for trade.

A clear priority is identifying key issues for consideration to promote agrobased industrialization in global (Europe, the United States, South Asia) and regional trade corridors in the Economic Community of West African States (ECOWAS). Studies on trade facilitation and logistics show that transport barriers are high, but also show the need for policies to develop finance and risk management instruments, upgrade production processes and competitiveness, build linkages to urban markets, and promote agribusiness-farmer linkages, as discussed more broadly in World Bank (2016d).

Investing in urban policies to stimulate demand and jobs in secondary towns would help reduce the jobs gap between major and minor cities and between regions. Urbanization in Ghana has not been restricted to Accra and Ashanti (GSS 2014). Additional research is needed to better understand the spatial jobs challenge and to identify secondary towns through which industrial and migration strategies could spread the gains of more and better jobs across the country, and in particular to northern regions that have benefitted less from the structural transformation that has occurred in the past few decades. Proximity to gold mines in Ghana is associated with positive agglomeration effects, off-farm employment, and increases in apprenticeships and wage employment (Fafchamps, Koelle, and Shilpi 2015). Cocoa production is also found to spawn many small towns (Jedwab 2014).

Micro, small, and medium enterprises (MSMEs) are less productive and seem to face greater constraints to expand, calling for upgrading technologies and financing policies specifically targeted to MSMEs. Entry costs do not seem to be the most binding constraint. Rather, targeted approaches are needed to address concerns once SMEs are up and running. In many cases, local business conditions may differ greatly from the national average (including practices of the informal sector, corruption, and access to land). Firms may also need direct advisory services and technological support, especially in areas outside the main commercial and financial centers in Ashanti and Greater Accra. A survey of establishments in Ghana's Brong Ahafo region showed that entrepreneurs did not consider generic issues (infrastructure, governance, regulations) to be the key constraints for small business. Instead, they cited the lack of business services and technological support (Mensah 2012).

Expanding producers' access to markets and connectivity from local and regionally based value chains to global ones would help increase the productivity of MSMEs. In particular, in agro-based industries, the development of value chains provides the opportunity to link smallholder farmers and MSMEs operating in processing and post-processing industries to local, regional, and possibly global food value chains. It also can provide more productive jobs to lower-skilled, female, and youth workers, thereby including the poorest and most vulnerable in the increased value added generated.

Facilitating access to finance and ensuring reliable basic infrastructure in terms of access to electricity and ICT are at the top of the policy priorities for private firms in Ghana, as in many other African countries. Credit in Ghana is prohibitively expensive and not accessible for most firms, particularly MSMEs. Facilitating access to credit and savings through subsidized credit and financial literacy and awareness are thus critical pathways for business development. Electricity and finance tend to be on the top of the list of complaints by private firms in African countries, and finance is the most important obstacle in most countries around the world, as it is in Ghana, according to the World Bank Enterprise Surveys and the Association of Ghana Industries (AGI 2015) Business Barometer.

Investment in the energy sector to ensure a consistent power supply would be a major step toward reducing constraints facing the industry sector, particularly manufacturing. This particular bottleneck has only worsened since 2013; the current energy crisis is deepening the problems related to a generally unreliable supply.

Finally, awareness about the government's initiatives needs to increase, and those initiatives need to be marketed more broadly. According to the AGI (2015) Business Barometer, 40 percent of the firms surveyed were not aware of three policies the government is pursuing to ease doing business, notably the Ghana Conformity Assessment Program (GCAP), Advance Shipment Information (ASHI) System, and the Common External Tariffs (CETs).[1]

Promote the Productivity of Agriculture, Especially of Smallholders and Family Farms

Improving agricultural productivity will be especially important to reach Ghana's poor. The agricultural sector, until recently the mainstay of Ghana's population and still the main source of livelihoods for the poor, will very likely continue to be a net job contributor in the foreseeable future. Ghana's jobs strategy needs to focus on how to make these jobs better. Ghana has significant agricultural assets and should be able to compete favorably with agricultural produce in West African and European markets. In spite of its significant potential, however, the agriculture sector remains highly volatile and is performing below potential. Agricultural growth has taken place on the extensive margin (by expanding land area) rather than the intensive margin (by increasing productivity growth); yields are poor by West African standards. The northern regions of Ghana in particular have few location-specific advantages and have not been able to fully capitalize on their abundance of less expensive access to land and proximity to trading partners north of the country.

Investing more in irrigation schemes could help build resilience in the agricultural sector. The impact of climate change is being felt in Ghana, as rainfalls have become less predictable than in the past. Strengthening resilience to climatic volatility is a significant challenge and requires further analysis. Output remains volatile because of the limited use of modern production methods, including outdated technology, lack of irrigation, and the low use of inputs. Climatic trends will only worsen vulnerability unless measures are taken to mitigate these risks. Drought-tolerant and shorter-duration crop varieties, improved water management techniques, and improved infrastructure would help (Jansen, forthcoming).

More productive agricultural jobs will hinge on commercialization, both by helping smallholder farmers enter value chains, and facilitating agribusiness investments—themselves a source of wage jobs. Agribusiness is currently under-developed in Ghana; most of the produce that is exported is unprocessed. The sector is undercapitalized and lacks modern technology and management approaches. More generally, there is a need to develop the system of land tenure to increase land property rights: currently, material investment in improving and upgrading land is held back by a lack of clear ownership rules (GIZ 2011).

There are already positive examples of policy approaches that could be developed further. Combining transfers of productive assets such as livestock or agricultural inputs with training in technical and management skills, regular visits from program staff/coaches, and subsidized access to savings through the integrated graduation approach implemented in six countries, including Ghana, by the Bangladesh Rural Advancement Committee (BRAC) had positive economic impacts one year after the program on several outcomes, including asset ownership, income and revenues, per capita consumption, food security, mental and physical health, financial inclusion, and the empowerment of women (Banerjee and others 2015).

Investment in technology needs to be matched by attention to physical infrastructure and skills, including literacy and numeracy. Much can, and should, be made of the potential for upgrading technology, including digital technology, to increase the productivity of agriculture. Mobile/digital technology, for example, can be used to provide extension services, coordinate distribution of inputs, provide early warning systems for climatic shocks, and reduce search costs related to sales. However, these investments need to be complemented by strong investments in physical infrastructure (permitting the transfer of knowledge through the Internet, and the physical distribution of produce, for example), as well as skills development (including both basic education and training) that can help farmers appreciate, understand, and use technology appropriately (World Bank 2015).

Stronger land ownership regulations would facilitate both agricultural investment and movements out of agriculture. Lack of property rights that define land ownership increases the risks of agricultural investment and thus deters potentially more productive enterprises. At the same time, insecure land rights discourage mobility: for example, if land cannot be safely leased or sold, smallholders cannot readily migrate.

Foster Productive Self-Employment and Entrepreneurship

Since diversification out of farm activities is a pathway to reducing poverty in rural areas, it is also important to increase the productivity of self-employment outside of agriculture. One-third of Ghana's workers are now self-employed, as their primary job, in nonagricultural sectors; unlike wage jobs, some 70 percent of those jobs are in rural areas. Some of these household enterprises may have the potential to expand, but a vast majority of such firms in Ghana are de facto livelihoods for one family, often involving only one person, and with very limited potential for employment and turnover growth. Nonetheless, they respond to a growing demand for low-cost goods and services, and play a significant role in reducing poverty through the earnings of each of these household enterprises. As shown in chapter 2, the earnings potential of self-employment is not much lower than that of wage work in Ghana (taking into consideration caveats regarding measurement and comparability).

The off-farm self-employment sector is included in Ghana's national development strategy and is explicitly acknowledged for its contribution to economic development and poverty reduction. Policy directions for the sector include (a) reducing vulnerability through strengthened infrastructure and secure sites for business in urban areas; (b) improving access to credit and business services; (c) raising productivity, especially by improving the apprenticeship system, which is a major provider of skills for this sector; and (d) finding and supporting social protection mechanisms that can reduce household vulnerability.

Despite high economic growth, the rate of formalization is low in Ghana and the share of workers engaged in household enterprises in small-scale entrepreneurship is increasing. More analysis, based on better firm data, is needed to better understand why firms do not formalize, as would be expected given the economic development in Ghana in the past decade. A larger formal sector is needed to boost exports and expand local value chains to regional and global markets. The analysis in this report points to severe constraints to formalization, however.

The costs of formalization do not seem to be a high barrier; interventions to reduce incentives for informal work and increase awareness of the benefits of formalization are more relevant, and would need to accompany policies to improve informal jobs productivity. The majority (87 percent) of household enterprises are not registered with any government agency, district assembly, or the Registrar General Department. The 2013 World Bank Enterprise Survey of informal firms, while not representative, offers insights to better understand very small firms' constraints and willingness to formalize. Lack of knowledge about the potential benefits (and costs) of formalization, rather than monetary and time costs, seems to keep microenterprises in the informal sector, and only half the respondents express a willingness to formalize. This evidence—coupled with a high share of microenterprises in the Enterprise Survey of formal firms (63 percent of registered firms are microenterprises)—suggests that the majority of informal and household enterprises operate that way *by necessity:* they seek to diversify their income, better manage risks, escape poverty, and cope with the urbanization process. This hypothesis places a priority on policies that help increase the productivity of informal jobs, as well as tax and regulatory reforms to reduce the costs of formalization. Enforcement of measures to increase compliance with regulation is also important, but may be not the priority in Ghana.

Many household enterprises and informal firms suffer from constraints similar to those facing formal firms, but in more severe forms, including lack of assets, no access to credit or modern technology, limited access to markets and value chains, lower skills levels and few opportunities to continuously develop skills, and no social security coverage. Reduced mobility and family duties add to the constraints faced by female entrepreneurs. Policies aimed at facilitating access to finance and savings and upgrading technical skills—as well as financial literacy, business management and practices, and socioemotional skills—through certified training and apprenticeships would help increase the productivity of the informal sector.

Along with increasing access to credit, helping informal microenterprises, households, and individuals save in more secure and profitable forms can help increase investment. Virtually no household enterprises have access to credit, and most investment is financed by household savings. Efforts to increase access to credit can be complemented with policy initiatives that help households save in more secure forms that earn more than cash savings kept at home.

Helping the self-employed upgrade their skills and business practices, as well as broaden their access to markets and value chains, can unleash productivity growth. To run a one-person business is to combine a great many job-relevant skills in one individual, including technical, marketing, financial, and accounting skills. At the same time, compared with larger firms, the self-employed have less access to information on training (including on assessment of training needs), face significant opportunity costs in attending training (because they need to work at the same time), and find it harder to afford training. Aside from quality basic education, the sector can be reached with information on the benefits of training and with training options that take into account financial and time constraints, help small firms identify skills constraints, and address the need for multiple skills (Adams, Johansson de Silva, and Razmara 2013). Providing government-sponsored business development services and training to entrepreneurs and expanding access to standards/certification systems are also possible interventions to foster the productivity of informal workers.

While important steps have been taken, expanding the coverage of the informal worker pension scheme, facilitating their access to the National Health Insurance Scheme, and improving their working conditions remain important challenges. The Social Security National Insurance Trust (SSNIT) created the Informal Sector Pension Scheme (ISPS) as part of the voluntary third tier. The scheme was formalized in 2008 and is open to workers who are not covered by the mandatory pension scheme under SSNIT. By the end of 2011, ISPS had about 91,000 members and had accumulated GH¢23 million in contributions, according to the Ghana News Agency.[2] Although the fund has grown very rapidly in recent years, coverage remains very low compared to the size of the informal sector (World Bank 2016b).

Urban policies should safeguard public space and property rights but not unduly constrain household enterprises operating in urban areas. Urban development policies affect the freedom of enterprises—especially microenterprises in the services sectors (such as street vendors)—the transport and communications infrastructure, and protection against crime and abuse (including from local authorities) in the areas where they operate. Individuals and firms put up with risk of harassment and forceful eviction, lack of adequate facilities, and poor quality of infrastructure. Authorities need to take this sector into account as a source of livelihood for urban families and consider the space and infrastructure needed for them to thrive. An example of more inclusive policies is the application of flexible regulations for street vendors in cities. With the exception of Accra, local authorities in Ghana focus on creating space for household enterprises, rather than controlling their space (Filmer and Fox 2014).

Cross-Cutting Issues for Jobs and Productivity

Generate the Skills for the New Jobs Being Created

New kinds of jobs will require new kinds of skills. Skills are not foremost on the list of obstacles in Ghana, according to the World Bank's Enterprise Surveys. However, the skills issue is increasing in importance: the share of large firms (those with 100+ employees) that considered workforce skills a major obstacle grew from 1 percent in 2007 to nearly 25 percent by 2013. As the Ghanaian economy successively transforms toward more high-productivity jobs, skills are likely to become an issue in the not-too-distant future. Workers' skills result from cumulative years of education and training systems, and investments are needed now to avoid bottlenecks later. Globally, the mix of skills in demand in the labor market is changing from routine tasks to tasks that involve nonroutine cognitive skills—those that complement rather than compete with computerized tasks (Acemoglu and Autor 2011). Investments are needed now to build opportunities to develop adequate cognitive, socioemotional, and job-specific skills.

Increasing the access to digital technologies and the skills needed to make the most of them would help workers (and job seekers) acquire a competitive advantage in the job market. The ICT sector is small in terms of employment and value added in Ghana. However, digital technologies have a potential to boost job creation indirectly in the way they can increase productivity and efficiency of firms, and more directly by increasing the access of the jobless to information, technology, markets, and even finance. Digital technologies also hold promise for smallholder agriculture, as discussed. Digital technologies have spread rapidly on the African continent. In Ghana, there are 115 mobile subscriptions, and 18 Internet users per 100 people. As outlined in the *World Development Report 2016: Digital Dividends*, reaping the full potential of ICT requires a clear agenda on investments, regulations, and skills (box 5.2) (World Bank 2015).

Ghana faces the challenge of sustaining gains in access to basic education, increasing quality, and responding to increasing demand for post-basic education. Ghana has successfully increased access to basic education, but there are many problems with quality. Basic education provides the general cognitive and other skills that are needed for further learning. Educational attainment has improved significantly over time, but attending basic education is not a guarantee for acquiring even basic functional skills in Ghana. Education and training policy needs to consider how best to strengthen the quality of basic education, reduce dropouts and repetition, and translate class attendance into valuable learning.

Attention needs to turn to post-basic education, including technical and vocational training and education (TVET). Previous work has shown that investments in TVET result in favorable labor market outcomes compared to higher secondary general schooling (Adams, Johansson de Silva, and Razmara 2013; GIZ 2014). The impact of TVET can be improved both by increasing the quality of training and involving employers in the design, implementation, and certification of training programs. Moreover, opening pathways between general and vocational education programs increases the flexibility of the education system at large.

Box 5.2 Harnessing Digital Technologies to Address Information Asymmetries

Digital technologies have spread rapidly in much of the developed and developing world

More households in developing countries own a mobile phone than have access to electricity or clean water. Even among the poor, nearly 70 percent of the bottom quintile own a mobile phone. The number of Internet users has more than tripled in a decade, to an estimated 3.2 billion at the end of 2015. The immediate benefits of the increased use of information and communications technology (ICT)—the Internet, mobile phones, and all the other tools for collecting, storing, analyzing, and sharing information—include expanding the access to information (inclusion), reducing the costs of economic and social transactions (efficiency), and promoting new ideas (innovation).

Has the increased use of digital technologies generated development benefits—so-called digital dividends—in the form of faster growth, more jobs, and better services?

In many instances around the world, digital technologies have boosted growth, expanded opportunities, and improved service delivery. While there are many success stories, the aggre-gate impacts of digital technologies have so far been smaller than expected and unevenly distributed. Firms are more connected than ever before, but global productivity growth has slowed. Labor markets have become more polarized, and inequality is on the rise within many countries. New jobs are being created, but the automation of mid-level jobs has helped hollow out the labor market. And because the economics of the Internet favor natural monopolies, the absence of a competitive business environment is resulting in more concentrated markets, benefitting incumbent firms. Not surprisingly, the better educated, the well-connected, and the more capable have received most of the benefits—and the gains from the digital revolu-tion have not been widely shared.

Why do benefits often remain unrealized?

The "digital divide" is still wide, in terms of both access and capability. Nearly 60 percent of the world's people are still offline and cannot participate fully in the digital economy. Nearly 2 billion people do not have a mobile phone. Moreover, access to ICT is unequal across income, gender, age, and geographic lines. In Africa, the richest 60 percent are almost three times more likely to have Internet access than the bottom 40 percent, and the young and urban have more than twice the access of older and rural citizens. Among those connected, digital capabilities also vary greatly. In the European Union, three times more citizens use online services in the richest countries than in the poorest, with a similar gap between the rich and the poor within each country.

How can digital dividends be reaped?

Making the Internet universally accessible and affordable remains an urgent priority, but greater digital adoption will not be enough. To get the most out of the digital revolution, coun-tries also need to create the right environment for technology and work on what the report calls the "analog complements"—by strengthening regulations that ensure competition

box continues next page

Box 5.2 Harnessing Digital Technologies to Address Information Asymmetries *(continued)*

among businesses, by adapting workers' skills to the demands of the new economy, and by ensuring that institutions are accountable. For example, the shift of income from labor to capital and the decline in the share of midlevel jobs in many countries is at least in part due to rising automation, even of many white-collar jobs. When workers have the skills to leverage technologies, they become more productive and their wages increase. When they do not, they compete with others for low-level jobs, pushing wages even lower. The skills agenda needs to respond to labor markets that demand different skills and are more flexible; depending on the level of adoption of digital technologies, the focus should be on teaching advanced cognitive and socioemotional skills, offering more opportunities for lifelong learning to reduce the digital divide for older workers, and preparing for careers rather than specific jobs—since fewer than half of today's schoolchildren can expect to work in an occupation that exists today.

Source: World Bank 2015.

Workplace training can be expanded and made more efficient. A majority of formal firms do not provide further training to their staff. Incentives for firms to take on less experienced workers and train them can be part of a package to develop skills. At the same time, most training for self-employment comes from apprenticeships. Those who become self-employed tend to enter the job market relatively early (they have lower education than wage employees) and thus are in need of further skills development while they are running their businesses. As discussed, they need flexible options, both in terms of financing (in-kind, or combining jobs with production, as is the case for apprenticeships), and in terms of time (providing training after business hours and/or in flexible, modular form) (Adams, Johansson de Silva, and Razmara 2013).

There is a lack of finance for initiatives to support skills development; financing can be leveraged through innovative partnerships. These can include demand-driven funds to support public-private partnerships. An example of a Skills Development Fund with a window for public-private partnerships is the World Bank Ghana Skills and Technology Development project, in partnership with Council for Technical and Vocational Education (COTVET). Similarly, the Ghana Skills Development Initiative supports the provision of demand-oriented further training courses to increase employability of apprentices and employees in MSMEs. In the medium term, the project plans to introduce a voucher system via the national Skills Development Fund under COTVET (GIZ 2014).

Address the Gender Gap

Helping women enter more productive jobs is important, as gender differences in job opportunities are significant in Ghana. More in-depth analysis is needed to determine whether the low participation of women in wage jobs and higher-return activities primarily reflects constraints on the demand side (firms hesitate to hire female workers) or the supply side (women have less education, face more constraints on their time and money, and so on). Experience shows that prevailing social norms that constrain women's options can be changed by information, advocacy, and the provision of role models. For example, an experiment in Kenya showed that informing girls and young women of the opportunities and returns to occupations typically dominated by males, and encouraging them to consider these options, helped reduce some of the gender segregation in occupational choices (Hicks and others 2011).

Addressing women's lack of rights on property, including land, will be necessary to promote investment and expansion. The lack of access to land and other property is exacerbated by social norms establishing women's role as family caretakers and men as the main decision makers in businesses—even those run by their wives. This constitutes a major obstacle for women's investment in their businesses (GIZ 2011). Lack of land ownership holds back women's investment in agricultural production, but may also hinder more significant investment in off-farm activities, as it means land cannot be sold or used as collateral for their independent activities.

A recent study of microenterprises in urban Ghana suggested that household enterprises run by women are very heterogeneous and will respond very differently to incentives. More specifically, providing access to capital per se was not sufficient to enhance growth of household enterprises run by women, as other constraints—notably, low human capital and behavioral characteristics—also mattered. By contrast, firms run by males did benefit from access to capital. In a majority of enterprises, the options for expanding business were limited because of the nature of the business and/or personal considerations. Shifting into wage employment would help these women increase their earnings; this would be more effective than efforts focusing on helping their firms grow. However, in a group of women-led microenterprises with higher profitability, women did benefit from capital if given in-kind assistance, rather than cash (cash was too fungible and too readily absorbed into general household expenditures) (Fafchamps and Woodruff 2014).

Make Migration Pay Better

Migration is a strong feature of Ghana's jobs landscape, and improving the outcomes of labor mobility needs to be part of Ghana's agenda. Rural-to-urban migration is often viewed as a cause of rising urban poverty and a force for uncontrolled urban development, including growth of slums and excessive pressure on infrastructure, the environment, and employment. However, rural-to-urban migration is likely to continue, and has manifest benefits for those who move, as well as for the families left behind that receive remittances. Policy should focus on reducing the negative impacts and strengthening the positive impacts of migration, rather than on attempting to stem the flows. Urban planning policies are necessary to ensure sustainable urban expansion, including those policies that affect conditions for informal self-employment—which is where a vast majority of urban in-migrants end up.

Strengthening remittances systems increases the returns to migration. Urban migrants send remittances home but tend to use informal means. The costs associated with formal transfers are particularly important for the poor, who tend to send smaller amounts and face higher fixed costs. Mobile technology holds significant potential for lowering the cost and reducing the risks associated with transfers. In other countries, entry of digital competition in systems for international remittances transfers has lowered costs significantly (World Bank 2015).

As discussed, the weak and unclear system of land rights is in itself an impediment to migration. In northern areas, where agricultural employment and output is variable (due to seasonal and rain-dependent farming) and volatile (due to increased climatic variance and unpredictability of rainfalls), there are strong incentives to migrate temporarily to more promising agricultural zones in search of wage work or additional land. Land ownership rules may lead households to leave family members at home to protect their plot, even when there is no work to be done.

Improve the Flexibility of Labor Market Regulations

Labor regulations are not a binding constraint but may well become more significant if the formal sector expands. In order to encourage labor markets to function efficiently and meet the interests and needs of both employers and workers, labor regulation and institutions need to adapt to the economic contexts in which firms operate and the changing nature and risks of jobs prevailing in the labor markets. Labor market regulations include severance pay reform, changes in dismissal and hiring rules, reforms of the labor code, and setting the minimum wage. Employers require flexibility to adjust their workforce during economic downturns, for example, and workers require a guaranteed minimum level of income and protection from income losses while transitioning between jobs (box 5.3).

Increase the Coverage and Assessment of Active Labor Market Programs and Social Protection

Ghana has in place a set of active labor market programs (ALMPs), although their coverage is very limited and there is not yet evidence on their effectiveness. ALMPs include a series of programs and services to firms and job seekers to facilitate their adjustment to changing labor market conditions and facilitate the transition from school or unemployment to stable quality jobs. These services include labor market information; job search assistance; career counseling;

Box 5.3 Labor Market Regulations and Institutions

Set against international comparisons, and compared to other constraints like access to finance, markets, and technology, labor regulations do not appear to be the key binding constraint to job creation in Ghana. Ghanaian firms rate labor regulations the lowest among 13 possible obstacles in the 2013 World Bank Enterprise Survey. Ghanaian executives surveyed for the purpose of the *Global Competitiveness Report* rate Ghana somewhere in the middle—neither

box continues next page

Box 5.3 Labor Market Regulations and Institutions *(continued)*

good nor bad—in terms of collaboration in labor-employer relations, flexibility in determining wages, and hiring and firing practices. From an international perspective, however, Ghana ranks among the very lowest of 144 countries in firing practices (WEF 2015). In particular, severance pay is high (equivalent to nearly one year of salary) (World Bank, Doing Business).

Minimum wages serve to guarantee workers a minimum level of fair income for their job. Minimum wages that are too high may nonetheless have negative effects on job creation, especially for less productive workers, and/or may shift job creation into the informal sector. There is only one official minimum wage in Ghana. It is set by the National Tripartite Committee, headed by the Minister for Employment and Social Welfare, for all workers, with only a few exceptions (armed forces personnel, police, and workers in free trade zones). In general, the minimum wage is anchored in cost of living estimations and thus fluctuates with inflation. The national minimum wage nonetheless constitutes a floor, and minimum wage rates may be determined under collective agreements. To compensate for inflation, the daily minimum wage was increased from 6 to 7 cedis in January 2015, and from 7 to 8 cedis in October 2015—an increase by one-third, in total, bringing the daily minimum wage to an equivalent of US$2. In spite of this significant hike, minimum wages appear not to be binding in Ghana. Set in relation to 2012 cash earnings (as calculated based on Round 6 of the Ghana Living Standard Survey, GLSS6), the minimum wage is quite low: it reaches about 50 percent of the mean wage in private wage work (both formal and informal) and self-employment, and only 20 percent of public wage workers. This is consistent with a study by Bhorat, Kanbur, and Stanwix (2015), which looked at minimum wages across Africa and concluded that the ratio of the minimum rate to the mean wage (the Kaitz ratio) in Ghana is among the lowest in Africa, and that the minimum wage, in the African context, is lower than expected for the GDP per capita. Ghana's high levels of informality in wage work are not likely to be explained by the minimum wage.

By law, employees have the right to organize themselves into unions: two or more workers employed in the same undertaking may form a union. Ghana has a long tradition of tripartite negotiations, and ranks 85th out of 144 countries in the Global Competitiveness Index on cooperation in labor-employer relations. The Trades Union Congress (TUC) of Ghana is the main umbrella organization for trade union activities in Ghana and is made up of 18 national unions. Union density in the formal sector is 68 percent, the International Labour Organization (ILO 2006) estimates. Given the low level of formality in Ghana's jobs landscape, this nevertheless amounts to low levels of unionization in the private sector. According to the GLSS6, only 17 percent of private wage workers worked in workplaces where there was a trade union, compared to 70 percent of public wage workers.

Sources: ILO 2006; Aryeetey and Baah-Boateng 2015; Bhorat, Kanbur, and Stanwix 2015; WEF 2015; World Bank Doing Business and Enterprise Survey databases.

and skills development programs for the unemployed, underemployed, and specifically for youth, as they face unique constraints transitioning to labor markets (lack of experience, smaller networks, lack of credit history), in addition to skills and credit constraints. In Ghana, the Ministry of Employment and Labor Relations (MELR) has the mandate to coordinate government employment initiatives (box 5.4). The MELR is in the process of developing an implementation plan for the NEP. The Ministry of Youth and Sports (MoYS), on the other hand, spearheads the National Youth Policy agenda. More work is needed to evaluate the effectiveness of these programs (World Bank 2016c).

Social protection policies to ensure income stability should complement labor market policies to increase productivity and earnings. In poor countries, employment rates are high because people cannot afford to be unemployed or inactive. Thus, broad, inclusive social insurance not restricted to social protection for wage

---

Box 5.4 Improving Existing Skill Development and Active Labor Market Programs to Facilitate the Transition of Youth to Productive Jobs in Ghana

The government and several nongovernmental organizations[a] (NGOs) in Ghana offer a number of small and fragmented programs to promote skills development, entrepreneurship, and access to jobs. Ghana has a large number of public and private programs that provide skills upgrading and technical and vocational and educational training (TVET) and over 200 public and 450 private TVET institutes through the country. The Ministry of Employment and Labor Relations (MELR) administers over 60 employment centers throughout the country. However, labor market information is recorded manually and cannot help match job seekers and firms in a timely manner. In the area of publicly funded programs targeted to vulnerable youth,[b] four major programs operate beyond the fragmented initiatives run by NGOs.

The National Apprenticeship Program (NAP). The NAP has increased its scale, yet its effectiveness in terms of labor market outcomes has not been evaluated. The NAP started in 2011 to improve informal apprenticeship by providing junior high school graduates with one year apprenticeship training with master craftsmen. The program, which covered about 7,000 youth in 2015, provides tools to the trainees and pays a stipend to the master craftsman (GH¢150 per trainee per year). After the training, beneficiaries are encouraged to start their own businesses. The U.S. Agency for International Development (USAID) is financing a randomized control trial to evaluate the effectiveness of the program, which is being conducted (from 2012 to 2017) by the Jamel Poverty Action Lab.

The Local Enterprises and Skills Development Program (LESDEP). Training and financing support for small-scale entrepreneurship through LESDEP have also not been evaluated in terms of job creation and sustainability, and program eligibility could be improved. The LESDEP was created in 2011 in partnership with the private sector to improve the skills of informal sector workers and promote viable small enterprises nationwide, with a special focus on youth. The program, which supported 15,005 youth in 2014, provides 6 months of entrepreneurial skills development through apprenticeship training with a master craftsman and start-up funding of GH¢1,000 in the form of a loan, access to credit, and support following the start-up. Demand for the program is high, but there are no clear eligibility criteria for selecting those who are ultimately enrolled in the scheme.

The Youth in Agriculture Program. This program, launched in 1999 under the Ministry of Food and Agriculture (MoFA), is the largest government intervention that seeks to promote

box continues next page

Box 5.4 Improving Existing Skill Development and Active Labor Market Programs to Facilitate the Transition of Youth to Productive Jobs in Ghana (continued)

youth employment in the agricultural sector. Under this program, the government aims to provide "youth with necessary inputs to take on farming as a life time vocation." The program has never been subject to a rigorous review of its effectiveness.

The National Service Scheme. The National Service Scheme (NSS) is a one-year mandatory employment program for all tertiary graduates under the age of 40 in the country. Participants receive a monthly allowance and are posted to work in public or private sector organizations. The NSS secretariat acts as an employment office matching students graduating from all tertiary institutions in the country to public and private firms that are invited to submit vacancies.

More investment is needed to develop the capacity of and the coordination of national and local governments to support the transition of youth to work. The *Youth Employment Agency* was established in 2015 to support about 600,000 disadvantaged youth by providing job placement, skill training, and seed capital to establish microenterprises. It targets graduates from junior and senior high school and from technical and vocational schools, as well as school dropouts and illiterate youth. The program is being redesigned under the MELR. It includes the following components: skills training and internship through the formal and informal structures; entrepreneurial training; assistance to form cooperatives/trade associations; and support services (financial support, tools, equipment) for organized and registered cooperatives and trade associations.

Sources: Ghana, Ministry of Employment and Labor Relations 2014; World Bank 2016b.
a. These organizations include the Don Bosco Technical Institute, Ghana Skills Development Initiative (GIZ, German International Cooperation), GRATIS Foundation, Innovations for Poverty Action, the Junior Achievers Trust International, Meltwater Entrepreneurial School of Technology (MEST) and the MEST incubator (international nonprofit economic development organization), and Technoserve.
b. "Vulnerable" includes poor youth, school dropouts, recent graduates who are jobless or unemployed, and low-productivity workers.

---

employees is needed, along with social safety nets. This includes the establishment of safety nets that help poor households deal with earnings volatility, whether expected (for example, seasonal) or unexpected (for example, due to shortfalls in income). The government is undertaking important reforms to modernize and scale up existing social safety nets programs, notably the country's flagship cash transfer program, Livelihood Empowerment Against Poverty (LEAP); the Labor-Intensive Public Works (LIPW) program providing temporary employment to rural poor youth and adults; and the national health insurance subsidized programs. It is important for the government to continue supporting such safety net programs to ensure minimum income and nutrition, and to avoid deprivation, especially in households with no member who is able to work.

Improve Access to Reliable Labor Market Information

Although Ghana's main jobs constraints lie outside the realm of labor market intermediation and skills mismatches, labor market information systems can be a cost-effective tool to influence labor market outcomes, especially in urban areas. In particular, Internet-based and other tools and services may increase the efficiency of job search in larger urban areas. In addition, the government can provide or encourage the provision of impartial assessments of educational institutions, guidance to educational pathways, and relevant labor market information, including on labor market prospects, actual vacancies, skills needs, and projected sectoral growth. As experience from Kenya, Madagascar, and Malawi shows, helping students and workers identify educational and occupational pathways that offer higher employability and higher potential earnings can reduce early school dropouts and increase investment in nontraditional occupations (Nguyen 2008; Dizon-Ross 2014). The MELR is currently developing the vision and framework for a Ghana labor market information system that would collect, analyze, and disseminate indicators on labor demand and supply based on different sources.

Ghana has improved data collection and data management for results-based policy making. Ghana is fairly unique among Sub-Saharan African countries in its availability of compatible household-level microdata over time. This has made it possible to analyze labor market trends over more than two decades in this report. The detailed labor force module and the additional household enterprise module in the last round of the Ghana Living Standards Survey have been especially helpful. On the labor demand side, regular collection of representative firm-level data will be needed to document employers' needs. The last available census data are dated 2003 and could not be used in the analysis of this report. Recently, the Ghana Statistical Service (GSS) has undertaken an extensive project to establish a registry of formal and informal establishments through an enterprise census, and to collect detailed survey data for a selected sample; however, results were not available at the time of the writing the report (GSS 2016). Thus representative firm-level data were the biggest data gap.

Notes

1. Ghana's Conformity Assessment Program ensures that imported products conform with the applicable Ghanaian standards or approved equivalents and technical regulations. The Advance Shipment Information System enables importers to fill out documentation online to expedite the cargo clearance process; it has been active since March 1, 2015. Under the Common External Tariff, all member-states of ECOWAS, including Ghana, will charge one another the same import tariff. It has been effective since February 1, 2016.

2. See the Ghana News Agency website at http://www.ghananewsagency.org/economics/ssnit-informal-sector-mobilises-more-than-91-000-members-38132.

References

Acemoglu, D., and D. Autor. 2011. "Skills, Tasks and Technologies: Implications for Employment and Earnings." In *Handbook of Labor Economics*, Vol. 4, Part B, edited by D. Card and O. Ashenfelter, 773–1823. Elsevier.

Adams, A. V., S. Johansson de Silva, and S. Razmara. 2013. *Improving Skills Development in the Informal Sector: Strategies for Sub-Saharan Africa*. Directions in Development: Human Development. Washington, DC: World Bank.

AGI (Association of Ghana Industries). 2015. *Business Barometer, 1st quarter 2015.* www.agighana.org.

Aryeetey, E., and W. Baah-Boateng, 2015. "Understanding Ghana's Growth Success Story and Job Creation Challenges." WIDER Working Paper 140/2015, UNU-WIDER.

Banerjee, A., E. Duflo, N. Goldberg, D. Karlan, R. Osei, W. Pariente, J. Shapiro, B. Thuysbaert, and C. Udry. 2015. "A Multifaceted Program Causes Lasting Progress for the Very Poor: Evidence from Six Countries." *Science* 348 (6236): 1260799.

Bhorat, H., R. Kanbur, and S. Stanwix. 2015. "Minimum Wages in Sub-Saharan Africa: A Primer." IZA Discussion Paper 9204, Forschungsinstitut zur Zukunft der Arbeit (IZA, Institute for the Study of Labor), Bonn.

Dizon-Ross, R. 2014. "Parents' Perceptions and Children's Education: Experimental Evidence from Malawi." Unpublished Manuscript. Massachusetts Institute of Technology. http://economics.yale.edu/sites/default/files/dizon-ross_jmp.pdf

Fafchamps, M., M. Koelle, and F. Shilpi. 2015. "Gold Mining and Proto-Urbanization: Recent Evidence from Ghana." Policy Research Working Paper 7347, World Bank, Washington, DC.

Fafchamps, M., and C. Woodruff. 2014. "Identifying Gazelles: Expert Panels vs. Surveys as a Means to Identify Firms with Rapid Growth Potential." CAGE Online Working Paper Series 213, Competitive Advantage in the Global Economy (CAGE).

Filmer, D., and L. Fox. 2014. "Youth Employment in Sub-Saharan Africa." Africa Development Forum Series. World Bank and Agence Française de Développement.

Ghana, Ministry of Employment and Labor Relations. 2014. *National Employment Policy.* Vol. 1. Accra, Ghana: MELR.

Ghana Statistical Service (GSS). 2014. *Ghana Living Standard Survey Round 6 (GLSS6). Main Report.* Accra, Ghana: GSS.

———. 2016. *Ghana Integrated Business Establishment Survey, Summary Report. Summary Report.* Accra, Ghana: GSS.

GIZ (Deutsche Gesellschaft für Internationale Zusammenarbeit, German International Cooperation). 2011. *Financing Agricultural Value Chains in Africa: Focus on Pineapples, Cashews and Cocoa in Ghana.* Eschborn, Germany: GIZ.

———. 2014. *Ghana: An Employment and Labour Market Analysis.* GIZ Programme for Sustainable Economic Development and the GIZ Sector Project for Employment-Oriented Development Strategies and Projects.

Hicks, J. H., M. Kremer, I. Mbit, and E. Miguel. 2011. *Vocational Education Voucher Delivery and Labor Market Returns: A Randomized Evaluation among Kenyan Youth.* Report for Spanish Impact Evaluation Fund (SIEF) Phase II, World Bank, Washington, DC.

Hsieh, C.-T., and P. J. Klenow. 2014. "The Life Cycle of Plants in India and Mexico." *Quarterly Journal of Economics* 129 (3): 1035–84. doi:10.1093/qje/qju014.

ILO (International Labour Office). 2006. *Ghana: National Labor Laws* (accessed January 31, 2016), http://www.ilo.org/ifpdial/information-resources/national-labour-law-profiles/WCMS_158898/lang--en/index.htm.

IMF (International Monetary Fund). 2016. *Ghana: Second Review under the Extended Credit Facility Arrangement and Request for Waiver for Nonobservance of Performance Criterion.* IMF Country Report No. 16/16. Washington, DC: IMF.

Jansen, J. G. P. Forthcoming. *Ghana Agriculture Sector Brief.* Ghana Country Office, World Bank.

Jedwab, R. 2014. *Urbanization without Structural Transformation: Evidence from Consumption Cities in Africa.* George Washington University, Unpublished.

Mensah, M. S. B. 2012. "Local Business Climate in Ghana–Insights for Policy Direction." *International Journal of Business and Management* 7 (2): 17–35.

Nguyen, T. 2008. "Information, Role Models and Perceived Returns to Education: Experimental Evidence from Madagascar." MIT Working Paper, Massachusetts Institute of Technology.

UN (United Nations). 2014. *World Urbanization Prospects: The 2014 Revision (Database).* Population Division, Department of Economic and Social Affairs (accessed September 2015–January 2016).

———. 2015. *Probabalistic Population Projections based on the World Population Prospects: The 2015 Revision.* Population Division, Department of Economic and Social Affairs, http://esa.un.org/unpd.ppp/.

WEF (World Economic Forum). 2015. *The Global Competitiveness Report 2015–2016.* Geneva: World Economic Forum.

World Bank. 2012. *World Development Report 2013: Jobs.* Washington, DC: World Bank.

———. 2015. *World Development Report 2016: The Digital Dividend.* Washington, DC: World Bank.

———. 2016a. *Ghana Public Expenditure Review 2016. Fiscal Consolidation for Growth and Employment.* Washington, DC: World Bank.

———. 2016b. *Ghana: Social Protection Assessment and Expenditure Review.* Washington, DC: World Bank.

———. 2016c. "Harnessing Youth Potential in Ghana: A Policy Note." Report No. 106877, World Bank, Washington, DC.

———. 2016d. *Promoting Agro-based Industrialization in ECOWAS Trade Corridors.* Washington, DC: World Bank. Unpublished.

———. Enterprise Surveys (database). www.enterprisesurveys.org.

———. Doing Business 2016 (database). www.doingbusiness.org.

———. WDI (World Development Indicators) 2016 (database). World Bank, Washington, DC, http://data.worldbank.org/data-catalog/world-development-indicators.

Environmental Benefits Statement

The World Bank Group is committed to reducing its environmental footprint. In support of this commitment, the Publishing and Knowledge Division leverages electronic publishing options and print-on-demand technology, which is located in regional hubs worldwide. Together, these initiatives enable print runs to be lowered and shipping distances decreased, resulting in reduced paper consumption, chemical use, greenhouse gas emissions, and waste.

The Publishing and Knowledge Division follows the recommended standards for paper use set by the Green Press Initiative. The majority of our books are printed on Forest Stewardship Council (FSC)–certified paper, with nearly all containing 50–100 percent recycled content. The recycled fiber in our book paper is either unbleached or bleached using totally chlorine-free (TCF), processed chlorine-free (PCF), or enhanced elemental chlorine-free (EECF) processes.

More information about the Bank's environmental philosophy can be found at http://www.worldbank.org/corporateresponsibility.

green
press
INITIATIVE

www.ingramcontent.com/pod-product-compliance
Lightning Source LLC
Chambersburg PA
CBHW080424270326
41929CB00018B/3156